HOW TO
END THE NUCLEAR
NIGHTMARE

HOW TO END THE NUCLEAR NIGHTMARE

STUART M. SPEISER

Published in Cooperation
with
THE COUNCIL ON INTERNATIONAL AND PUBLIC AFFAIRS

North River Press, Inc.
CROTON-ON-HUDSON, NEW YORK

Library of Congress Cataloging in Publication Data

Speiser, Stuart M.
  How to end the nuclear nightmare.

  Bibliography: p.
  Includes index.
  1. Stock ownership—United States. 2. Atomic weapons and disarmament. I. Title.
HG4910.S62 1984   332.6'5   84-8017
ISBN 0-88427-057-2

Manufactured in the United States of America

For information on how to order additional copies of this book, write to:

North River Press, Inc.
Box 241
Croton-on-Hudson, NY 10520

11,10, 9, 8, 7, 6, 5, 4, 3, 2, 1

CONTENTS

Acknowledgments

The author wishes to acknowledge the editorial and research assistance of Elaine Gibbs, Lisa Gibson, Jo Kaufman, and Sharon Morgan. The author is especially indebted to The Reverend Erskine White, a minister of the United Church of Christ, for assistance in the portion of Chapter 9 dealing with the Protestant churches.

The views expressed in this book are entirely those of the author.

To the Reader:

This book is about a radical idea—radical in the primary sense of that term: going to the root or source of a problem. This radical idea goes to the roots and sources of humanity's two gravest problems: the threat of nuclear war, and economic stagnation. But unlike other radical ideas, this one probably will not appeal to extremists at either end of the political spectrum. Instead, it will appeal to the vast majority of people throughout the world whose principles lie between those extremes.

You will readily agree that the idea of solving the nuclear and economic problems with a single change is radical. Before reading the details of the idea and the historical evidence that supports it, you will probably jump to the conclusion that the idea is also far-fetched. I thought so myself, until I faced up to the question: How else are we going to end the nuclear nightmare and solve our economic problems?

Unless you have a satisfactory answer to that question, please don't jump—just read on.

Chapter 1

A Startling Proposal:
One Change That Can End Both Economic Stagnation and the Nuclear Nightmare

The unleashed power of the atom has changed everything except our thinking. Thus, we are drifting toward a catastrophe beyond conception. *We shall require a substantially new manner of thinking if mankind is to survive.* [Italics mine]

—ALBERT EINSTEIN

From now on, it is only through a conscious choice and through a deliberate policy that humanity can survive. The moral and political choice that faces us is putting all the resources of mind, science and culture at the service of peace and building up of a new society.

—POPE JOHN PAUL II
at Hiroshima, 1981

The spectre of nuclear holocaust is the great nightmare of our age. That nuclear war of any kind—whether "limited" or all-out—would be a catastrophe beyond conception is a point few of us would care to argue. Even as the Soviet and American governments strain their economies to the breaking point to expand their bulging nuclear arsenals, each acknowledges that neither side could possibly win a nuclear war. In his 1981 farewell address to the nation, Jimmy Carter stated: "The survivors, if any [of a nuclear holocaust], would live in despair amid the poisoned ruins of a civilization that has committed suicide." In that same year, a Soviet government booklet proclaimed: "The Soviet Union holds that nuclear war would be a universal disaster, and that it would most probably mean the end of civilization." All of humanity hopes and prays that this mutual recognition of nuclear war as a no-win situation will prevent both superpowers from ever launching the first missile. But is this enough? Can our civilization produce no better solution to the gravest problem it has ever faced?

This book is an outgrowth of my own increasing lack of faith in the various solutions proposed to date, all of which seem either unreliable at best (deterrence, no-first-use pledge); incapable of practical implementation (freeze, arms control treaties, nuclear-free zones); or antithetical to human nature (world government and other so-called utopian solutions). None of these solutions addresses what I believe is the root of the problem—the basic enmity and distrust that exist between the United States and the Soviet Union. In view of the paranoia that characterizes our relations, is it likely that either nation would put its faith in a non-proliferation treaty, a move toward actual disarmament, or a promise of no-first-use—to say nothing of the goodwill required to create a genuine world government? Present-day deterrence strategies acknowledge this basic dilemma, but certainly provide no solution for it. Indeed, as we shall see when we examine these solutions in greater detail in Chapter 2, deterrence actually nourishes mutual distrust and promises us nothing more comforting than an endless buildup of American and Soviet nuclear arsenals.

Must we then throw up our hands in despair and ignore the problem, as most of the world has done since 1945? That, I believe, would be even more disastrous. As Jonathan Schell points out in his remarkable 1982 book, *The Fate of the Earth,* "A society that systematically shuts its eyes to an urgent peril to its physical survival and fails to take any steps to save itself cannot be called psychologically well" (p. 8). If we are to avoid the unimaginable horror of a nuclear holocaust, we must think about the unthinkable.

Too Frightening to Contemplate/Too Terrifying to Ignore

Since the dawn of the nuclear age, most of us have dealt with the problem in the time-honored tradition of "out of sight, out of mind." After all, how can we get any joy out of life if we spend our time contemplating the fact that nuclear missiles could blow us all to kingdom come in the next few minutes? This understandable apathy is fed by some common assumptions about nuclear war, including: "Nuclear war is too terrifying to contemplate"; "you have to be an expert"; "our national leaders know best"; "it's too big a problem for me to make a difference."

Recent events, however, have forced a reappraisal of these assumptions, which in turn has led to a massive public outcry for nuclear disarmament. The impetus for this sudden reawakening of concern was the 1979 announcement that the United States planned to station its new Pershing II missiles and cruise missiles on NATO soil, manned by American crews and trained on Soviet targets. This move came as a response to a request by NATO ministers who recognized their inability to withstand an attack by the Soviet Union's superior conventional forces, and who sought a less costly way of deterring a Soviet thrust into western Europe. That such a move would open their countries to immediate annihilation in a Soviet nuclear counterattack was, they believed, a necessary evil. What they didn't anticipate was the public response, which was fueled by the recognition that Europe would in effect become a sitting duck, wide open to nuclear obliteration even without a Soviet move on western Europe. Any nuclear exchange between the United States and the Soviet Union, even if it arose from a conflict in the Middle East or Latin America, would force the Soviets to destroy the European-based missiles before the United States had a chance to use them against the USSR. As British anti-nuclear activist Edward P. Thompson wrote in his 1982 book, *Beyond the Cold War,* "In every crisis someone else's finger will be upon 'our' trigger" (p. 53).

With the possibility of nuclear holocaust becoming less remote, it is hardly surprising that this announcement spawned a powerful peace movement in Europe, which continued to spread as the time for deployment of the Pershing II and cruise missiles approached. In December of 1982, thousands of British women linked arms to form a nine-mile human chain around the U.S. air base at Greenham Common, the chosen site for 96 American cruise missiles. By

Easter, 1983, the Greenham Common "peace force" had become a permanent encampment, and on Easter Sunday the human chain stretched over a fourteen-mile length. Similar demonstrations were being held all over Europe, with crowds many times larger than had marched before, and their impact was being felt in the parliaments of the NATO nations.

On this side of the Atlantic there was a similar surge of anti-nuclear sentiment, spurred on in part by the breakdown of détente in the late 1970s, and the coming to power of Ronald Reagan in 1981. With the Soviets accelerating the buildup of their nuclear and conventional forces at an alarming rate and, at the same time, backing Cuban military adventures in Angola, Ethiopia, and South Yemen and sending their own troops into Afghanistan, Reagan took a tough stance in his 1980 campaign. Seemingly intent on recapturing the global clout we lost during the Vietnam and Carter years, he made it clear that he would bolster our nuclear arsenal and implied he would use nuclear force against the Russians if necessary.

Reagan's hard line speeches naturally raised anxiety that he might try to restore American military supremacy through reckless use of nuclear weapons, especially since it was clear to the world that our conventional forces were not up to that task. Moreover, his administration's insistence on increasing military expenditures (including those for nuclear weapons) in the face of continued recession and inflation heightened fears that his policies would topple the uneasy nuclear standoff. Under Reagan, the National Security Council and other sensitive government posts were staffed by nuclear hawks, more than 50 of whom were members of the Committee on the Present Danger, a group organized in 1976 to work for a much tougher military stance against the USSR.

In the wake of these events, it no longer seemed prudent to believe "our leaders know best." According to pollster Louis Harris in an interview in the August/September 1982 *Bulletin of the Atomic Scientists,* the single most important factor in the mushrooming of the anti-nuclear movement was "a growing distrust of the rulers of the two superpowers." In Harris's view, people throughout the world had become "genuinely frightened, in an activated as opposed to a passive way, by the perception that the leaders of the Soviet Union and the United States are heading toward a nuclear confrontation." In a poll he conducted in 1982, 69 percent of the American people believed that Soviet leaders would not hesitate to use nuclear arms if they were desperate enough. Considering the fact that the United States used two atomic bombs—our entire arsenal of nuclear weapons—at a time when we were already winning the war against

Japan, can anyone really doubt that any nation having nuclear weapons would use them if driven to desperation?

With the stakes so high, silence became a luxury we could no longer afford. And on a sunny, magic Saturday in June, 1982, three-quarters of a million people, from every state and from many foreign nations, marched from the United Nations to New York's Central Park in support of world peace and disarmament. It was the largest—and most orderly—demonstration in American history, and it was marked by the absence of any opposition. Over 750,000 people demonstrating in New York, yet they left hardly any garbage. There were no riots or injuries, even though the police had set up several hospitals in the park and many hardened New Yorkers had left town for the day in anticipation of chaos. Journalists noted that the marchers seemed to be a cross section of humanity, rather than a typical protest group dominated by one class or style. As reported in *Newsweek* magazine on June 21, 1982: ". . . the gigantic turnout was a remarkable reminder of the extraordinary speed with which anti-nuclear sentiment has swept the world." At the close of the demonstration, 3,000 bomb-shaped balloons were released as the huge throng chanted, "Goodbye to nuclear weapons!"

While it is heartening to see that millions of people now want to articulate their concern about nuclear weapons, thus far the outpouring of sentiment in Central Park, Greenham Common, and in dozens of similar demonstrations throughout the world has produced little in the way of tangible results. What it has produced is a question: *What can we do—individually and collectively—to end the threat of nuclear holocaust?*

That is what I want to explore in this book. How can we harness all the energy, dedication, and fear that the nuclear nightmare has inspired in millions of people? What can we *do* to make a difference? How can we transform the spirit of Central Park and Greenham Common into political action?

A New Angle on an Old Problem

Taking my cue from Albert Einstein, whose pioneering work made possible the splitting of the atom and ushered in the nuclear age, I began to ponder the problem from a new angle. Is it possible to cut through the atmosphere of fear, distrust, and enmity that shrouds our relations with the Soviet Union? The answer to that question forms the core of this book and will, above all else, require you to consider the problem in an entirely new way.

What this book proposes is a basic change in our capitalist economic system. The plan itself, which I call SuperStock, is not new and is in fact a modification of ideas proposed by other writers. It was originally conceived of as a way to preserve capitalism by building on its strengths and minimizing its weaknesses. SuperStock, quite simply, is a system of "universal" capitalism, whereby *everyone* in this country could become a true capitalist—an owner of the means of production—via ownership of corporate stock. SuperStock is not a Marxist or socialist system, since it would preserve free enterprise, democracy, and the other advantages of our American system. How is this possible? Like any writer, I'm not going to give away essential "plot" details this early in the book. SuperStock will be explained in detail in Chapter 5. For now, indulge yourself in a brief bit of fantasy. Imagine every American household being able to own a significant amount of stock in the 2,000 strongest American corporations, without having to win the lottery or inherit a trust fund to pay for it. Imagine how much brighter the future would be if each household could acquire, *without any personal investment,* $100,000 worth of corporate stock that would produce income of about $20,000 a year, over and above salary. All households that owned less than $100,000 worth of stock would be eligible, since SuperStock is much broader than current plans that distribute stock only to a company's employees.

Sound too good to be true? Not to the Joint Economic Committee of Congress (JEC), to whom I presented the concept in 1976 and who found it promising. Not to the 35 economists, financial experts, and government officials who attended an all-day seminar at the Brookings Institution in 1977, none of whom were able to find any fatal flaws in the plan. I have been an ardent supporter of the SuperStock plan since the mid 1970s, and I have gone public with it in *The New York Times* (1977), *The Journal of Post Keynesian Economics* (1979), and in a 1977 book, *A Piece of the Action,* in which I argued that universal capitalism might be the only practical solution for our ailing welfare state and our increasingly severe economic problems.

But, you're probably ready to ask, how can a change in our economic system affect our relations with the Soviets and lessen the chance of nuclear holocaust? That brings us to the central point of this book: SuperStock is not only capable of solving our domestic economic woes, but may be the most practical approach to rapprochement with the Soviet Union.

To understand how this might be possible, let's return to the fact that none of the nuclear arms solutions put forth to date really addresses the bottom line issue: the enmity between the United

States and the Soviet Union. What lies behind this enmity? From the American point of view, it is Soviet expansionism, their commitment to worldwide communist revolution. But I doubt many of us believe the Soviets seek literal expansion, that they actually want to occupy American soil. What we really fear is the spread of Marxist ideology and what that might mean to our way of life under the capitalist system. On the other side of the coin, the Soviet leadership fears the spread of capitalist ideology and the free enterprise system. Essentially, then, what we have is a clash between two economic systems—capitalism and communism—although we usually prefer to describe the confrontation in more heroic terms: democracy vs. totalitarian communism, or freedom vs. slavery. Whatever name we use, however, what we're fighting to protect is *capitalism.* What we're fighting to protect it from is the appeal of an *idea,* not necessarily Russian-style communism, but the Marxist ideology. And we fear its appeal largely because of the failings of our own capitalism.

In the broadest sense, both our domestic and international crises stem from one economic root—inequitable distribution of capital ownership and income. This fact will come as no surprise to those readers who are struggling to get by on salary alone, who, if they're lucky, may own 50 or 100 shares of one or another blue-chip stock, and who often ponder the injustice of a system that allows a Rockefeller to continually increase a fortune that couldn't be spent in several generations. Ours is *not,* in truth, an affluent society. Wealth in this country remains highly concentrated, especially corporate stock; the richest 1 percent of the people own more than half of all individually owned shares. The present system of taxation and corporate finance perpetuates this overconcentration, so that ownership of newly created capital is piped into the already overflowing coffers of the wealthy, while those who own no capital get none. Can we expect this vast group of have-nots to support indefinitely a system that blocks their access to the wealth of the nation?

While it is true that we have over the years rectified some of capitalism's abuses, we have done little to close the gap between the haves and the have-nots. Our attempts to do so—to make capitalism viable for the 94 percent of our population who do not own substantial amounts of stock—have not only created a massive welfare state we can no longer afford to sustain, but have also forced us to adopt our "better dead than red" posture. How else but by decrying the evils of Soviet communism and expansionism can we stave off the natural appeal Marxism has for the have-nots of our society? But consider: if capitalism could be made universal, if we could *in one generation equalize the wealth of the nation* as SuperStock is designed to do, what threat would Marxism pose to the United States? If the system worked for everyone, why would voters seek to alter it? If everyone becomes an owner, there would be nobody left to exploit; thus, capitalism and Marxism would no longer be divided over the central issue of class struggle to overcome exploitation.

Universal capitalism is a startling idea at first, but its logic is overpowering. If it can be implemented, it could become the economic counterpart of political democracy, combining the emotional appeal of Marxism with the self-betterment drive and productive power of Adam Smith's laissez-faire, while preserving all our treasured American principles.

In the Soviet Union, as in the United States, 94 percent of the population is denied access to their nation's wealth. Although technically the state owns the means of production, in practical terms the 6 percent of Soviet citizens who are members of the Communist Party control all of the nation's capital, creating a similar chasm between the haves and have-nots. To the average Russian waiting in line for two hours to buy groceries, decadent capitalism must hold some appeal. How, but by pointing to the evils of American capitalism and glorifying Marxism, can the Soviet leadership maintain their ideological grip on this vast underclass? In an article in the *Wall Street Journal* of May 23, 1983, journalist David Satter, who lived and worked in the Soviet Union, notes that unlike Americans whose goals are tangible—career success, a private home, a car, expensive clothes—"the Soviet citizen, who has no access to these things, dedicates his life to the service of abstract goals—the eventual victory of world communism and an end to the exploitation of man by man."

It is a central irony of American-Soviet relations that the failings of both capitalism and communism have created similar internal problems—inequitable distribution of wealth, income, and power. It is perhaps an even greater irony that both nations attempt to deal with this problem by assuming an adversarial stance against the other, rather than by making internal changes that would achieve more equitable distribution. It may be human nature to avoid examining one's own faults by pointing an accusing finger at someone else's seemingly worse faults. But in my view it is precisely this attitude that has brought us to the brink of nuclear holocaust, forcing both superpowers to deal from a position of fear and weakness and to defend their systems by brandishing an increasingly lethal array of nuclear weapons. As Father Robert F. Drinan concludes in his 1983 book, *Beyond the Nuclear Freeze:*

The only real hope, therefore, for the lessening of the possibility of a nuclear war is for the lessening of the tensions and hostility that brought it about in the first place—the fear of communism by the American people and the fear of American imperialism by the leaders of the Kremlin. [p. 122]

I believe SuperStock can be the means of eradicating that fear. It may also be our last opportunity to ensure the survival of capitalism and democracy in America. With the spectre of pension fund socialism moving across Europe, with much of the world already under socialist governments, and with capitalism no longer able to provide enough employment, it is only a matter of time before voters in all democratic countries will choose collective ownership—*unless they can participate in capitalism as capitalists.*

How might a plan like SuperStock be implemented? How can we make SuperStock appeal to the Soviets' self-interest? How might the Soviets respond? Can we be sure the Soviets won't try to force communism down our throats whether we have universal capitalism or not? Is Marxist ideology really important to the Kremlin rulers, or is it merely a stalking horse for their dream of world domination? These are some of the questions I will be addressing in this book.

My aim in writing it is not to proclaim the infallibility of the SuperStock plan. In fact, I perceive it as no more than a starting point, the broad outline of a solution to the two gravest problems we face—nuclear confrontation and economic chaos. Because SuperStock is radical, it will be controversial, but I hope that controversy will at the very least lead to further study and development of the idea.

Is SuperStock too radical an idea to be taken seriously? Some will undoubtedly think so; history is filled with examples of ideas that were initially scoffed at simply because they were unconventional. But surely if a conventional solution were possible, it would have surfaced by now. For over twenty years, the best and brightest among us have proposed an array of solutions, none of which has yet proved more than a stop-gap measure. Our experts have been rounding up the usual suspects, but in the end their "cures" have proved the equivalent of prescribing aspirin for cancer. It is time for us to broaden our perspective and consider a solution that matches the staggering scope of these problems. It is time, as Einstein warned us, to develop that "substantially new manner of thinking."

It is also time to recognize the link between our economic problems and the threat of nuclear holocaust. It has been our practice to discuss these as separate issues, to be treated by different sets of "experts." One of my aims is to demonstrate that economic stagnation and the nuclear nightmare are closely related, that neither problem can be solved by conventional remedies, and most important, that a single change in our economic system can produce a solution for both problems. Failure to perceive this connection is, I believe, one of the main reasons why no solutions for either have surfaced, despite constant efforts by leaders in government, economics, and strategic analysis throughout the world.

Some Information about your Guide

By now you may be wondering: who is this fellow Speiser and why does he think he has the answers that have eluded all the "experts"? To answer that perfectly valid question, I offer below some information about my background and possible biases.

I would classify myself as a frightened capitalist who believes that capitalism has enabled America to achieve much that would not have been possible under any other system. I am a capitalist for the most reliable of reasons: materialism, self-interest, (or if you insist, greed). I organized my own law firm as well as other businesses, and once served as the chairman of a company whose stock was publicly traded. I have achieved far greater success within the capitalist system than I ever dreamed I would, and I now have a respectable share of capital ownership I would like to retain. So I am also frightened for the most reliable of reasons: I believe our capitalist system is running down and unlikely to survive in a democracy where the voters, most of whom are denied the principal benefits of capitalism, are rapidly learning how to achieve their increasingly high expectations through the ballot box. I would prefer to become part of a system that affords *everyone* access to capitalist ownership, rather than stand by and watch America drift to socialism.

I am not a professional economist, although I have written several books on economics. My knowledge of the subject is actually a direct outgrowth of my legal practice, which involved me in accident cases where people were seriously injured or killed. In such cases, the loss of future wages suffered by accident victims and their families must be figured into compensation demands, which required me to project the earning power of these individuals twenty-five or more years into the future. This in turn led to my study of the likely structure of our economy many years into the future. I found it necessary to consider industry and company employment histories, earning levels likely to prevail in various jobs, and the effects of inflation. The end result was that I was virtually forced to immerse myself in economics and in the even more sophisticated field of econometrics—the statistical measurement of economic theories. However, unlike professional economists, I did not have the luxury of remaining in the ivory tower, confining myself to theoretical analysis. The rigid courtroom rules of evidence restrict testimony to matters of relative certainty and exclude speculation and conjecture.

Along with other lawyers in this field, I helped to pioneer the practice of using economists and their economic statistics to prove in court the value of lost earnings. I wrote the first textbook on this subject, which has since been quoted by the U.S. Supreme Court and many other courts throughout the country. As a result of my writings on economics, I was named an honorary editor of the *Journal of Post Keynesian Economics*.

I offer this information not to blow my own horn, but to demonstrate that I am simply a concerned citizen with some degree of economic expertise, yet an outsider vis-à-vis the economic and political establishments and therefore someone with no axe to grind. I do not depend on book royalties to make a living, nor am I under the academician's pressure to publish or perish. I have no political ambitions. I am writing this book for only one reason—nobody else has written it.

Since I cannot avoid thinking like a lawyer, this book will reflect some of the lawyer's methods of reasoning. We are trained to separate fact from opinion, and the relevant from the irrelevant. We try to line up the evidence in a cause-and-effect sequence, searching for what the courts call "causation." We are accustomed to dealing with opinions of technical experts who differ sharply in their conclusions. When all this has been done, we try to sum up the case in a way that will convince the jury that our client should prevail. I hope to convince you that there is a way out of the nuclear nightmare. This is one case I can't afford to lose.

Chapter 2

Why None of the Proposed Solutions Can End the Nuclear Nightmare

Each year, the number of bombs has grown, until now there are some fifty-thousand warheads in the world, possessing the yield of roughly twenty billion tons of TNT, or one million six hundred thousand times the yield of the bomb that was dropped by the United States on the city of Hiroshima . . .

—JONATHAN SCHELL
[The Fate Of the Earth, page 3]

Above all, while defending our own vital interests, nuclear powers must avert these confrontations which bring an adversary to a choice of either a humiliating retreat or a nuclear war.

—PRESIDENT JOHN F. KENNEDY,
speech at American University, June 10, 1963

The single most terrifying aspect of nuclear weapons is that no one really knows how devastating their effects could be. Depending on your source of information, you might be cheered by some predictions that we could recover from a nuclear war in several years. Or, you might be terrified by the more likely possibility that a nuclear exchange would mean not only the end of civilized life but planetary life as well. It is becoming more difficult for anyone to buy the optimist's point of view. Yet for years now, millions of people have comforted themselves with the belief they had a reasonably good chance of surviving a nuclear war. Is that a rational assumption? Answering this question seems a logical place to begin an examination of the nuclear crisis and the various solutions proposed to prevent a holocaust.

The Face of Devastation

Current predictions are of necessity based on our only real source of knowledge—the damage to Hiroshima and Nagasaki. In *The Fate of the Earth,* Jonathan Schell describes Hiroshima immediately after the bombing, using survivors' eyewitness accounts and a report compiled by a group of Japanese scientists. From this latter source, we learn, "It is no exaggeration to say that the whole city was ruined instantaneously" (p. 37). In Schell's own words, we discover:

> In that instant [of the bombing] tens of thousands of people were burned, blasted and crushed to death. Other tens of thousands suffered injuries of every description or were doomed to die of radiation sickness. The center of the city was flattened and every part . . . was damaged. . . . The number of people who were killed outright or who died of their injuries over the next three months is estimated to be a hundred and thirty thousand. Sixty-eight percent of the buildings in the city were either completely destroyed or damaged beyond repair . . . [p. 37]

Yet the bomb dropped on Hiroshima was, by modern standards, a rather small weapon, with an explosive force equivalent to about 12,000 to 15,000 tons of TNT. In the parlance of nuclear weaponry, the explosive force of 1,000 metric tons of TNT is known as a *kiloton,* so the World War II bombs had yields of about 12 to 15 kilotons. The hydrogen bombs in our 1980s missiles measure their force in *megatons,* and one megaton is the equivalent of one million metric tons of TNT. Therefore, a one-megaton nuclear warhead is 70 to 80 times more powerful than the atomic bombs used in 1945. Yet it, too, is a relatively small weapon in the current arsenals of the superpowers. Many warheads are in the 20-megaton range, which means they have a force equivalent to 20 million tons of TNT and are thus 1600 times more powerful than the bombs dropped on Hiroshima and Nagasaki. Does this mean that the damage resulting from a 20-megaton bomb would be "only" 1600 times greater than the damage Hiroshima sustained? Not necessarily, for there are immeasurable compounding factors and side effects.

Schell describes the various effects of nuclear explosions in great detail. They include what he calls the *local* primary effects:

initial nuclear radiation, electromagnetic pulse, thermal pulse, blast wave, and local fallout. In addition, there are *global* primary effects, which are especially significant when many nuclear weapons are detonated all over the earth: worldwide fallout, the general cooling of the earth's surface, and at least a partial destruction of the ozone layer surrounding the earth. This layer is crucial to life on earth because it shields us from what would otherwise be harmful, if not deadly, levels of ultraviolet radiation in sunlight.

Schell does not claim that a full nuclear exchange would kill everybody on earth directly through local effects. But he documents a case for the earth becoming uninhabitable over a period of weeks following such an exchange. As he puts it:

> Nuclear weapons are unique in that they attack the support systems of life at every level. And these systems, of course, are not isolated from each other but are parts of a single whole: ecological collapse, if it goes far enough, will bring about social collapse, and social collapse will bring about individual deaths. [p. 23]

Remember that Hiroshima was hit with a single bomb that had less than one-thousandth (1/1000) the force of a 20-megaton thermonuclear weapon. In any present-day war scenario, cities the size of Hiroshima are likely to be attacked by dozens of bombs from the thousands stockpiled by both superpowers. Thus, to fully gauge the effect, we must try to visualize devastation hundreds of thousands— or millions—times worse than that of Hiroshima.

One way to translate this unthinkable disaster into human terms (if you have the courage) is to visualize the exploding of a hydrogen bomb on your hometown. Were the Soviets to attack my hometown of New York City, they would probably use a 20-megaton bomb (with 1,600 times the force of the Hiroshima bomb). The blast wave would flatten everything within a radius of 12 miles, an area of more than 450 square miles stretching from the middle of Staten Island through all of Manhattan to the northern edge of the Bronx and most of Queens. The fireball would be about four-and-one-half miles in diameter. People as far as 23 miles from ground zero—the point on the ground directly below the explosion—would be burned to death. The mushroom cloud would be 70 miles in diameter. New York City and its suburbs would be destroyed in a few seconds. Counting the fallout effects, this single bomb would probably kill about 20 million people—and there are thousands of such bombs in the Soviet arsenal.

Coupling the facts at our disposal with scientific speculation, it isn't hard to conclude, as Schell does, that a 10,000-megaton attack on the United States would simply wipe out the country and its people. Tens of millions of Americans would go up in smoke immediately. Soon, fires would, in Schell's words, "simply burn down the United States." And as he points out, the killing power of the local fallout would be far greater than the initial blast effect.

In densely settled Europe, the effects of a nuclear barrage would be even worse. It is unlikely that there would be many survivors left in all of Europe after the detonation of several hundred megatons, and most European nations could be wiped out by as little as tens of megatons. But the most chilling image offered by Schell is the effect of a 10,000 megaton exchange, which is fully within the capability of present arsenals: it would bring an end to all meaningful life on the earth.

A somewhat more "optimistic" view is presented in a detailed report by Herbert L. Abrams, M.D., and William E. Von Kaenel, published on November 12, 1981, in the *New England Journal of Medicine*. Using the Federal Emergency Management Agency's 1976 model, which assumed a 6,559-megaton attack (equal to 524,720 Hiroshima bombs), these prominent Harvard Medical School researchers estimated the physiological and pathological effects of a nuclear war on the American population. Here's what they tell us:

> Moments after the attack, 86 million people—nearly 40 percent of the population—will be dead. An additional 34 million—27 percent of the survivors—will be severely injured. Fifty million additional fatalities are anticipated during the shelter period for a total of 133 million deaths. Many of the millions of surviving injured will have received moderate to high radiation doses. Approximately 60 million may survive and emerge from the shelter period without serious injury and with relatively limited radiation exposure.

In addition, they project a great increase in the risk and severity of infection and the spread of contagious diseases, as a result of the effects of radiation. Bubonic plague, carried by wild rodents, would become a widespread danger. Under prevailing conditions—millions of corpses and the swarms of flies attracted to them; the hoarding of available grain; the lack of disease control, quarantine facilities, medical and laboratory services, water and sewage purification—there would be a rapid spread of plague-carrying rodents who are themselves highly resistant to the disease.

If you are cheered by the news that 60 million Americans might survive, I am afraid I must take on the role of bearer of bad tidings.

The Abrams-Von Kaenel report was based on a 1976 government study, which assumed a much milder attack than the level probable today. The real killing power of our latest weapons remains a closely guarded secret. And while we devote billions of dollars to increasing this killing power, we virtually ignore any development that might reduce casualties. Furthermore, studies by teams of authors representing many scientific specialties, published in the December 23, 1983 edition of *Science,* indicated that an all-out nuclear exchange would probably produce a "nuclear winter" in which most of the world would be plunged into darkness, and global environmental changes would threaten extinction of the human race. A major 1983 study by the Congressional Office of Technology Assessment, *The Effects of Nuclear War,* concluded "the effects of nuclear war that cannot be calculated in advance are at least as important as those which analysts attempt to quantify."

At this writing (1983), efforts to contain devastation are limited to two nuclear defense strategies—sheltering and evacuation. Can we rely on these methods? Numerous observers say no and document their case with frightening credibility. Schell, for example, notes that fallout shelters would be virtually useless against the heat, radiation, and fires occurring in areas directly attacked, particularly since most existing shelters lack some or all of these essentials: adequate radiation shielding; a filtration system to screen out radioactive particles; independent heating systems; medical supplies; counters to measure surface radiation levels; and a means of dealing with the bodies of those who die during the shelter period.

There is also the very real question of how many people could even reach a shelter before an attack. According to the Arms Control and Disarmament Agency, it would take a *minimum of 15 minutes* after a Soviet launch for earliest warnings of an impending attack to reach the general public, and it's unlikely that most people would hear or respond immediately to that first warning. But it would take *no more than 10 minutes* after firing for Soviet submarine-based missiles to reach American targets, and another 15 or 20 minutes for the ICBMs launched from within the Soviet Union. Depending on your location, you might have no more than 10 to 15 minutes to seek out a shelter that might or might not be stocked with the necessary supplies. Although shelters might save some lives in places receiving relatively light amounts of fallout, such places are not likely to be located in the heavily populated areas of the United States or the Soviet Union. And in an all-out nuclear war, given the global ecological effects mentioned above, it is unlikely that anyone initially saved by sheltering would eventually survive. In fact, those surviving a massive nuclear exchange might wish they had died in the original blast wave. As the former chairman of the Joint Chiefs of Staff, General Maxwell Taylor, said in a 1981 interview:

> In any major strategic exchange, the reciprocal damage would create conditions that would make victory and defeat virtually indistinguishable, save perhaps that the victors might survive a bit longer than the vanquished.

In his 1982 book, *With Enough Shovels: Reagan, Bush and Nuclear War,* journalist Robert Scheer examined the Reagan administration's civil defense strategy, which he notes is based on the Soviet model. From discussions with Thomas K. Jones, Reagan's Deputy Under-Secretary of Defense for Research and Engineering, Strategic and Theater Nuclear Forces, Scheer learned that "the United States could fully recover from an all-out nuclear war with the Soviet Union in just two to four years . . . and that nuclear war was not nearly as devastating as we had been led to believe." On what basis does Jones make this assertion? "If there are enough shovels to go around," said Jones, "everybody's going to make it." The shovels would be used to dig holes in the ground, which would be covered with doors and three feet of dirt. These holes, according to Jones, would provide adequate sheltering for the millions of Americans who had been evacuated to the countryside. As Jones explained to Scheer: "It's the dirt that does it" (p. 18).

Scheer concludes that both Soviet and American civil defense plans are absurd on their faces and that it is dangerous to lead people to believe they could survive a nuclear attack through such measures. He points out that it would take at least three days to evacuate major cities, evacuation would furnish early warning of intent to launch a nuclear strike, missiles could be re-aimed to strike evacuation areas, and eventually radiation would kill early survivors anyway.

It is tempting to mock these desperate plans, but given the superpowers' determination to match and outdo one another in every nuclear arena, is it surprising that some gesture toward civil defense must be made? The reasoning goes like this: If the Soviets are doing something about civil defense, we must assume they have not written off the possibility of a first strike. Clearly, our strategy must be similar. How can Scheer—or any of us—expect Jones, in his role as administration representative, to ridicule such preparations when it is his job to match every Soviet move and countermove, eyeball to eyeball? As Jonathan Schell points out, ". . . the civil-defense issue is a strategic, not a humanitarian, question" (p. 35). In other words, within the parameters of current nuclear strategy, it is vital that each superpower preserve—or appear to preserve—its ability to devastate the other in the wake of a nuclear attack.

That each has the firepower to do so, that victor and vanquished can (and probably will) go down together, is the chief horror of the nuclear age. Although it remains an unrealized horror, that is small comfort in view of our increasingly sophisticated and lethal nuclear arsenals and our minuscule chances for survival. Civil-defense strategy notwithstanding, there is only one way to survive a nuclear war—to prevent it from ever starting.

Proposed Solutions: How Do They Stack Up?

What follows is in the nature of a guided—and necessarily encapsulated—tour through the entire spectrum of nuclear politics, based on my study of both popular and technical literature about the nuclear arms problem, the solutions proposed by various individuals and organizations from the political left, right, and center, and the efforts of government bodies, including the United States Congress and the United Nations. This bird's-eye view will, I hope, allow you to draw your own conclusions (with perhaps a bit of gentle nudging from me).

Spy vs. Spy: The Escalating Game of Deterrence

Deterrence through mutual assured destruction. Its very name (and acronym MAD) makes it an unlikely choice for a peace-keeping strategy. Yet it has been our chief means of preventing nuclear war for almost 40 years, and despite the various wars and "police actions" that have occurred since 1945, no nuclear weapons have been fired in battle. Therefore, argue its proponents, we must maintain MAD deterrence until something better comes along. The problem is that the logic of MAD creates ever-increasing tension, and nobody can foretell at what point the MAD "solution" may become the actual trigger of nuclear war.

MAD deterrence brings to mind Antonio Prohias's "Spy vs. Spy" cartoons, published (appropriately enough) in *MAD* magazine. Both spies have the faces and beaks of crows; their only distinguishing characteristic is that one is dressed in white, the other in black. Each is dedicated to thinking up fiendish schemes for disposing of the other. This eternal confrontation is epitomized by Prohias's drawing of both spies balancing on one tightrope, staring each other down at beak-to-beak range. The spy in white is attempting to cut the rope behind his adversary with a huge hunting knife. The spy in black follows suit with a large pair of scissors. The tightrope, symbolizing civilization's lifeline, is held in place by no more than a few thin threads. Should either spy succeed in completely severing it, both will go down together.

The certainty of retaliation is the key to deterrence. Says Edward P. Thompson in *Beyond the Cold War:* "[Deterrence] is at heart a very simple, and simple-minded, idea, which occurred to the first cave men when they got hold of clubs" (p. 3). For both sides, the equation is basic: an enemy is lurking outside your "turf," threatening your way of life, armed with a club (or machine gun, or nuclear bomb). What recourse have you but to fashion your own club or, better yet, 2 clubs, and hope that the mere presence of these clubs will dissuade him from attacking? The next step then becomes inevitable: when he reappears with a party of friends and 10 clubs, you will have to find 20 friends and make 20 clubs. And on it goes, in an endless cycle of escalation and counterescalation.

In view of the basic distrust between the United States and the Soviet Union, neither side ever feels secure enough to rest on its current deterrent force. Every improvement in America's ability to avoid a crippling first strike is seen by the Soviets as a new offensive thrust, and vice versa. The end result is the kind of escalation game that has characterized the entire history of the nuclear age, beginning after the 1945 bombing of Japan, when the Truman administration made some effort to avoid an arms race with Stalin's Russia. A graphic summary follows:

1946

MOVE: Bernard Baruch, head of the American delegation to the United Nations Atomic Energy Commission, proposes that all nuclear fuel and weapons be placed under an international atomic development authority. This plan is rejected by the Soviets who perceive it as a ploy to give the U.S. worldwide control over atomic development. The Russians object particularly to the stipulation that personnel of the international authority "should be recruited on the basis of proven competence," albeit "as far as possible on an international basis." Since the Russians have far less "proven competence," they view this as a means of assuring American control.

COUNTERMOVE: At the second meeting of the UN Atomic Energy Commission, Soviet representative Andrei Gromyko proposes a treaty to outlaw production and use of all atomic weapons. The U.S. rejects this plan since it is the only nation that has usable nuclear weapons.

1948

MOVE: The U.S. introduces long-range aircraft for intercontinental bombing.

1949

COUNTERMOVE: The Soviets explode their first atomic bomb.

1954

MOVE: The U.S. explodes the first hydrogen (thermonuclear) bomb, which has a force equivalent to 15 million tons of TNT.

1955

COUNTERMOVE: The Soviets respond by building their own hydrogen bomb, with a force of about one million tons of TNT. In the same year, they also put their own intercontinental bombers into service.

1957

MOVE: The Soviets deploy the first intercontinental ballistic missiles (ICBMs) and pave the way for the space race by orbiting Sputnik I.

1958

COUNTERMOVE: The U.S. matches these developments, deploying its own ICBMs and launching its first space satellite.

1960

MOVE: The U.S. produces the first nuclear-powered submarine, the *Polaris*, capable of firing long-range missiles while submerged.

1968

COUNTERMOVE: The Soviets develop their own nuclear-powered sub.

1966

MOVE: The U.S. begins deployment of multiple warhead missiles (MRVs). These missiles carry three warheads, each of which had 16 times the explosive power of the Hiroshima bomb.

1968

COUNTERMOVE: The Soviets catch up with their own MRV missiles.

1968

MOVE: The Soviets pioneer development of the anti-ballistic missile (ABM), deploying 64 defensive missiles around Moscow.

1969

COUNTERMOVE: The U.S. begins construction of its own Safeguard ABM system, but by 1972, in one of the few successful anti-nuclear diplomatic efforts, both nations sign a treaty restricting development of the ABMs. Their willingness to do so is based in large part on the fact that existing systems are both ineffective and prohibitively expensive.

1970

MOVE: The U.S. develops the first multiple independently targetable reentry vehicles (MIRVs), capable of hitting a dozen or more targets as far as 100 miles apart.

1975

COUNTERMOVE: The Soviets respond by putting their own MIRVs into service.

And so it goes. In the war of nerves that is MAD deterrence, a move by either superpower is matched by the other. As Mahatma Ghandi put it, "The Americans do not arm the United States, and the Soviets do not arm Russia; it is the Americans who arm Russia, and the Soviets who arm the United States!" Where will it end? According to elder statesman Averell Harriman, it won't. In his foreword to *Freeze!*, the 1982 book authored by Senators Ted Kennedy and Mark Hatfield, Harriman writes:

> My reading of the Soviet experience—and I have met with every Soviet leader from Stalin to Brezhnev—indicates that Moscow will make whatever sacrifice it takes to remain equal—as we will too. The conclusion will not be superiority; the end will be an arms race without end. [p. xiv]

An attempt to appraise current American and Soviet arsenals is something like comparing apples and oranges, especially since recent developments are surrounded by a wall of military secrecy. The many weapons' categories and methods of comparison make it impossible to judge relative strength simply by the number of missiles or warheads each possesses. However, it is sufficient for us to know that as of December 1982 the United States had about 30,000 nuclear warheads and the USSR had about 20,000. These totals include strategic (long-range or intercontinental) missiles; tactical (short or intermediate range) missiles; and those launched from the ground, from aircraft, and from submarines.

The USSR is considered to have about a two-to-one superiority in total megatonnage, but even this statistic does not speak for itself. Soviet warheads are heavier than those of the U.S., but American weapons are considered to be more accurate. Indeed, the U.S. replaced its heavier Atlas and Titan ICBMs with the lighter and more accurate Minuteman III in order to take advantage of America's lead over the USSR in microminiaturization. Therefore, many observers believe that we are now as close to rough parity as we are ever likely to get, given the Soviets' ability and determination to match any future American buildup.

In 1982, President Reagan claimed that the Soviets had achieved nuclear superiority because their 5,500 land-based warheads could destroy our 2,000 land-based warheads in a first strike, leaving us powerless to retaliate. But this ignores our clear superiority in submarine-based warheads (approximately 4,750 to the USSR's 1,900), which would enable us to retaliate with submarine-based missiles that are not vulnerable to a first strike—assuming, of course, there would be anyone left in the U.S. to give the necessary launch orders. The U.S. also has a ten-to-one edge in warheads carried by intercontinental bombers (3,000 to fewer than 300 owned by the Soviets), although they would take hours rather than minutes to reach Soviet targets.

Although the logic of MAD deterrence demands such mind-numbing inquiries (even to the point of considering whether NATO missiles should be counted in the totals), for our purposes it is enough to know that differences between the superpowers' arsenals are largely the result of design choices, and that each nation has the power to destroy the other many times over. That would be true even if we froze warheads and missiles at present levels and developed no new weapons. The end result of 40 years of reliance on MAD was described with mocking vividness by Dr. Mischio Kaku, professor of physics at the City University of New York, in a 1982 speech at the New York City Bar Association:

> Imagine the United States and the Soviet Union as two pyromaniacs who are standing up to their noses in high octane gasoline. One of the pyromaniacs has 30,000 matches and the other has 20,000 matches. And one says to the other, "Do you want a light?"

Although in theory, deterrence will prevent that match from being lit, a growing number of observers believe the escalation that is built into MAD deterrence is incendiary by itself. Or, to put it more bluntly, in a world already possessing 50,000 nuclear warheads and fast developing newer and deadlier weapons, isn't it likely that some coming event—whether an intentional first strike, an international crisis, or an accident—will trigger use of those weapons, ending not only the arms race but the world itself?

Possibility of a First Strike: Since MAD demands that each side perpetually increase its deterrent force in order to postpone disaster, the delicate balance upon which deterrence rests is in a constant state of flux. And, according to Edward P. Thompson, the resultant shifts in equilibrium can become dangerously addictive. In *Beyond the Cold War,* he notes:

> Deterrence theory proposed a stationary state: that of MAD. But history knows no stationary states. As deterrence presides, both parties change; they become addicted . . . uglier and more barbarous in their postures and gestures. They turn into societies whose production, ideology, and research is increasingly directed towards war. . . . This is the reason . . . why nuclear war is probable within our lifetimes. It is not just that we are preparing for war; we are preparing ourselves to be *the kind of societies which go to war.* [pp. 22–23]

Moreover, says Thompson, the belief with which we comfort ourselves—that no one in their right minds would wage nuclear war—has little validity, given the psychological strains of deterrence and the state of panic likely to prevail in a clash of any kind. As he puts it: "When a course of military confrontation is embarked upon, statesmanship gives way before military exigencies, and after a few days none of the operators are in their right minds any more" (p. ix).

According to a 1976 Brookings Institution study, American presidents brandished the nuclear threat 33 times during the period from 1945 through 1975—an average of more than once a year. And that coming from the nation commonly supposed to be the more peaceful and less volatile of the two superpowers. In light of the terrifying tension generated by MAD deterrence, it isn't hard to imagine an incident that could induce leaders on either side to act on such threats. In its 1982 book, *Common Security,* the Independent Commission on Disarmament and Security Issues points out that:

> On more than one occasion, the danger of nuclear war has arisen because an international situation has developed in which one or both of the great nuclear powers indicated a preparedness to escalate the confrontation beyond the nuclear threshold. . . .

It is claimed that there have been around thirty such incidents, involving either the United States or the Soviet Union or both, and in one instance the United Kingdom. . . .

Any such incident could get out of hand. The way that governments typically make decisions under pressure deviates considerably from models envisioning the rational contemplation of events and careful evaluation of alternatives. [pp. 46–7]

Evidence to support these conclusions may be found in the records of America's response to France's desperate pleas for aid near the end of its regime in Indo-China. In *The Foreign Relations of the United States, 1952–1954,* Vol. 13 (published in 1982), it was revealed that in 1954, the National Security Council considered giving France three atomic bombs to wipe out Vietnamese communist insurgents. Fortunately, a majority of the Joint Chiefs of Staff voted against this proposal. Had they not, we might have set a dangerous precedent for the use of nuclear weapons in colonial warfare. Even so, in view of the volatile political situation in the Middle East and Third World nations, an unprovoked first strike could easily result from an international crisis that does not initially involve the superpowers, but eventually draws them in.

While both superpowers vehemently deny any intention to use nuclear arms, American and Soviet military handbooks and instructions to their field commanders reveal that they are ready and willing to use these weapons if necessary. In his 1968 Soviet text, *Military Strategy,* Marshall V.D. Sokolovsky says, "The essential nature of war as a continuation of politics does not change with changing technology and armaments." This view is echoed in the 1971 U.S. Army Field Manual, *Tactical Nuclear Operations:*

The introduction of tactical nuclear weapons onto the battlefield neither negates the principles of war described in FM 100-5 [the basic Army field manual] nor causes the development of new ones. The intensity of a tactical nuclear conflict emphasizes the importance of these fundamental truths and demands the competent application of these principles by those who would succeed in battle.

Another U.S. Army Field Manual, *Nuclear, Biological, and Chemical (NBC) Reconnaissance and Decontamination Operations (1980),* states that "The U.S. Army must be prepared to fight and win when nuclear weapons are used."

Certainly, the credibility of the nuclear deterrent would be severely weakened if such instructions did not exist. Yet the willingness of both nations to wage war if necessary not only feeds continuing escalation, but intensifies the climate of paranoia, making it more likely that the slightest shift in the balance of power will push either nation beyond the threat-making stage. And the various possible war scenarios are chilling. As George Kennan points out in *The Nuclear Delusion,* should the Soviets misinterpret some action on our part and conclude that we believe war is inevitable, they, too, will be forced to adopt that view. Which, says Kennan, makes "war inevitable by assuming its inevitability." Nor does he believe MAD definitely rules out a Pearl Harbor-type first strike by either side, particularly as the arms race accelerates. In his words:

> It is sobering to remember that modern history offers no example of the cultivation by rival powers of armed forces on a massive scale which did not in the end lead to an outbreak of hostilities. [p. 143]

At the other end of the political spectrum, Herman Kahn foresaw in the shifting balance of power the possibility of a preemptive first strike. In his 1982 book, *The Coming Boom,* Kahn compared our mutual fear of surprise attack to the classic gun battles in cowboy films, in which the cowboy who shoots first—and accurately—walks away unharmed. This, he noted, "obviously puts a great premium on shooting first and accurately." With the Soviets for the moment holding the upper hand, might this not lead them to consider the advantageous timing of a preemptive first strike in which they could fire first and accurately? Nor would a first strike necessarily be the result of aggression. Kahn points out that the very "existence of vulnerable ICBMs is dangerous in itself; during an acute crisis, the Soviet Union might attack them simply to prevent the United States from using them first" (p. 165). These possibilities would, in turn, force the United States to consider more seriously the possibility of mounting its own preemptive strike.

Strike Caused by Accident: Perhaps the most frightening aspect of MAD escalation is the possibility that our increasingly sophisticated deterrent forces could trigger an otherwise unintended strike. As Richard Barnet points out in *Real Security:*

> Anyone who ponders the elaborate system of war prevention we have erected—people in submarines submerged for months waiting for the word to destroy three hundred cities or more with the touch of a button, banks of computers that are expected to behave significantly better in communicating critical information than those that produce the billing foul-ups in department stores, cool rational leaders whom we expect to make the most agonizing decisions in a crisis without information or sleep—can understand why a growing number of scientists state flatly that if the arms race continues nuclear war is now inevitable. [p. 102]

According to the *Stockholm International Peace Research Institute 1982 Yearbook,* there were 32 major accidents involving nuclear weapons between 1950 and 1980. These include the accidental dropping of nuclear bombs from aircraft and explosions at storage installations. These accidents involved only U.S. nuclear weapons; there is no information available about similar Soviet incidents. But it is clear that human error is just as great a hazard in nuclear weapons' management as it is in any complicated technological undertaking. And when coupled with the psychological strains of nuclear deterrence, the chances of a fatal mistake are greatly increased.

On at least three occasions in recent years, relatively minor human errors have brought us to the brink of nuclear holocaust. Twice there were malfunctioning computer chips in the North American Air Defense Command's warning system, and once a test tape of a Russian missile attack was mistakenly inserted in the system. Because nuclear warfare is so complicated, systems are run by computer, which increases the chance of a crisis caused by misinformation. This is especially true when modifications are made or new equipment is installed, as in the scenario of the 1964 film *Fail-Safe,* based on the novel by Eugene Burdick and Harvey Wheeler. Unfamiliar signals from the United States were wrongly interpreted by the USSR, thus setting in motion a chain of responses and counter-responses that placed a U.S. nuclear bomber beyond the "fail-safe" point, its crew believing they had been ordered to bomb Moscow. When the aircraft drops two nuclear bombs on Moscow, the American president is forced to get on the hot line to the Soviet chairman. Under great stress, the president (played by Henry Fonda) convinces the chairman that the bombing of Moscow was an accident, only by agreeing to drop a similar load of nuclear bombs on New York. When the president's order to destroy New York is heard at SAC headquarters, a top scientist there says, "He can't do it!" But a visiting congressman asks, "What else can he do?"

As new generations of nuclear weapons come off the drawing boards, the chances of a *Fail-Safe*-type scenario becoming a reality multiply, because each new system destabilizes the existing counter-system and reduces the time within which the "receiving" nation must decide whether a real attack is under way. We have already moved far beyond the *Fail-Safe* scenario by substituting 10,000 mile-per-hour missiles for aircraft. Both sides also have submarine-launched missiles that can reach enemy territory in ten minutes or less. And the Pershing II missiles that are to be stationed in the NATO countries could reach Russian targets in about six minutes. With both sides developing new weapons that will further reduce missile flight time, American and Soviet leaders will have only a few minutes (and sometimes really only seconds) to react to an apparent threat.

The narrowing of decision time has given rise to a frightening new concept: *launch on warning.* In 1982, both nations were reported to be considering plans to launch their ICBMs at a given "reliable" stage of computerized warning, instead of waiting for verification of an actual attack. With only minutes in which to evaluate and react to a warning signal, neither side can afford to wait; final verification might come too late to launch an effective retaliatory attack.

If we ever reach this hair-trigger stage, the fate of civilization may rest with the least accurate of the rival computer systems. Unfortunately, there is no totally reliable method of obtaining electronic warning of a Soviet attack. According to a 1982 report published by the Congressional Office of Technology Assessment, we would have to spend billions of dollars and years of intensive work to upgrade our satellite and radar warning systems. Even then, we could not completely rule out the possibility of accident or error. Lightning and electrical noises can interfere with these systems, creating signals that indicate an attack is under way, and flocks of birds sometimes appear on radar as missiles.

Nor can Americans take much comfort in the fact that our detection equipment is more sophisticated than that of the USSR. This only means the Soviets are more likely to be deceived by a false or accidental signal and thus more likely to retaliate by mistake. Fear of such a catastrophic error was intensified in 1983 when the Soviets shot down a Korean Air Lines Boeing 747, possibly because Soviet air defenses were unable to identify it as a civilian aircraft. In the contorted world of nuclear deterrence, we are forced to rely on the accuracy of *Soviet* command and control systems to prevent the accidental destruction of the United States. One wonders whether it would not be wise for us to supply the Soviets with our most advanced detection technology to avoid just that possibility.

As a means of forestalling accidental war, Senator Henry M. Jackson suggested in the September 3, 1982 *Wall Street Journal* the establishment of a permanent Soviet-American Joint Consultation Center—"a new institution for facilitating immediate information exchange and consultation between the two countries when events occur that could trigger a nuclear war not intended or desired by either side." Senator Jackson pointed out that the only instrument for direct consultation is the 20-year old Washington-Moscow hotline, a mere teleprinter system that requires composing, encrypting, transmitting, decrypting, translating, and digesting of written messages. Recognizing what a communication delay could mean, President Reagan in 1982 proposed adding voice communication to the hotline. This came as a surprise to those who remember that in *Fail-Safe,* Henry Fonda, playing the American president, spoke directly to the Soviet chairman by telephone. One can only hope that in this case, life will soon imitate art.

If the inherent dangers of MAD deterrence aren't frightening enough, MAD seems to be taking us into an even more bizarre stage: NUTS.

Beyond Deterrence to "Nuclear War-Fighting"

While classic MAD deterrence holds that we must simply stockpile enough clubs to deter aggression, the NUTS (nuclear use theorists) maintain we must be ready, willing, and able to swing those clubs in battle. The NUTS position was best explained by the late Herman Kahn, a jolly man with white chin whiskers who would have had no trouble getting a job as a department store Santa Claus, had he not already been employed as chairman of the Hudson Institute, an extremely influential strategic think-tank. To many people, however, Herman Kahn would have been better cast as The Grinch Who Stole Christmas, because he advocated since the 1960s that the realities of the nuclear age require Americans to "think about the unthinkable." In his 1960 book, *On Thermonuclear War,* he labeled MAD deterrence theory as "Type I," and argued that it would not deter the Soviets. To accomplish that, we would have to adopt Type II, which required us to prepare to fight and win a nuclear war. Kahn's position is best summarized in the following excerpt from his 1982 book, *The Coming Boom:*

> I am a reasonably well-known member of one NUTS group whose own version of the doctrine goes as follows: we must be prepared to use nuclear forces to deter and correct the use or threat of use of nuclear forces by others but should not use our nuclear forces for positive gain—e.g., should not threaten nuclear escalation against conventional threats. . . . There are other NUTS doctrines in which nuclear concepts might be considered less justifiable, e.g., those that accept nuclear weapons as just another weapon. But given the present global situation, I have no apologies regarding the moral aspects of maintaining large and usable nuclear forces. However, to maintain these forces just to save money, or to solve problems associated with having inadequate conventional forces, is both immoral and impractical. The crucial point is that every position—MAD, NUTS, unilateral or world disarmament, world government (or world empire)—has serious problems. I argue that the NUTS position I propose is the least unacceptable. [pp. 166–7]

Despite my initial revulsion to Kahn's suggestion that we must prepare to fight and win a nuclear war, I was forced to agree with his logic. How can Type I deter the Soviets unless they think of us as potential nuclear-war fighters? The mere brandishing of a nuclear arsenal is meaningless; it is the willingness to use that arsenal that gives it credibility as a deterrent force. Although I don't like the image of the U.S. as a nation of nuclear-war fighters, I have to conclude—albeit reluctantly—that our adoption of MAD deterrence as national policy carries us inescapably to the second stage of NUTS.

That conclusion has been reached by every American administration since the 1960s, whether Democratic or Republican, liberal or conservative. Robert McNamara, who served as secretary of defense in John F. Kennedy's administration, announced in 1962 that U.S. strategy in a nuclear war would be the same as in past wars. And President Kennedy himself made it clear that the U.S. might strike first if threatened.

Of course, in the early 1960s the U.S. had clear nuclear superiority over the Soviets, and Kennedy was able to outbluff Krushchev in the 1962 Cuban Missile crisis for that reason. But even after the missile buildup started by Kennedy was matched and then surpassed by the Soviets, every American administration eventually came over to Kahn's NUTS strategy, although under more palatable labels, such as "flexible response." In 1973 and 1974, Secretary of Defense James Schlesinger announced that the U.S. would seek a wide range of nuclear strategic options rather than relying on Type I deterrence. And Schlesinger's successor, Donald Rumsfeld, also embraced Herman Kahn's nuclear warfare theories.

The election of Jimmy Carter raised the hopes of the anti-Kahn forces, particularly since his secretary of defense, Harold Brown, had condemned plans for nuclear-war fighting because he thought they increased the likelihood of catastrophe. But soon after assuming power, when forced to look straight into the face of MAD deterrence, Brown (and Carter) swung over to the Kahn strategy. In the Department of Defense annual report prepared in 1978, Brown said:

> We cannot afford to make a complete distinction between deterrence forces and what are so awkwardly called war-fighting forces.

Yes, the term "war-fighting" is awkward; but unless we view nuclear weapons as war-fighting forces, where is our nuclear deterrent?

The Carter Administration went on to adopt Presidential Directive 59 (PD59), which increased the President's options in responding to nuclear crises, instead of limiting his choices to an all-out launch or surrender. Because it embraced the concept of limited nuclear war and thereby undercut MAD deterrence, PD59 was condemned by anti-nuclear activists. But the Carter Administration argued that it merely codified the flexible response strategy the U.S. had been developing for years.

The Reagan Administration's adherence to PD59 has generated even more concern because Reagan's men seem to be committed to using nuclear options, rather than just talking about them. In other words, they are better at the deterrence game than the Carter team was because their commitment to the use of nuclear weapons appears more credible. The question is: Are Reagan's men too deeply committed, too credible, and therefore likely to upset the delicate MAD-NUTS balance of deterrence by frightening the Soviets into a destabilizing countermove?

In 1982, Secretary of Defense Caspar Weinberger caused an uproar by releasing a five-year defense plan *(Fiscal Year 1984–1988 Defense Guidance)* that included this statement:

> The primary role of U.S. strategic nuclear forces is deterrence of nuclear attack on the U.S., its forces, and its allies and friends. Should such an attack nevertheless occur, U.S. nuclear capabilities must prevail even under the condition of a prolonged war.

This brought an immediate barrage down on Weinberger: Was he really advocating a prolonged nuclear war, and did he really think the U.S. could win it? He then had to explain that although he did not believe either side could win a nuclear war, preparing for one would be another form of deterrent, without which a Soviet nuclear attack was more likely. To his critics, he threw back the ultimate question: "Do you expect the U.S. Secretary of Defense to plan to *lose* a nuclear war, if all our deterrent efforts fail?"

Thus, the concept of MAD deterrence, which leads inescapably to NUTS deterrence, forces us to adopt contingency plans for nuclear strikes aimed solely at Soviet missile installations (limited nuclear war); for first strikes (the NATO policy to counteract our disadvantage in conventional forces); and for civil defense. If we are trying to convince the other side we mean business, we cannot walk away from any of these distasteful, if not ludicrous, preparations, especially when there is clear evidence that the Soviets have also formulated such plans.

While many of us (myself included) abhor the NUTS doctrine and recognize its potential to cause as well as to prevent war, it is nonetheless unproductive (and perhaps foolhardy) to hurl epithets at those Americans who advocate preparations for nuclear warfare, space warfare, civil defense, or any of the escalations embraced by the Soviets. After soul-searching review of MAD deterrence, NUTS proponents have come to the compelling conclusion that we must anticipate or match the Soviet move to NUTS and every other strategy which escalates the pressure of deterrence if we hope to force them to bargain seriously for disarmament. Books and articles that attack the motives and rationality of American officials responsible for nuclear policy are sometimes unfair in their approach. It is easy for anti-nuclear activists and organizations to attack MAD, NUTS, and any other policy that even hints at the use of nuclear weapons. The subject itself is so obscene that no government official can discuss nuclear policy without becoming defensive. Yet these officials have to deal with the reality of present-day confrontational politics; they cannot afford to assume the Soviets do not intend to use their nuclear weapons to dominate the world.

Why would any president want to accelerate the arms race except on evidence that it is necessary to avoid a nuclear Pearl Harbor? Boosting military expenditures inevitably busts the budget and makes it almost impossible for the American economy to perform well. This creates havoc for any administration. It runs up huge deficits, puts upward pressure on inflation and interest rates, forces cuts in social programs, interferes with tax-reduction plans, and threatens to make the incumbent a one-term president. It creates some jobs, but not as many as could be created by using the money for non-military purposes. It pleases military contractors, but does anyone claim that all our presidents from Truman through Reagan (and their leading advisers) have been pawns of the munitions makers?

Thus, until we can find a solution that ends Soviet-American enmity (and I hope this book will be the first step toward such a solution), how can we afford to abandon NUTS deterrence? Can we be sure that Herman Kahn, Caspar Weinberger, Eugene Rostow, and other well-known "hawks" are not the Paul Reveres of the nuclear age? We cannot afford to dissipate the spirit of the anti-nuclear movement in pointless attacks. Instead, let's band together to work for a solution that *will* permit us to abandon deterrence safely.

The Dark Side of Deterrence: Nuclear Proliferation

In his 1979 report to Congress, the then secretary of defense, Harold Brown, asked:

It is all well and good to say that we want both deterrence and stability. But how do we know when we are strong enough to deter, but not so strong as to drive the other side to actions detrimental to both?

How do we know, indeed? Or, to phrase it another way, how much is enough, and how much could become too much? From the standpoint of those responsible for American defense, we can never have enough weapons because we don't know how many would be knocked out in a first strike, we don't know how many would work properly under the chaotic conditions of a nuclear exchange, and we don't know how many of our commanders would survive to give the complicated chain of orders necessary to launch a retaliatory attack in the few minutes available. Yet, from the standpoint of those of us who seek an end to the nuclear nightmare, production and deployment of new weapons threaten to destabilize the very peace that deterrence is designed to protect. In fact, too many weapons can be even more dangerous than too few.

Vertical Proliferation—The Destabilizing Effect of New Weapons: If the presence on earth of 50,000 or more nuclear weapons is not terrifying enough, we are pouring billions of dollars into the development of more "advanced" weapons, deployment of which would raise a number of frightening possibilities. For one thing, many experienced observers believe by 1985 these new weapons will be so fast, accurate, and impervious to detection that it will become almost impossible to negotiate a verifiable arms reduction treaty. Furthermore, these new weapons will hasten the onset of the hair-trigger launch-on-warning policy, which, as we've seen, increases the chances of a false signal sparking accidental war.

Despite these obvious dangers, the Reagan Administration is committed to the development of new weapons that are likely to destabilize the delicate equilibrium of deterrence. In justification, it is said that these new weapons provide bargaining chips with which we can force the Soviets to negotiate in good faith for arms reductions. But the history of the nuclear arms race has moved in the other direction. For example, we developed MIRVs in the 1960s, well ahead of the Soviets, but instead of playing them as a chip at the SALT I negotiations, we built them and deployed them. And of course, the MIRVs came back to haunt us when the Soviets caught up and MIRVed their own larger missiles, which are capable of destroying our land-based ICBMs.

Will our upcoming generation of nuclear weapons—cruise missiles, the Pershing II, Trident submarines and missiles, or the MX missiles—be used as bargaining chips? Unfortunately, they will probably go the way of the MIRV. To make them credible threats, they must be built and deployed; once that occurs, the Soviets will deploy similar weapons in the almost inevitable countermove. Even more ominous is the possibility that the Soviets may feel so threatened by this new generation of weapons (in which they are at least five years behind us) that they may be panicked into firing their ICBMs to avoid an ultimatum or a crippling American first strike. Remember that the Soviets have concentrated their forces in land-based missiles, which are especially vulnerable to the new weapons.

Thus, proliferation is destabilizing in several ways. While our new weapons are intended to destabilize Russian defenses and nuclear strategy, they also destabilize the already uneasy prospects for peace; they provoke the Soviets into dangerous countermeasures; they raise questions about American compliance with existing nuclear arms treaties; and they threaten to destabilize the entire NATO alliance because of their demoralizing effect on the European people and parliaments. On a more basic level, each new weapons system has its own inherent dangers and problems. Cruise missiles, for example, can fly at very low altitudes and can be programmed to follow the contours of the terrain, making radar detection difficult. They can be launched from the air, the ground, or the sea. Because they are only about 20 feet long and highly mobile, verification of their numbers and locations will be virtually impossible. They could be hidden in trucks, cargo ships, or commercial aircraft; a single DC-10 could carry more than a dozen cruise missiles, and every Russian fishing trawler could become a major missile delivery system. Once the world is full of cruise missiles, it will even be difficult for a nation under attack to determine whose missile is on its way to a target. Not only do they make satellite verification of arms treaties impossible, they also increase the chances of accidental nuclear war by reducing reaction time to a very few minutes. They will put the Soviets at least five years behind us in an important new weapons race, and the Soviets have already announced they will not consider any reduction in their ICBM force if we deploy cruise missiles. Yet the Reagan Administration plans to deploy more than 10,000 cruise missiles.

Then there is the famous MX (for "missile experimental"), dubbed the "Peacekeeper" in 1982 by Ronald Reagan. The MX program was devised in 1974 by Secretary of Defense James R. Schlesinger as an answer to the developing Soviet advantage in silo-busting missile power. The MX is intended to be the most powerful and accurate missile ever built, giving the U.S. the ability to knock out all Soviet ICBMs in a first strike. It is expected to be ready for production and deployment by 1986. But long before it went into production, it became the subject of the most intensive debate in U.S. weapons history, focused on the question: How and where will the MX be deployed?

The U.S. Air Force considered more than 30 options, and during the Carter Administration it favored a "racetrack" basing system that would have shuttled 200 MX missiles on trailers to and from over 4,000 shelters in Nevada and Utah. This $34 billion shell game plan attracted little public support and was finally abandoned in favor of the "Dense Pack" system endorsed by Ronald Reagan in 1982. Under Dense Pack, 100 MX missiles would be housed at Warren Air Force Base near Cheyenne, in fixed super-hardened silos 1,800 feet apart, spread over an area 14 miles long and 1½ miles wide. On its face, Dense Pack seems like a suicidal repetition of the bunching of American aircraft at our Hawaiian air bases in 1941 (in order to more easily guard them against sabotage), which made them sitting ducks for Japanese aircraft and resulted in only six American fighter planes getting off the ground during the Pearl Harbor attack. But Dense Pack's proponents claim that clustering the MX missiles so closely will have a "fratricidal" effect on enemy missiles. In other words, because the Soviets will have to aim all their ICBMs into one narrow area, the shock waves, debris, dust-cloud friction, and other effects produced by their early missiles will destroy or cripple their later missiles before they can damage any more MX silos. As a result, according to the fratricide theory, only a few of the Soviet ICBMs will destroy MXs, leaving a substantial number available for retaliation and thus reducing the chance of a crippling first strike against the U.S.

As with many other nuclear weapons questions, there is no way of fully testing or verifying the fratricide theory. However, say the opponents of Dense Pack, even if fratricide were valid, it could easily be avoided by programming ICBMs to explode under ground rather than in the fratricide zone. The 1982 Senate hearings on appropriations for Dense Pack revealed that the Joint Chiefs of Staff had found the proposal "very difficult to understand and very difficult to explain." As a result, three of its five members voted to delay their recommendations until "technical uncertainties" had been resolved. The JCS did not explain how technical uncertainties could ever be resolved, given the impossibility of testing the fratricide theory. But this did not stop Ronald Reagan from pushing for immediate approval of the $26 billion Dense Pack plan.

In response to Congressional doubts about the fratricide theory,

President Reagan appointed a special commission, headed by retired Air Force Lt. Gen. Brent Scowcroft, to settle the MX basing problem. In April of 1983, the Scowcroft Commission recommended that the U.S. build 100 MXs and deploy them in the silos that now house the older Minuteman III missiles, thus abandoning the search for invulnerable basing. In the summer of 1983, despite heated debate and a filibuster led by Senator Gary Hart, Congress approved the Scowcroft plan.

Opponents of the MX missiles do not limit their attacks to the question of deployment. They also contend that deployment of the MX would violate our treaty obligations. Although the SALT I treaty expired in 1977 and SALT II was never approved by Congress, both the U.S. and the USSR have agreed informally to be bound by their provisions, one of which bans new "fixed" launchers for ICBMs. The Reagan Administration claims that the MX launcher will not be a new fixed launcher because it will be a canister that can be moved from one shelter to another. However, this technical distinction isn't likely to defuse contentions by the Russians and other opponents of MX that the new system violates at least the spirit of SALT.

Perhaps the most bizarre aspect of vertical proliferation are plans for the development of outer space weaponry. Both the Soviets and the Americans have started work on systems designed to destroy the communications satellites that now operate in outer space. These satellites are the eyes, ears, and nervous systems of nuclear warfare. We rely on them for early warning and many other functions that are vital to both verification of arms control agreements and to our ability to launch a retaliatory strike or actually fight a nuclear war.

The 1983 United States defense budget provides multi-million dollar expenditures for space weapons research because the Pentagon believes that the Soviets are hard at work on such weapons. It has been reported that in 1979 the Soviets launched their first "killer satellite," designed to put American satellites out of commission. In both countries, work on these systems is proceeding despite the existence of a 1967 treaty that limits military activity in outer space.

Space weapons may well lead to a "use it or lose it" approach, forcing one side to launch its nuclear weapons before an enemy attack on its satellites renders such weapons useless or uncontrollable. Thus, the possibility of a real *Star Wars* is no longer very remote. In the Heritage Foundation's publication, the *National Security Record,* a June 1982 lead story headlined "High Frontier: A New Option in Space," noted that:

We can escape the brooding menace of "balance of terror" doctrines by deploying defensive systems in space. . . . We visualize a layered strategic defense. The first layer would be a spaceborne defense which would effectively filter a Soviet missile attack in the early stages of flight. The second layer would be a broader space protection system, perhaps using advanced beam weaponry to further reduce the effectiveness of a missile attack and to defend other space assets from a variety of attacks. The third layer would be a ground based point defense system capable of removing any Soviet assurance of success of a first strike against our missile silos—even *before* a space system is deployed—and of intercepting Soviet missiles which later might leak through the space defenses. A passive fourth layer would be civil defense, which becomes a valuable aspect of strategy in conjunction with these active defense layers.

On March 23, 1983, President Reagan sent shock waves throughout the world when he proposed that the United States develop just the sort of *Star Wars* defenses suggested by the Heritage Foundation. At a later briefing, White House aides explained that the President was speaking only about a preliminary feasibility study to assess the possible use of laser beams and particle beams to destroy or deflect Soviet missiles before they reached their targets. Reagan's aides also indicated that no such defenses were likely to be produced before the year 2000, and they declined to make cost estimates.

While talk of new defensive measures usually receives a sympathetic reception by those interested in peace, the opposite is true in the strange game of nuclear deterrence. Many scientists and military analysts reacted negatively to the Reagan speech, pointing out that such a program would increase the probability of a preemptive first strike by the nation in a position to ward off a retaliatory attack. In their view, pursuing the *Star Wars* scenario would also increase the probability of a nuclear exchange in outer space, since each side would seek to destroy the other's defenses. Even more frightening, perhaps, is the likelihood of a massive offensive buildup, since this is the automatic response to any new defensive system. How do you suppose the Soviets would respond if the U.S. built defenses that could stop 90 percent of their missiles? Obviously, they would build thousands of additional missiles to make sure the 10 percent that do penetrate American defenses will destroy the United States. So the arms race would be accelerated beyond any semblance of reason, with the cost of new defensive and offensive weapons overwhelming both superpowers.

With deterrence resting on an increasingly unstable seesaw, which, as we have seen, can easily be unbalanced by too great a show of strength, can we safely rely on the judgment of the government officials who must decide how much is enough?

This question was explored in a 1982 television program entitled "How Much Is Enough?" hosted by ex-Congresswoman Barbara Jordan. According to the program's narrator, in 1960, President Eisenhower had budgeted for 200 of our first ICBMs, the Minuteman I. However, the Kennedy Administration decided to build 1,000. Interviews with officials responsible for this decision revealed that the number 1,000 was practically picked out of a hat. Herbert York, who was director of research and engineering for the Pentagon during the Eisenhower-Kennedy transition period, said he believed the 1,000 figure was used hypothetically to simplify unit cost calculations, and that it somehow survived the decisionmaking process. Here is a key excerpt from the television program:

HERBERT YORK: . . . You can find a letter in the files where somebody asks someone else—someone asks a colonel to cost out an ICBM system. And he starts out by saying, "Well, let's assume there will be 1,000." And then he costs it out. That number 1,000 [laughs]—that is the origin of the figure of 1,000 Minutemen.

GENERAL MAXWELL TAYLOR [former chairman of the Joint Chiefs of Staff]: My recollection would be that [Secretary of Defense] Bob McNamara picked that number out as a good number. A thousand of the new missiles plus 54 of the old. He certainly asked me did that sound like enough, and I said, "It certainly does." . . . Whether any further scientific research was made on the subject, I don't know, and I doubt it.

HERBERT YORK: One thousand is a good, round number in our culture. A hundred seemed to a lot of people to be too small, and 10,000 seemed to be beyond what we could afford, so it comes out 1,000.

Consider another chilling example, this one from the 1970s. In a 1982 *Washington Post* interview, Roger Molander, nuclear strategy adviser to presidents Nixon, Ford, and Carter, told of his earlier job with a Washington defense think-tank, soon after he had earned his doctorate. The young scientist made theoretical studies of nuclear exchanges, based mostly on guesswork. Then he went to work for the National Security Council, and to his surprise he found that officials at the highest level of our government were ready to rely on the nuclear strategy developed from his minuscule experience:

I was at the White House's National Security Council only a few months when it was time for a SALT negotiating session to begin in Geneva. One of Secretary of State Kissinger's division heads asked me to draft a set of instructions for the American delegation. I asked what to put in the instructions—and was told just to do a draft on my own, with one cover memo to Kissinger and another from Kissinger to the president.

Three days later I got the package and the instructions back. The person who had asked for the draft had not changed a word. Nor had Kissinger. Nor had the president. The instructions were on their way to Geneva. I swallowed hard.

Those people above me who were supposed to be thinking about the Big Questions were relying on me to think about those things. I was to make decisions in the nuclear war trade, not just stick in pins. . . . I thought about the fact that nobody else around the White House seemed to understand nuclear war issues better than I did; knowing my limitations, that did not reassure me. . . . I had discovered that most of the senators on the Armed Services and Foreign Relations committees—those making critical decisions, to say nothing of endless speeches—lacked even a rudimentary understanding of the nuclear war business.

Does this mean that the three presidents whom Molander served were stupid or poorly staffed? I don't think so. I believe that the decisions involved are beyond the degree of competence that we have the right to expect in any president. Our presidents must make many guesswork decisions when they take on this brand new and temporary job. Often their advisers are even more transitory. In a field where most of the information is necessarily secret, most conclusions are not verifiable, and the deadly game is to be played only once and without practice—how can we rely on them, or anyone, to make all the right guesses?

These jarring examples illustrate just how desperate the situation is. The problems of the nuclear age cannot be solved by conventional political processes and remedies. The stakes are simply too high. Yet as long as deterrence holds sway, guesswork will be necessary. We must, therefore, seek a solution that allows us to avoid the necessity of guessing how many nuclear weapons are enough.

Horizontal Proliferation—The Spread of Nuclear Weapons to Other Nations: Unfortunately, the destabilizing effects of American-Soviet proliferation extend throughout the world. To date, France, Great Britain, China, and India have exploded nuclear weapons, and U.S. intelligence surveys published in 1982 estimate that at least 25 other nations will follow suit by the year 2000.

To deal with this menace, the United Nations General Assembly adopted a resolution that led to the 1968 Treaty on the Non-Proliferation of Nuclear Weapons (NPT). It has been adopted by 116 nations, including the U.S., the USSR, and Great Britain. However, France, China, and India have not signed it, nor have the three other nations thought to be close to developing nuclear weapons—Israel, Pakistan, and South Africa.

The Non-Proliferation Treaty prohibits both the transfer of nuclear weapons to any nations and the manufacture or receipt of nuclear weapons by non-nuclear weapon states. It also established the International Atomic Energy Agency (IAEA) to prevent diversion of nuclear fuel to weapons manufacture. Unfortunately, the IAEA has not been very effective. Black and grey markets have sprung up to supply weapons-grade uranium and other materials needed for making bombs, and the world has lost faith in the ability of the IAEA to control this traffic. This was made quite clear in 1981, when the Israelis attacked an Iraqi research reactor which had allegedly been diverted to military use. Absolute control of such material on a worldwide basis would be impossible even if all reactors were under IAEA scrutiny, which they are not.

The nuclear arms race between the U.S. and the USSR further undermines the effectiveness of the Non-Proliferation Treaty. Smaller nations have little incentive to abide by the restrictions of the NPT while the superpowers continue to make nuclear weapons the hallmark of national security. In a world where the nuclear missile is a status symbol, there is great pressure on nations such as Argentina to develop their own nuclear weapons. As dangerous as nuclear weapons are in the hands of the superpowers, they are even more likely to be used by smaller nations driven to desperation or ruled by unstable leaders. Imagine another Falkland Islands war with macho pressure on Argentina's leaders to nuke the British forces. Imagine the next Idi Amin armed with nuclear missiles! These nightmares can easily become reality. Controlling the threat of horizontal proliferation will require the combined strength of the U.S. and the USSR, and that strength cannot be applied until the two superpowers end their own nuclear arms rivalry.

When Alva Myrdal won the 1982 Nobel Peace Prize, she commented in her acceptance speech on the wide-ranging and serious effects of nuclear proliferation. Her message is disturbing:

> War and preparation for war have acquired legitimacy, and because of the tremendous proliferation of arms through production and export, they are now available more or less to all and sundry, right down to handguns and stilettos. The cult of violence has so far permeated relations between people that we are compelled to witness as well an increase in everyday violence. These are the examples we give to our young people. The crimes of violence committed on the streets are to a large extent a result of the spread of arms.

Freeze

The most widely supported improvement on MAD and NUTS is the nuclear freeze. As embodied in the congressional resolution introduced on March 10, 1982, by Democratic Senator Edward Kennedy and Republican Senator Mark Hatfield, it provides:

> 1. As an immediate strategic arms control objective, the United States and the Soviet Union should:
> (a) pursue a complete halt to the nuclear arms race;
> (b) decide when and how to achieve a mutual and verifiable freeze on the testing, production, and future development of nuclear warheads, missiles, and other delivery systems;
> (c) give special attention to destabilizing weapons whose deployment would make such a freeze more difficult to achieve.

The freeze, like many great ideas, is beautiful in its simplicity. Instead of requiring a series of complicated negotiations, it simply stops everything in place. It could be put into effect very quickly; indeed, Soviet Foreign Minister Andrei Gromyko virtually agreed to it in his address to the U.N. General Assembly on June 15, 1982. While it still leaves the world with 50,000 nuclear warheads to worry about, it would provide a breathing spell, during which further steps toward disarmament could be taken in a much more hospitable atmosphere than the present one. With a freeze in effect, the U.S. and the USSR could jointly, and with greater credibility and moral authority, work out plans to enforce against other nations the Nuclear Non-Proliferation Treaty. A breathing spell would also forestall the build-up of tensions that would otherwise accompany the introduction of the new destabilizing weapons, such as the cruise missile and the killer space satellites. Once that next generation of weapons is deployed, a freeze will not be nearly as promising a step toward nuclear disarmament.

The Kennedy-Hatfield freeze resolution came to a vote in the House of Representatives on August 5, 1982, and was defeated by the narrow margin of 204 to 202. It probably would have won by a comfortable margin but for the introduction and passage of a rival resolution, which was backed by the Reagan White House. This resolution said:

> The Congress supports the initiation of the strategic arms reduction talks and urges the Soviet Union to join with the United States in concluding an equitable and verifiable agreement which freezes strategic nuclear forces at equal and substantially reduced levels.

"Equal and substantially reduced levels" is the key phrase of the Reagan freeze concept. By emphasizing the reduction of nuclear arsenals, it appears to be a greater step toward disarmament than the

Kennedy-Hatfield measure. By specifying "equal" levels, it nullifies the Reagan Administration's primary objection to the Kennedy-Hatfield plan: that it would freeze nuclear arsenals at a time when the USSR had the upper hand, locking the U.S. into a position of permanent inferiority and thus inviting the Soviets to make brutal use of their superiority. In opposing the freeze, U.S. Air Force General David C. Jones, who served as chairman of the Joint Chiefs of Staff from 1978 to 1982, said, "The Soviets have essentially completed major modernization programs, while we are still living off the investments of the 1960s."

Unfortunately, waiting until strategic forces are at equal levels is at best a futile gesture since in all probability equality will never occur. If we deploy the MX, the cruise missiles, and our other new weapons to regain what we call "parity," it will be the Soviets' turn to refuse a freeze until they have spent billions more catching up. This seesaw game would delay a freeze for at least 5 to 10 years, to say nothing of its destabilizing effect on the delicate balance of MAD-NUTS deterrence. During that period, reaction time would be reduced to a few minutes, and the economies of both superpowers would probably be in shambles—conditions that could trigger a war. Furthermore, any attempt on our part to achieve superiority (if that can ever really be measured) would involve heavy political strife to justify such peacetime expenditures, as the Reagan Adminstration learned in its futile efforts to sell the Dense Pack MX program to Congress in 1982. The Soviets, however, would not be tied down by the constraints of the democratic process; the Kremlin could simply direct Russian factories to produce missiles instead of their regular output.

While the Reagan Administration insists that a freeze at present levels would seriously curtail its disarmament negotiating leverage, most Americans apparently disagree. Freeze resolutions on the ballots in the 1982 midterm elections were approved in 8 out of 9 states and 28 out of 30 counties, indicating that American voters rejected not only the "inferiority" argument, but also the Administration's other objections to a freeze: that it was Soviet-inspired, and that we could not trust the Soviets to conform even if we did agree to a freeze. Obviously, to most Americans, the Soviet Union's willingness to agree to a freeze was reassuring since it indicates that efforts to obtain one would not be wasted. As to trusting the Soviets, the word "verifiable" in the Kennedy-Hatfield resolution means that only what can be verified will be frozen.

In 1983, Congress again voted on a freeze resolution. Its proponents were unable to gain approval of the language in the Kennedy-

Hatfield plan, but the House passed a modified version calling for a freeze that would be revoked automatically unless it was followed by negotiated arms reductions within a specified reasonable period of time. This freeze resolution was defeated in the Senate, thanks to the backlash of the Korean Air Lines disaster and intensive pressure from the White House. But even if Congress passes a pure freeze resolution and local freeze resolutions continue to gain support in state elections, the Reagan Administration is not likely to adopt the freeze strategy. Sitting at their council tables with secret information that cannot be made available to us, Reagan's staff believes it is their duty to delay a freeze until the cruise missiles and Pershing IIs are deployed and plans for the MX have been solidified.

Thus, while a freeze would obviously be a major step in the right direction, implementation is extremely unlikely in view of the Administration's commitment to MAD-NUTS deterrence. Nor is a freeze really a practical alternative to deterrence, since it leaves both powers with huge arsenals that they must continue to brandish at each other in order to maintain the requisite credibility. Disarmament is the only real solution to the nuclear nightmare, and a freeze is not so much a step toward disarmament as a halting of the march in the opposite direction.

No-First-Use Pledges

The NATO plan for the defense of Europe against a Soviet non-nuclear attack rests on a triad of strategies: first, use of conventional forces; then, if conventional forces cannot hold, the "limited nuclear war" concept of using tactical (short-range) nuclear weapons against the attacking Soviet forces; then, if necessary, use of U.S. strategic (long-range) nuclear weapons to hit Russian targets. This flexible-response strategy was developed during the 1960s at the request of the European NATO nations, in recognition of the superiority of Soviet conventional forces. It places NATO in the position of openly threatening to be the first to use nuclear weapons.

By 1982, many of those who supported this first-use threat had begun to have second thoughts. Among them were four high-ranking former U.S. officials: McGeorge Bundy, George F. Kennan, Robert S. McNamara, and Gerard Smith. They published a landmark paper, "Nuclear Weapons and the Atlantic Alliance," in the spring 1982 edition of *Foreign Affairs* and were especially negative about the prospects for limiting nuclear exchanges to the battlefield area once NATO made its first strike:

It is time to recognize that no one has ever succeeded in advancing any persuasive reason to believe that any use of nuclear weapons, even on the smallest scale, could reliably be expected to remain limited. Every serious analysis and every military exercise, for over 25 years, has demonstrated that even the most restrained battlefield use would be enormously destructive to civilian life and property. There is no way for anyone to have any confidence that such a nuclear action will not lead to further and more devastating exchanges. Any use of nuclear weapons in Europe, by the Alliance or against it, carries with it a high and inescapable risk of escalation into the general nuclear war which would bring ruin to all and victory to none.

But contrary to popular conception, these distinguished authors did not flatly condemn the NATO first-use strategy. Rather, they recommended a reevaluatiuon of this policy as a way of finding a less dangerous defense strategy.

Shortly after publication of this article, Soviet Foreign Minister Andrei Gromyko delivered this message from President Brezhnev at the June 1982 U.N. Special Session on Disarmament: "The Soviet state solemnly declares the Union of Soviet Socialist Republics assumes an obligation not to be the first to use nuclear weapons." The Soviets immediately made strong propaganda use of this initiative. In the June 26, 1982 *Soviet Weekly,* published in London, the banner headline on page 1 read: "WE WILL NEVER BE FIRST TO USE NUCLEAR WEAPONS." The lead article went on to say:

> The Soviet Union has pledged officially that it will never be the first to use nuclear weapons. . . . The pledge, made on behalf of the 260 million Soviet people, becomes effective immediately.
>
> The USSR has thereby taken yet another unilateral initiative in what is the most urgent and important concern of all mankind—halting the endless build-up of ever more destructive types of weapons.
>
> The Soviet Union has taken this step although NATO makes no secret of the fact that its military doctrine not only doesn't rule out making a nuclear first strike, but is actually based on that concept.

So, right on the heels of the stirring march to Central Park, here was a chance to end the nuclear nightmare! Brezhnev had pledged before the world never to use nuclear weapons first; if Ronald Reagan gave the same pledge, nuclear war couldn't occur because nobody would ever fire the first missile. Therefore, both sides could begin to dismantle their nuclear arsenals. Right?

Wrong. That same old stumbling-block—the deep-seated distrust on both sides—makes these no-first-use pledges meaningless. As U.S. Air Force General David Jones, former chairman of the Joint Chiefs of Staff, said in a July 1982 article in *Defense* magazine:

> The no first use proposal fails to account for the conventional force imbalance. . . . If in a political crisis the Soviets believed that they could launch a successful conventional attack against NATO without fear of a possible nuclear response, their incentive to do so—and thus the probability of armed conflict—would be greatly increased.

***

> Furthermore, it is unreasonable to expect that promises made with cool reason in peacetime will be kept in the heat of battle when a nation is threatened with military conquest. Either a defensive nuclear response to conventional attack or a preemptive nuclear strike by the aggressor would still remain possibilities regardless of declaratory policies. Paradoxically then, a declaratory policy of no first use may well lead to the very outcome its proponents seek to avoid—an increased likelihood of conflict and escalation to nuclear warfare.

***

> Rather than a declaratory policy of no first use of nuclear weapons, therefore, NATO has a more comprehensive policy of no first use of military force.

Thus, the no-first-use pledge, like all other disarmament proposals, is a two-edged sword. In the mind-boggling game of deterrence, it might either lead to disarmament or bring on a nuclear war. For that reason, the U.S. has never made a no-first-use pledge, either in connection with NATO or any other theater.

Nuclear-Free Zones

The concept of a nuclear-free zone was first discussed in 1956, when the Soviets proposed to the U.N. Disarmament Subcommittee that a zone of "arms limitation and inspection" be established in Central Europe. No nuclear weapons could be deployed in this zone, which was to include East and West Germany as well as neighboring states. At the time, the Soviets had superior conventional forces and decidedly inferior nuclear forces; thus a nuclear-free zone (NFZ) would have strengthened their position in Europe. For those reasons, NATO refused to negotiate for a European NFZ unless conventional forces were also eliminated or reduced.

After 1956, there were many attempts to establish NFZs outside of Central Europe. In 1957 there was a Romanian proposal to denuclearize the Balkans. In 1959, Ireland called for denuclearization of the entire planet, region by region; the Chinese People's Republic also spoke out for a nuclear-free Pacific Ocean and Asia. In 1960, several African nations proposed an agreement to denuclearize the whole continent.

In 1961, the Swedish government presented the Unden Plan to the U.N., proposing a "non-atomic club," but it was rejected for the same reason that defeated the 1956 Soviet NFZ plan: NATO would not agree to an NFZ without simultaneous reductions in conventional forces. Other unsuccessful attempts to create nuclear-free zones include the Nordic NFZ suggested by Nikita Khrushchev in 1959, and New Zealand's proposal for a nuclear-free South Pacific in the wake of India's "peaceful" nuclear explosion.

Finally in 1967 came the first treaty establishing an NFZ. Most of Latin America has ratified the Treaty of Tlatelalco, which prohibits "possession, transportation or production of nuclear weapons in Latin America or the establishment of military bases there for nuclear weapons." However, this treaty has little practical value, since Cuba, the most likely base for Soviet nuclear missiles, has refused to join, and Argentina and Brazil—the two Latin American nations most likely to develop their own nuclear weapons—have not effectively joined it. Argentina has signed but not ratified the treaty; Brazil has ratified it, but has refused to implement it until Argentina and Cuba are fully bound by it.

The European NFZ idea was revived in the 1980s by Olof Palme, when he headed the Independent Commission on Disarmament and Security Issues, an unofficial international group with many prominent members. When Palme regained the office of Prime Minister of Sweden in 1982, his first foreign policy move was to propose that NATO and the Warsaw Pact nations establish a 186-mile wide NFZ on the border between East Germany and West Germany. At the same time, many local European governments took it upon themselves to declare their own territories nuclear-free zones. More than 120 cities in Great Britain, including Birmingham and Manchester, have adopted resolutions proclaiming local nuclear-free zones. These actions have no legal effect, but they demonstrate the strong grass-roots opposition to the deployment of nuclear weapons on European soil.

Although an NFZ might be a useful first step in decelerating the arms race by opening up a corridor of daylight and gradually expanding it, given the great range and speed of nuclear missiles, the zone would have to be quite wide to be an effective peace-keeping measure. Nor is NATO likely to agree to the establishment of a European NFZ unless the Soviets agree to reduce their conventional forces. Which brings us right back to the one stumbling block that bedevils all these proposed remedies: the distrust between the Soviet Union and the Western alliance. As long as both sides perceive these measures as mere bargaining chips in the escalation game, none is likely to be of much practical value.

Arms Control and Disarmament Treaties

America's move toward nuclear arms control and disarmament began during the 1950s, when President Eisenhower took the initiative and opened negotiations with Soviet Premier Khrushchev. Eisenhower's first goal was a comprehensive treaty that would ban all testing of nuclear weapons, and by 1960, U.S. and Soviet negotiators had actually agreed on the basic principles of such a treaty. Shortly thereafter, an American U-2 spy plane was shot down in the act of spying on Russian territory, and the subsequent cooling of Soviet-American relations not only forced cancellation of the Vienna summit at which negotiations were to be concluded, but also killed the test ban treaty for the remainder of Eisenhower's term in office.

When John F. Kennedy took office in 1961, he renewed negotiations. However, the Test Ban Treaty that was finally approved in 1963 was far from comprehensive; although it prohibited tests in the atmosphere and the oceans, underground testing remained permissible. Thus, while the 1963 Partial Test Ban Treaty helped to save the world's population from the effects of atmospheric fallout, it did little to slow down the arms race. In fact, since 1963 the nuclear powers have stepped up underground nuclear testing, and attempts to revive the Comprehensive Test Ban Treaty have been unsuccessful. With both sides committed to MAD-NUTS deterrence, the military must have a means of testing new weapons.

The most recent and strongest thrusts for arms control and reduction have been the Strategic Arms Limitations Treaties of 1972 and 1979. SALT I, signed in Moscow in May 1972, came into force on October 3, 1972, and set a five-year freeze on the aggregate number of fixed land-based ICBM launchers and submarine-based missile launchers. As to strategic defensive weapons, it restricted deployment of antiballistic missile (ABM) systems to one site in each nation. This provision was largely meaningless, however, since the treaty was limited to the ABM systems existing in 1972, which were all ineffective, and did not prohibit development of new defensive systems, such as laser beams. This once again demonstrates the difficulty of achieving any significant arms control breakthrough in the current climate of American-Soviet relations. Nevertheless, the ABM agreement was considered an enormous achievement, even though the inadequacy of existing systems was the main reason why both nations were willing to sign the treaty.

SALT I's expiration date was 1977, at which time it was to be replaced by SALT II. However, in September of that year, both the U.S. and the USSR voluntarily agreed to continue to respect the SALT I provisions.

SALT II, signed in Vienna on June 18, 1979, has never come into force because it has never been ratified by the United States. Opposition to it was led by Washington Senator Henry Jackson, who argued that it placed the United States in an inferior position because it left intact the heavy ICBM systems, an area in which the USSR had (and has) the advantage. In addition, in the wake of Soviet and Cuban military adventures in Afghanistan, Angola, Ethiopia, and South Yemen, neither Carter nor Reagan was in a position to submit SALT II to the Senate for ratification. There were, in any case, grave doubts about its effectiveness in limiting the arms race. The numerical limits placed on strategic nuclear weapons were very high, practically in line with both nations' future defense budgets. Indeed, during SALT II's six-year life, deployment of many of the most destabilizing weapons would have been permitted to increase by 50 to 70 percent.

In place of SALT II, President Reagan initiated a treaty process that he called START—Strategic Arms Reduction Talks. START is more ambitious than SALT because it provides for the actual elimination of nuclear weapons. For this reason, however, it is not considered likely to result in any agreement, since it would involve negotiators in painstaking comparisons of apples versus oranges, in order to evaluate their respective arsenals. Nor are the Soviets likely to agree to the U.S. proposal that opened START talks on June 30, 1982. This proposal calls for a reduction of strategic missiles to approximately one half of current U.S. levels, and would therefore require the Soviets to discard a lot more of their weapons than would the United States. And if past experience is any guide, START's future is dubious at best; in the entire history of the nuclear age, not a single weapon has been scrapped as a result of a treaty.

During this same period, the Reagan Administration began efforts to deal with the increasingly tense situation in Europe. In December of 1979, NATO ministers had met in Brussels to discuss the Soviet military buildup that had widened the Warsaw Pact's superiority over NATO forces. As noted earlier, because NATO was unable to match this conventional buildup, the ministers decided unanimously that the U.S. should bolster their defenses by deploying 108 Pershing II missiles and 464 ground-launched cruise missiles in Europe. These intermediate-range missiles, which were capable of obliterating important targets in the Soviet Union, would be owned and controlled by the U.S., with the European NATO allies merely supplying the sites. All 108 Pershing IIs were to be based in West Germany. The cruise missiles were to be deployed as follows: 160 in Great Britain; 112 in Italy; 96 in West Germany; 48 in Belgium; and 48 in the Netherlands. Deployment was scheduled to begin in December of 1983, and it would be at least four years before all 572 were in place.

In 1979, the U.S. already had 7,000 nuclear warheads deployed in Europe, but they were short range battlefield-type weapons that did not threaten targets in the Soviet Union. Thus, the 1979 NATO decision dramatically increased the stakes in the deterrence game, and the reaction to it created new political forces that threatened to paralyze European parliaments and to destroy NATO.

In practical terms, deployment meant that the people of Western Europe would be held hostage to both the U.S. and the Soviet deterrence game players. The decision to send Warsaw Pact forces into Western Europe would be made in Moscow; the decision to retaliate with nuclear weapons would be made in Washington. And right in the middle of this deadly crossfire would be the millions of people of Western Europe whose lives would be snuffed out in the first few minutes of a nuclear exchange. In fact, a European holocaust could occur even without a Soviet move on Western Europe. Any nuclear exchange between the U.S. and the USSR—even if it arose from a conflict in the Middle East or Latin America or from a Pearl Harbor-type strike—would force the USSR to destroy the new European-based Pershing IIs and cruise missiles immediately; otherwise, they could be used by the U.S. to devastate the Soviet Union. The NATO ministers knew this, of course, but they felt they had to do something to counter the Soviet buildup of nuclear and conventional forces, and they were neither willing nor able to commit their nations to the only other alternative: a massive buildup of conventional forces.

The 1979 decision was made at least partly as a ploy in the deterrence game, in the hope that it would spur the Soviets to remove some of their medium-range missiles trained on European targets. In fact, concurrent with the deployment plan was a call for a renewal of Soviet-American arms control negotiations, in the hope that an agreement could render deployment unnecessary. To that end, American and Soviet negotiators met in Geneva on November 30, 1981, to discuss the reduction of intermediate-range nuclear forces (INF). The United States opened negotiations with Reagan's "zero option" proposal, offering to scrap its NATO deployment plan in exchange for Soviet dismantling of all the SS-4, SS-5, and SS-20 intermediate-range missiles they had trained on Western Europe. Although this proposal would have effectively reduced the nuclear threat in the European theater, it was not considered realistic since it would have required the Soviets to dismantle 600 existing missiles in return for a mere NATO promise to abandon future deployment plans.

In December of 1982, the Soviets announced a clever counterproposal to zero option. If NATO refrained from deploying the Pershing II and cruise missiles, the Soviets would remove all but 162 of their SS-20 intermediate-range missiles aimed at Europe. The figure of 162 was selected because Britain and France had exactly that many intermediate-range land-based missiles aimed at the Soviet Union. But Great Britain and France immediately denounced the Soviet proposal, arguing that because those missiles were under their own national control, they should not be considered part of NATO forces. The United States offered similar objections, refusing to use the British and French missiles as bargaining chips in the negotiations.

While the Soviet proposal was seen by some as a hopeful sign, total INF withdrawal from Europe would, in fact, have little practical impact on the nuclear threat. Europe would remain dependent on America's own strategic missiles to counter a Soviet movement into Western Europe, as stipulated under the NATO treaty. And NATO's only real deterrent to the USSR's superior conventional forces would continue to be its first-strike option. Furthermore, since the SS-20s are mobile enough to be returned to the European theater quickly, moving them from present launching sites would not bring any real measure of security to NATO nations.

In March of 1983 Reagan modified the zero option plan by offering to limit NATO's deployment of new intermediate-range missiles to whatever number the Soviets would scale down to in Europe and Asia, thereby giving each side the same total number of warheads. At the same time, Reagan indicated that the U.S. planned to deploy at least 100 of the new intermediate missiles. Even at this reduced level, it was impossible to tell whether the NATO governments would be able to gain parliamentary approval to deploy the new missiles when the moment of truth came. And that moment would last far beyond deployment of the first few missiles in December of 1983. The Kremlin is likely to exploit the divisive nature of these weapons throughout the four years it will take to deploy all 572 missiles, by placing its own new intermediate-range missiles in Czechoslovakia and East Germany; by continuing its anti-American propaganda and its support of European anti-nuclear groups; by breaking off arms control negotiations (as it did in December of 1983); and by threatening to sharply increase the number of missiles deployed on its submarines. If, under this continuing pressure, some or all of these European parliaments eventually balked at deployment of the new missiles, what would be left of NATO defense policy—and of NATO itself?

Would West Germany and other NATO members seek accommodation with the Soviet Union, reasoning that the U.S. would not really expose its own cities to Soviet missiles in order to defend Western Europe? Would they decide that in the end, "red is better than dead"? This skeptical, neutralist attitude toward the NATO defense position was illustrated by a joke making the rounds in Europe. A member of parliament suggested that the entire defense budget should be scrapped and replaced by a tape recording to be played the moment the first shot of World War III was fired. The recording would be in two languages, Russian and English, and it would consist of two words: "We surrender!"

Clearly, as long as the U.S. and the USSR remain wedded to deterrence, treaty negotiations will remain simply another ploy in the MAD-NUTS game. Even when negotiations produce some kind of an agreement, it is, in most cases, meaningless. In 1973, for example, the U.S. and the USSR signed an agreement "on the prevention of nuclear war," with each nation pledging to prevent incidents that would further strain their relations. They also pledged to avoid military confrontations and to "exclude the outbreak of nuclear war." But in the true macho style of MAD-NUTS deterrence, they inserted a clause reserving their right of self-defense, leaving both parties free to employ nuclear weapons for that open-ended purpose.

In his 1982 book, *The Nuclear Delusion*, George Kennan, one of the leading advocates of arms reduction negotiations, sums up the difficulties involved:

> . . . political communication between the Soviet and American governments . . . will not be successful unless it is based on a recognition of the perceived security interests of both partners (even those for which the other partner may have small sympathy), and unless

it rules out extraneous issues and sticks strictly to the question as to how those security interests can find dependable mutual recognition in a world devoid of the massive military sanction. [p. xxix]

Despite his awareness of this stumbling block, George Kennan has suggested a simpler method of arms reduction than the START process adopted by the Reagan Administration. He would propose to the Soviets an immediate, across-the-board arms reduction of 50 percent, which would apply equally to *all* forms of nuclear weapons and thus circumvent the need to match disparate elements in both arsenals and select suitable categories for reduction. This plan seems to be an ideal step toward nuclear disarmament, but as of this writing there has been no movement toward such a solution. Others have urged the Reagan Administration to negotiate for a return to single-warhead missiles, and to seek agreement on the "build-down" concept of destroying two old missiles for each new one deployed. But in the absence of any degree of trust between the U.S. and the USSR, there is little hope for any meaningful treaties, regardless of the negotiating methods employed. This reality was made painfully clear during the United Nations' two special sessions on disarmament, the first held in Geneva in 1978 and the second in New York in 1982. For despite the impassioned support of millions of people throughout the world, the UN-SSDs made no progress whatsoever.

Treaty negotiations, then, are less a solution than a prospective means of solidifying peaceful relations *once a foundation of mutual trust has been laid.* For only when both nations recognize the advantage of building that foundation can they hope to find, in George Kennan's words, "dependable mutual recognition [of their security interests] in a world devoid of massive military sanction." The nuclear nightmare will end either in a treaty or a holocaust. And if we hope to avoid the holocaust, we must ask ourselves: What will put us in a position to negotiate an effective treaty? How can we build a foundation of trust?

Roger C. Molander, a former Pentagon nuclear weapons expert and now executive director of Ground Zero, made this very point in an interview published in *The New York Times Magazine* on July 11, 1982:

> The freeze campaign is a good way for people to express their concern about the dangers of nuclear war. But the lesson we can learn from the last 20 years is that focusing exclusively on arms-control agreements or the development of new weapons is not enough. The hard thing to face up to is that you can't get real arms control without improving relations with the Soviet Union.

Unilateral Nuclear Disarmament

As fear of nuclear war intensifies, there is a growing feeling that unilateral disarmament may be the only way out. This fatalistic attitude is far more prevalent, at least publicly, in the West than in the Soviet bloc, although there are undoubtedly thousands of people in the USSR and its satellites who also feel that nothing is worth the destruction of civilization.

The most significant expression of the unilateral disarmament philosophy has come from the British Labour Party. At its annual conference held at Blackpool in September of 1982, the Labour Party committed itself to scrapping the Trident missile system, closing all nuclear bases in the United Kingdom, and cancelling the scheduled installation of American cruise missiles in the U.K. This proposal was approved by a margin of more than two to one and thus became part of the official party program. While party leader Michael Foot did not use the word *unilateral*, the dismantling of Britain's entire nuclear arsenal called for by the Labour Party resolution would take place *regardless of any reciprocal action by the Soviet Union.*

As the December 1983 deadline for deployment of the Pershing II and cruise missiles in NATO nations approached, there were strong expressions of the "better red than dead" philosophy from other Western European nations, such as the public opinion poll taken in Holland late in 1981 which indicated that 72 percent of the Dutch people favored unilateral nuclear disarmament. But such actions are not likely to affect American and Soviet commitment to MAD-NUTS deterrence. Nor would American adoption of unilateral disarmament eliminate the possibility of a holocaust. If we disarmed tomorrow, and even if the Soviets followed suit, both nations would still be at the mercy of Red China and possibly other nuclear powers. Similarly, an all-out nuclear exchange between the Chinese and the Soviets would probably destroy most or all of civilization whether or not we had disarmed. Therefore, unilateral disarmament does not really afford the United States a choice between red and dead. We might first become red and then end up dead anyway. Our only choice is to seek Soviet cooperation in finding a way to end the nuclear nightmare for *all* nations.

Nongovernmental Solutions

With treaty negotiations offering so little hope for disarmament, a growing number of antinuclearists have concluded that our only hope is to circumvent the militarism inherent in national sovereignty by forming a world government, or by inspiring people throughout the world to force disarmament against the wills of their governments. Albert Einstein believed that creation of a world government was the only hope of saving civilization. In his footsteps, such prominent antinuclearists as Jonathan Schell, Robert Jay Lifton, Richard Falk, and Edward Thompson have expressed similar views. While they support efforts to achieve disarmament through treaty negotiations, they have all recommended more radical steps in the likely event that treaty efforts fail.

In *The Fate of the Earth,* Jonathan Schell concludes:

> In sum, the task is nothing less than to reinvent politics: to reinvent the world. . . . I would suggest that the ultimate requirements are in essence the two that I have mentioned: global disarmament, both nuclear and conventional, and the invention of political means by which the world can peacefully settle the issues that throughout history it has settled by war. [pp. 226–7]

Schell drew inspiration from Mahatma Ghandi's principle of nonviolent action, but understandably he did not lay out any blueprint for global application of this principle. In the end, Schell rests his case on the absence of any hope for peace other than the elimination of the present world political system.

In their highly praised book, *Indefensible Weapons,* Yale psychiatry professor Robert Jay Lifton and Princeton international law professor Richard Falk reach similar conclusions:

> To get rid of war, however, requires a new type of world order, including a far stronger sense of human identity to complement and complete the various partial identities of nationalism, religion, race, and ideology. The end of war implies, in effect, the displacement of Machiavellianism by a holistic world picture. [p. 245]
>
> ***
>
> A holistic world picture defines group coherence positively by a capacity to satisfy basic human needs of all people without damaging the biosphere or weakening reverence for nature. [p. 255]

Webster's dictionary defines "holistic" as "emphasizing the organic or functional relation between parts and wholes." Lifton and Falk do not clearly delineate their "holistic world picture." Like Jonathan Schell, they disclaim any intent to present a concrete plan or blueprint for ending the nuclear nightmare. They do not support the creation of a world government or a superstate, but they describe their concept as a "potential constituency of the whole world."

British writer and activist Edward P. Thompson takes a slightly different view. His plan is not to eliminate governments, but to circumvent them by people-to-people action. As he says in *Beyond the Cold War:*

> I am talking of a new kind of politics which cannot (with however much goodwill) be conducted by politicians. It must be a politics of peace, informed by a new internationalist code of honour, conducted by citizens. And it is now being so conducted by the international medical profession, by churches, by writers and by many others. [p. 183]

The problem, of course, is that physicians, church leaders, and writers have neither the responsibility of defending their nations against a nuclear attack nor the power to order disarmament. It is easier for them to break out of the mold of nationalistic militarism than it is for the American president or secretary of defense. Yet wouldn't any American president embrace a bilateral disarmament plan that didn't threaten our national security? Unfortunately, to date, no one has presented such a plan.

Perhaps the strongest thrust toward a non-governmental solution can be seen in the efforts of America's National Conference of Catholic Bishops to draft a pastoral letter on nuclear war and to come to grips with the seemingly insoluble dilemma posed by MAD deterrence. Although many of the bishops felt the use and threatened use of nuclear weapons was morally indefensible, they recognized the potential usefulness of deterrence as a means of securing a negotiated disarmament. In fact, Pope John Paul II's June 1982 message to the United Nations Special Session on Disarmament said in part: "Under present conditions, deterrence based on balance, certainly not as an end in itself but as a step on the way toward progressive disarmament, may still be judged morally acceptable." Meeting in Washington in November of 1982 to discuss a draft of the pastoral letter, the bishops seemed to be heading toward a position that would allow the use of morally unjustified means to achieve desirable ends. However, their acceptance of the morality of deterrence was qualified by their staunch position against the use or threatened use of nuclear weapons against nonmilitary targets. The problem, of course, is that such a form of deterrence would lack the very element needed to spur disarmament negotiations: credibility.

Seeking to head off a moral censure of MAD deterrence, the Reagan Administration responded with a letter by National Security Adviser William P. Clark. Delivered to the bishops' conference in November, 1982, it included these statements:

It is our policy, and that of our allies, not to use any force, whether nuclear or nonnuclear, except to deter and defend against aggression. . . . our decisions on nuclear armaments, and our defense posture are guided by moral considerations as compelling as any which have faced mankind. The strategy of deterrence on which our policies are based is not an end in itself but a means to prevent war and preserve the values we cherish . . .

After three years of study and debate, and despite intensive lobbying by the Reagan administration, on May 4, 1983, the bishops issued a pastoral letter that boldly attacked the morality of maintaining a nuclear arsenal. They called for a nuclear freeze, denounced any intention to use nuclear weapons against civilian populations, and proclaimed that deterrence was justifiable only as part of a serious effort toward disarmament. Some of the bishops feel that the 155-page pastoral is, in effect, a condemnation of any and all uses of nuclear weapons, and some have even called on Roman Catholics in the American armed forces to disobey any order to launch a nuclear missile.

The bishops hope their historic letter will spur government action toward disarmament. It would seem, however, a largely futile hope. Since the bishops' actions can produce no change in Soviet policy, it is unlikely that we can abandon our present policy of deterrence, regardless of its morality. Our own government's response to date was embodied in the Defense Department's 1983 annual report to Congress, which attempted to further defuse the bishops' opposition to American nuclear policy with these words: "Under no circumstances may such weapons be used deliberately for the purpose of destroying civilian populations." But lest anyone believe that the government was seriously considering the bishops' position, Pentagon officials assured reporters that this wording did not really represent a policy change. Rather, it was merely a clarification for the bishops and those who read the pastoral letter.

Back to Square One: Where Do We Go From Here?

Having examined all of the proposed solutions to the nuclear crisis, it isn't easy to remain optimistic about our chances for peace and survival. Yet we must continue to support these remedies and try to make them work, from the simple concept of nuclear freeze, to Jonathan Schell's complicated idea for ending national sovereignty, to the even more elusive concept of "holistic world picture" painted by Lifton and Falk. However, none of these ideas is promising enough to permit us to discontinue the search for a more basic solution: one that can bridge Soviet-American hostility and lay the foundation for a positive relationship upon which a lasting peace can be built.

The very fact that all of the solutions offered to date are unworkable or impractical illustrates just how precarious the situation is and how far out we must reach for a realistic remedy. We will not find it in the grab bag of conventional diplomatic maneuvers designed for the prenuclear age. We will have to come up with something as revolutionary as the splitting of the atom itself, as Einstein warned us.

Just how desperate we are for a new idea became apparent on Sunday, November 20, 1983, when the ABC television program, "The Day After," was watched by more than 100 million Americans. Following the telecast of the fictionalized nuclear devastation of Lawrence, Kansas, ABC news commentator Ted Koppel chaired a discussion panel consisting of William F. Buckley, Jr., Henry Kissinger, Robert McNamara, Carl Sagan, Brent Scowcroft, and Elie Wiesel. For an hour and 20 minutes these six men, who span the entire political spectrum and collectively possess the highest degree of knowledge and insight that our nation can bring to bear on the nuclear problem, talked about the problem without once bringing forth the glimmer of a solution. To me, that spectacle was more frightening than the watered-down scenes of nuclear holocaust that had preceded it. For a moment, I thought Henry Kissinger was going to turn the discussion toward a solution, when he said that the problem was not the existence of nuclear weapons but "the underlying political tensions" that might cause them to be used. But there the subject was dropped, and the panel returned to discussion of the symptoms while ignoring the disease.

The orientation of this book is to accept the world as it is, recognizing that the hawks, the doves, and the nuclear theorists might be either right or wrong. We'll never have enough information to make the right guess, and it doesn't really matter, because no one has yet advanced a solution that can work in the present climate of tension and fear between the superpowers. As the American Committee on East-West Accord puts it:

> Simply to be against nuclear weapons is not enough. The basic problem over the long term requires changed attitudes between the U.S. and the USSR.

Roger Molander has dedicated his Ground Zero organization to changing those attitudes, starting by educating Americans on the Soviet Union through books and media articles. In 1983, Ground Zero began "pairing" cities of the U.S. and the USSR, in the hope of fostering individual contact, understanding, and friendship between American and Soviet citizens. Ground Zero is also sponsoring "Firebreaks: A War/Peace Game," which simulates international crises that can lead to nuclear war. Ground Zero lists improved Soviet-American relations as the firebreak most likely to prevent nuclear war, and hopes that its program of simulating nuclear crises will alert public opinion to the need for such improved relations.

Is this program likely to improve broad-scale Soviet-American relations? Will greater citizen-to-citizen contact produce any changes in government policy? I hope so, but I don't think the probabilities are strong enough for us to rely on Ground Zero alone. I believe we need the kind of radical solution that SuperStock offers: a structural change capable of defusing the main source of friction between the U.S. and the USSR, thus making it profoundly logical and in the selfish interests of the people *and the governments* of both nations to become friends or, indeed, partners.

Chapter 3

Why Are We Fighting Marxism?

Nations don't distrust each other because they are armed; they are armed because they distrust each other. And therefore to want disarmament before a minimum of common agreement on fundamentals is assured is to want people to go undressed in winter. Let the weather be warm, and people will discard their clothes readily.

—SALVADOR DE MADARIAGA,
League of Nations Disarmament Officer

Our relationship with Moscow is inherently ambiguous. Ideology implies an ineradicable conflict; nuclear weaponry compels co-existence.

—HENRY KISSINGER

Although the nuclear arms race has awakened the world to the dangers of American-Soviet confrontation, it has also to some extent obscured the true nature of our 65-year history of enmity. Our joint emphasis on maintaining arms superiority and credible deterrent forces has created the impression that the battleground is solely in the military arena and that firepower is both the problem and the solution. But by focusing on Soviet expansionism, we have come to ignore—or at least minimize—the driving force behind that expansionism: Marxist ideology. While the struggle for military supremacy may be the most visible manifestation of our mutual hostility, the root of that hostility is not militarism, but an ideological conflict that began in 1917 when the Bolsheviks succeeded in translating abstract Marxism into revolutionary action. Marxism was from the start, and continues to be, the sworn global enemy of capitalism, and as such poses a serious threat to the United States, the world's leading exponent of capitalism. (In this discussion of ideology, we shall follow the style of the historians and the propagandists by using the terms *socialism, communism, Marxism, Bolshevism,* and *international proletarianism* interchangeably.)

Certainly, no differences other than our ideologies can account for the depth of enmity existing between the United States and the Soviet Union. We are not neighbors haggling over boundary lines, nor does either nation have designs on the other's territory. There are no historical reasons for deep enmity between the two nationalities, as there are between the Turks and the Greeks or the English and the Irish. Russia is one of the few major powers against whom we have never gone to war, and in World War II we were, of course, allies in a victorious cause. Although American propaganda would have us believe that Soviet totalitarianism is the primary cause of friction, our much-publicized commitment to human rights has not prevented us from supporting any number of repressive regimes when it suited us. What we find so objectionable is less the Soviet political system than the anti-capitalist ideology which sustains that system. Indeed, our support of many other dictatorships—in Greece, Spain, Portugal, the Philippines, Chile, and Nicaragua, for example—has been a direct outgrowth of our fear of the spread of Marxism.

Even as we trade accusations about imperialistic aggression and expansionism, what we're really talking about is ideology. For the most part, modern expansionism isn't about territory anymore; it is about ideology. The erosion of the British empire and other colonial systems has demonstrated the unprofitability of territorial conquest, and while we are still trying to expand our influence throughout the world, we no longer desire to do this by colonizing or occupying territory. Rather, both we and the Soviets concentrate on building "spheres of influence," usually via overt economic aid and (often covert) military aid. On our part, this aid is designed to contain the spread of Marxism, while the Soviets use their aid programs for exactly the opposite purpose: to spread Marxism throughout the world. Although this sort of expansionism is one public manifestation of our power struggle, expansionist policies cannot be sustained on either side without a supporting ideology. As Edward Thompson points out in *Beyond the Cold War:*

> The confrontation of the superpowers has, from its origin, always had the highest ideological content: ideology . . . has motored the increment of weaponry, indicated the collision-course . . . In both camps, ideology performs a triple function: that of motivating war preparations, of legitimating the privileged status of the armourers, and of policing internal dissent. [p. 67]

Thus are the battle lines drawn between the superpowers, each of which is committed to an economic system that is the antithesis of the other. And in the name of ideology, each has escalated the contest, justifying both expansionism and the arms race as the key to each nation's very survival. When we slice through the cold war rhetoric on both sides, it becomes apparent that the worldwide power struggle between American capitalism and Soviet communism has not only shaped much of twentieth-century history, but has also laid the foundation for the present nuclear crisis. British historian Geoffrey Barraclough, a professor at Oxford and Cambridge, has made a particular study of the impact of Marxist ideology. His 1967 textbook, *An Introduction to Contemporary History*, contains a chapter entitled, "The Ideological Challenge: The Impact of Communist Theory and Soviet Example," in which he says:

> Ever since the Russian revolution of 1917 people have depicted the drama of contemporary history as a tremendous conflict of principles and beliefs, a *clash of irreconcilable ideologies*. They have compared it to the struggle between medieval Christianity and Islam or between Catholics and Protestants at the time of the Reformation and have seen in it "the most vital issue of our time," "the great continuing conflict of the twentieth century." [p. 199; Italics mine]

Let us not, however, be mesmerized by the lofty notion that either side is trying to purify the world (although each would have us believe so). Rather, let us recognize that each side is seeking to protect—and often actively promote—its way of life or, in other words, its ideology.

The Clash of "Irreconcilable Ideologies"

To many Americans, ideology is a word better suited to the college classroom than discussions of real-world events. Yet, as "the body of ideas reflecting the social needs and aspirations of an individual, group, class, or culture," ideology has been a major cause of war and conflict throughout history—from the religious wars of ancient times, through the bloody crusades of the Middle Ages, to present-day religious and ethnic clashes in Northern Ireland, Lebanon, and throughout the Middle East. In earlier times, wars were often fought over the interests of individual sovereigns, the sole motivation being acquisition of territory or wealth. But the modern era beginning with the French Revolution changed at least the external face of warfare. As combat grew more sophisticated, involving several nations and requiring mass conscription, it was no longer possible for rulers to raise an army simply to satisfy their greed. Ideological justification became vital, as in Great Britain's assumption of the "white man's burden" to justify its colonization of much of the world. Remember, too, how we Americans rationalized our own expansion with the slogan "manifest destiny." Even Hitler needed his "master race" ideology to mobilize Germany and plunge it into World War II. And however expedient these ideological explanations may have been, they were also accurate reflections of the temper of the times, giving a name to what people wanted to believe in.

Because ideology articulates a nation's way of life—the most cherished beliefs of its people which they are willing to fight and die for—it is a key factor in the ability of governments to unite and mobilize their people. In recent years, however, it has become fashionable to dismiss ideology as irrelevant; to view international conflict as the result of mere lust for power. Certainly the desire for power is a basic human characteristic that must play a role in relations among nations, but to stop short of probing for the ideology that underlies the power drive is both shortsighted and dangerous, particularly when applied to our relations with the Soviet Union. Why dangerous? Because until we recognize precisely who—or rather what—our enemy is, rapprochement with the Soviet Union will not be possible. We are not simply engaged in a power struggle with a nation whose "muscle" matches our own, but with a revolutionary idea that cuts across all geographical, social, economic, and ethnic barriers—an idea that has and will continue to have enormous appeal for the world's vast population of poor and disaffected people. Says Geoffrey Barraclough in *An Introduction to Contemporary History:*

> ... in spite of its identification between 1917 and 1949 with the Soviet Union, Bolshevism was from the start, and never surrendered its claim to be, universal in approach and appeal. At the heart of communism ... was a deeply ethical concern for social justice, for equality between man and man.... Marx and Lenin spoke not for one country against others, but in the name of oppressed groups and classes all over the world, and this universality was beyond all doubt a main factor in ensuring their influence.... The emergence of a new world was matched by the emergence of a new ideology. Scarcely less important was the fact that, for the first time in history, it was an ideology which overstepped all geographical boundaries. [pp. 206, 214]

It is Marxist ideology—and the Soviet Union as its leading proponent—that poses a direct threat to the American way of life, which is based on private ownership and the free enterprise system. Yet we dare not raise the banner of capitalism to counter this threat, particularly since capitalism in its present form can no longer promise the good life to the vast majority of people. What choice, then, but to move the battle to safer ground, to focus on Soviet totalitarianism and repression? But however reprehensible Soviet disregard for human rights may be, exposing it does not reach the heart of the dilemma: that we are engaged in a death struggle of antagonistic economic ideas. It is within ideology—specifically the clash between two rival socio-economic systems—that we find not only the root of Soviet-American hostility, but the reason it appears to be a permanent condition.

As we move on to analyze the Soviet and American ideologies, bear in mind that while our other differences—nationality and political systems—*may* cause enmity, they do not *compel* us to be enemies. That compulsion comes only from the constant global conflict between capitalism and communism, each of which requires destruction of the other in order to survive. And remember too that of all the potential causes of Soviet-American enmity—ideology, nationalism, political systems, and human lust for power—ideology is the only one we can remove.

To put it graphically, let us chart the potential causes of Soviet-American enmity:

Factor:	*Nationality*	*Political System*	*Lust for Power*	*Ideology*
U.S.A.	American	Democracy	Human	Capitalism
USSR	Russian	Dictatorship	Human	Communism
Compels enmity	No	No	No	Yes
Can be eliminated	No	No	No	Yes

Ideology Russian-style: "Workers Of The World, Unite"

Those who dismiss the relevance of Marxism ignore the central role it plays in virtually every aspect of Soviet foreign and domestic policy. Remember that the Soviet Union itself was born in an ideological struggle to free Russia from Tsarist oppression and establish a government that would serve the interests of its vast peasant/ worker class. Whether or not Russian communism has succeeded is really not the germane point. What is important is that Marxist ideology not only provided the impetus for revolution, but has continued to serve as the Kremlin's chief means of legitimizing its power and offering to the Russian people a rationale for continuing sacrifice.

David Satter, formerly Moscow correspondent for the *Financial Times* and now an editorial writer for *The Wall Street Journal,* lived in the Soviet Union for six years. In a May 23, 1983 essay published in *The Wall Street Journal,* entitled "Soviet Threat Is One of Ideas More Than Arms," he offered some illuminating comments about the key role Marxism plays in the lives of Soviet citizens. To the average Russian, says Satter, communism is not unlike a religion, an article of faith that gives life meaning. Because the Russian citizen has no access to the kind of material possessions and goals most Americans take for granted, participation in a "great historical enterprise . . . gives a sense of purpose to what otherwise would be an unrelievedly bleak life." Moreover, notes Satter:

> What we have consistently failed to recognize—and what every Soviet citizen takes for granted—is that the power of the Soviet Union and its ability to expand do not owe principally to the military and political instruments that have built empires in the past but rather to *the success of an idea* and the desire of people to find a system of explanation that gives purpose to their lives. . . . As absurd as communist ideology may appear from the outside, it provides a consistent view of history to those who adhere to it and makes even the simplest citizen feel as though life has meaning, thus fulfilling, albeit falsely, a basic spiritual need. [Italics mine]

The essence of this "great historical enterprise"—and the main obstacle to any sort of trust between the USSR and the West—is the Soviet commitment to *worldwide* communist revolution, which Marxists see as the inevitable outcome of social evolution. Cooperation with the capitalist West, therefore, can at best be no more than a temporary condition, since the laws of Marxist class struggle cannot be circumvented by any Western notion of détente or "friendly" rivalry. With the eventual victory of world communism not only inevitable but irreversible, there can be, in Soviet eyes, no middle ground between capitalism and communism—and therefore no possibility of peaceful co-existence. As Thomas E. Larson, former chief of the U.S. State Department Division of Research on Soviet and Eastern European Affairs, points out in his excellent 1978 book, *Soviet-American Rivalry:*

In Soviet discussion of ideological and social systems the choice is said to be either socialism or capitalism. No third alternative is possible. According to this view nonalignment in ideology is ruled out; there is no intermediate system, no "zone of peace" in ideological struggle. [p. 159]

Given this sort of "either/or" thinking, it is not surprising that the Soviets view tensions between the superpowers as an inevitable product of ideological differences. This point is corroborated by sixty professional Sovietologists and national security experts in the 1983 Ground Zero book, *What About The Russians—And Nuclear War?* According to these experts: "The U.S.-Soviet conflict, and the cold war that developed between the two superpowers, was, in the Soviet view, a natural outgrowth of the clash between the socialist and capitalist camps each led" (p. 119). Little wonder, then, that generations of American diplomats serving both Democratic and Republican administrations have failed to halt the arms race despite the use of all known methods of negotiation. Ideological differences of this magnitude are simply not negotiable.

As a progressive revolutionary movement, Marxism was designed to free the world from the oppressive yoke of capitalist imperialism. Although Marx did not foresee the first use of his theories in a nonindustrialized nation like Russia, Lenin and his followers immediately embraced the worldwide revolutionary thrust of Marxism, which was designed to sweep away capitalism and the bourgeois democracies. As Thomas Larson put it in *Soviet-American Rivalry,* "They saw themselves as inaugurating a new era of world history just as surely as the Americans of 1776 saw themselves in the vanguard of human progress" (p. 28). This "new era" would, of course, witness the demise of capitalism, a notion decidedly uncongenial to the United States and its Western allies. That the global thrust of communism proved to be a major cause of Soviet-American antagonism is made clear in the firsthand observations of George Kennan, who was on the scene as a U.S. diplomat in Moscow in the 1930s. In *The Nuclear Delusion,* he writes:

The most important cause [of antagonism] was . . . the fact that the Bolshevik leaders looked upon the political and social system of [the United States] as a misconceived, regressive, iniquitous one . . . deserving of violent overthrow; and they conceived it as their duty, however poor the prospects for success, to encourage such an overthrow and to contribute to its realization wherever they could. [pp. 54–55]

Thus, from its very inception Soviet policy was built upon the duty to obliterate capitalism, perceiving in what Lenin defined as its inherent "imperialism," the natural enemy of progressive communism. This notion was and is central to Marxist ideology and serves to explain, in part, why peaceful ideological rivalry is impossible. For capitalism is not simply a rival economic system, but the major obstacle to creation of a worldwide classless society—an obstacle that *must* be destroyed if Marxism is to fulfill what it sees as its historic mission. According to the Marxist view, capitalism is the misguided way of the past; communism is the wave of the future. The inevitability of international revolution remains a basic tenet of Marxist ideology. This view is confirmed in the 1982 Program of the Communist Party USA, the concluding section of which states:

> Marxism-Leninism is the world outlook of the working class, the theoretical instrument essential for achievement of working-class political power. Nowhere has the working class achieved victory without it. This explains the phenomenal spread of Marxism. . . .
>
> Like Darwin's theory of evolution and Einstein's theory of relativity, Marxism illuminates mankind's true place in nature. By showing for the first time the laws governing the succession of the social systems, and proving the transient character of capitalism, Marxism qualitatively raises the level of self-awareness of mankind. [pp. 69, 71]

To the world outlook of Marxism-Leninism must now be added the Brezhnev doctrine. Promulgated in 1968 to provide ideological justification for the Soviet invasion of Czechoslovakia, it holds that all communist revolutions are permanent and irreversible; the USSR thus has the right to invade any communist nation to prevent anti-Marxist forces from trying "to turn the development of a given socialist country in the direction of the capitalist system." The Brezhnev doctrine is, of course, a one-way street, because all capitalist nations remain fair game for the forces of communist world revolution.

Importance of Marxist Ideology to The USSR

Soviet dedication to Marxist ideology and the price that dedication exacts—global conflict with the United States—is brought home dramatically in a fascinating book by General Sir John Hackett, *The Third World War: The Untold Story*. Although technically classed as fiction, it is based on the facts and insights Hackett gathered in high command posts in the British Army and NATO, as well as the views of half a dozen other military and political experts, including two former Russian officials. In the novel, Hackett posits the Soviets' "ultimate objective" of communist world control as the cause of World War III, which is "won" by the West. Writes Hackett:

> Had the USSR offered any convincing gesture of willingness to accept peaceful co-existence the Soviet Union might still be a great power today. It did not because it could not. Acceptance of the legitimacy of capitalist democracy was a contradiction wholly intolerable to the Marxist-Leninist ideology. [pp. 344–345]

Why intolerable? Because, as numerous Sovietologists and political observers have pointed out, such acceptance would cast in doubt the very legitimacy of the Kremlin's rule. Their role as keepers of the ideological faith is the basis of their authority, and any deviation from rigid orthodoxy would threaten that authority.

Roy Medvedev is a prominent Russian historian who has written many books and articles critical of the Soviet regime. He likens Marxism to a religion, so that consideration of the Soviet Union without Marxist ideology would be rather like looking at a Christian church without the New Testament or a Jewish synagogue without the Ten Commandments. The building would remain, as would the clergymen, but there would be no rational basis for their authority. In his 1980 book, *On Soviet Dissent,* Medvedev writes:

> . . . the Soviet regime isn't founded on a majority or a total consensus, but on ideology. Only Marxists, whatever that may mean today, have the right to rule; conversely, the ruling class justifies itself only by reference to the country's ideological foundations. It's a vicious circle, a religion, if you like. The USSR is the last great religious state on earth . . .
>
> Ideology is enormously important in the USSR, but much depends on how an ideological concept is interpreted at any given moment. That's because only those who command real power over the state and the ideological apparatus may carry out the function of authentic interpreting. [pp. 66, 145–6]

The rulers of the Kremlin were not elected to office, nor did they inherit a throne through the right of royal succession. Their grip on the reins of power is based entirely on the unique position of the Communist Party in the Soviet system, as embodied in the Soviet Constitution, the latest version of which was adopted in 1977. Some key excerpts follow:

CONSTITUTION
(FUNDAMENTAL LAW)
OF THE UNION OF
SOVIET SOCIALIST REPUBLICS

The Great October Socialist Revolution, made by the workers and peasants of Russia under the leadership of the Communist Party headed by Lenin, overthrew capitalist and landowner rule, broke the fetters of oppression, established the dictatorship of the proletariat, and created the Soviet state, a new type of state, the basic instrument for defending the gains of the revolution and for building socialism and communism. Humanity thereby began the epoch-making turn from capitalism to socialism.

After achieving victory in the Civil War and repulsing imperialist intervention, the Soviet government carried through far-reaching social and economic transformations, and put an end once and for all to exploitation of man by man, antagonisms between classes, and strife between nationalities. The unification of the Soviet Republics in the Union of Soviet Socialist Republics multiplied the forces and opportunities of the peoples of the country in the building of socialism. Social ownership of the means of production and genuine democracy for the working masses were established. For the first time in the history of mankind a socialist society was created. . . .

Socio-political and ideological unity of Soviet society, in which the working class is the leading force, has been achieved. The aims of the dictatorship of the proletariat having been fulfilled, the Soviet State has become a state of the whole people. The leading role of the Communist Party, the vanguard of all the people, has grown.

***

Chapter 1.
THE POLITICAL SYSTEM

***

Article 6. The leading and guiding force of Soviet society and the nucleus of its political system, of all state organisations and public organisations, is the Communist Party of the Soviet Union. The CPSU exists for the people and serves the people.

The Communist Party, armed with Marxism-Leninism, determines the general perspectives of the development of society and the course of the home and foreign policy of the USSR, directs the great constructive work of the Soviet people, and imparts a planned, systematic and theoretically substantiated character to their struggle for the victory of communism.

***

Chapter 2.
THE ECONOMIC SYSTEM

Article 10. The foundation of the economic system of the USSR is socialist ownership of the means of production in the form of state property (belonging to all the people), and collective farm and cooperative property. . . .

Thus, the CPSU controls the Soviet government through Article 6 of the constitution, which makes the head of the party—the General Secretary—the most powerful man in the Soviet Union. Josef Stalin never bothered to hold the presidency of the USSR; he ruled as a dictator from his position as Party Secretary. Leonid Brezhnev eventually added the title of president, but his real power came from his position as General Secretary of the CPSU. Also ranking high in the Kremlin hierarchy is the post of Supreme Party Ideologist, a position held by Mikhail Suslov during the first 17 years of Brezhnev's rule and later taken over by Yuri Andropov, who shortly thereafter succeeded Brezhnev as head of state. On Andropov's death in February of 1984, he was succeeded by Konstantin U. Chernenko, who also moved to the top from the position of Supreme Party Ideologist. On that occasion, *The New York Times* said of Chernenko, "The cures for all Soviet ills, he teaches, are ideology, propaganda, and party discipline." And in its edition of February 27, 1984, *Time* magazine quoted this excerpt from Chernenko's collected writings:

It is sometimes claimed that peaceful coexistence and détente, as well as cooperation, are impossible in conditions of continued ideological struggle. Some go still further, demanding that we renounce ideological confrontation. Nobody, however, can abolish the ideological struggle at will. This is an objective, historical category in a world where social classes and different social systems exist.

For these Soviet leaders, Marxist ideology is not only a symbol of their power, but the very platform on which they stand and from which they govern. As *New York Times* correspondent Serge Schmemann noted in a December 19, 1982 article: "The Kremlin rulers' claim to legitimacy rests largely on their pretensions as successors to Marx and Lenin, sole arbiters of the 'science' of Marxism-Leninism, and ordained keepers of orthodoxy."

This view is shared by many other qualified observers, among them George Kennan. In *The Nuclear Delusion*, Kennan explains why the Kremlin must protect its image as the center of worldwide revolutionary communism at all costs: its loss would raise doubts about the legitimacy of the regime both at home and abroad. As a result, in Kennan's eyes, the Soviet Politburo are virtual prisoners of Marxist-Leninist ideology (pp. 88–90, 153). British author Robert Conquest also confirms the vital importance of Soviet ideology to the USSR. In *Present Danger,* he says:

> The very acceptance of a closed ideology of absolute certainties provides the justification of rule, the mortar for the bricks of power and ambition. It is a further profound reason for their attitudes being so different from our own. [p. 13]

Even if the Kremlin leaders no longer believe in Marxist ideology and use its rhetoric only as a smokescreen, that does not make Marxism irrelevant. As Thomas B. Larson wrote in *Soviet-American Rivalry:*

> Although ideologies often serve a perceptual function for leaders as well as for the masses, concern here centers on the instrumental uses that the two ruling groups make of ideology to aid them in efforts to consolidate strength at home and gain influence abroad. For this reason, there is little need to bother about questions of sincerity, i.e., whether or not the ruling elite really believes in the propositions at the core of the established ideology. It does not matter all that much. [p. 118]

In 1976, two outstanding American journalists, Hedrick Smith of *The New York Times* and Robert Kaiser of the *Washington Post,* published books about their stints as Moscow correspondents during the early 1970s. Each delved into Marxist ideology, and they reached similar conclusions. In *The Russians,* Hedrick Smith uses an anecdotal approach to describe life in the USSR. In his long chapter on ideology, Smith recounts many conversations with Russians from all walks of life. He concludes:

> So, belief or nonbelief in ideology is not the vital issue, so long as the individual submits and does not challenge ideology openly. The system prevails, and along with it the ideological rituals which affirm and legitimize and perpetuate it. [p. 401]

And in *Russia,* Robert Kaiser observes:

> For Soviet communists the safe refuge is ideological orthodoxy. Those who demonstrate it prove that they are with us, not against us. In societies whose leaders rule with self-confidence, this kind of ostentatious display of loyalty is superfluous, but not in the Soviet Union. [p. 147]

In essence, then, Marxist ideology functions as the Kremlin's mandate to rule, and preservation of that mandate is the guiding principle of all Soviet policy. In his 1979 book, *The Unfinished Revolution: Marxism and Communism in the Modern World,* Harvard professor Adam Ulam points out that ideology has become an "indispensable servant of Russian nationalism" because the centralized control exercised by the Communist Party is its only means of forging any kind of unity among the USSR's fifty-odd national groups. He also notes that the USSR clings to outmoded farming practices which wreak havoc on food production, because any move away from collectivism—such as returning the farms to individual operation—might be interpreted by farmers (and even industrial workers) as a sign of the breakdown of communist ideology (pp. 231–251). For similar reasons, in the 1960s the Kremlin rejected economist Evsey Liberman's suggestion that Soviet industry might be better served by the injection of the profit motive and competition; this, too, was seen as a threat to the ideological orthodoxy that is the source of the Kremlin's power.

In *The Third World War: The Untold Story,* General Sir John Hackett dramatizes the methods the Soviet army would use to prepare its soldiers psychologically for battle:

> There was a completely unprecedented intensity of ideological work. Political commissars of every rank were conducting hundreds of individual and group discussions about the bestial face of capitalism and its blood-sucking nature, about unemployment, inflation and aggressive capitalist intentions. This went on, of course, during any training exercise, but not with such high intensity. . . .
> A message was then read out from the Government of the Soviet Union. NATO forces, it said, had treacherously attacked forces of socialist countries with no prior warning. All ranks, the message ended, soldiers, sergeants, warrant officers, officers and generals must now do their duty to the end, to crush this imperialist aggression by destroying the wild beast in its den. Only thus could the peoples of the world be kept free from capitalist enslavement. The soldiers enthusiastically shouted 'Hurrah!' as was expected of them. [pp. 9–10]

General Hackett's insight was confirmed in a 1980 nonfiction book by John Barron, *MiG Pilot,* the story of Soviet Air Force Lt. Viktor Belenko, who defected to the West in 1976 by flying his MiG-25 to Japan. From his early school days, Viktor learned that capitalism, while an essential stage in human evolution, "created an inherently defective socioeconomic environment based on selfishness, greed, and exploitation of the many by the few." And in such an environment, of course, "aberrant behavior" could be expected to flourish; thus, the "criminality, alcoholism, acquisitiveness, indolence, careerism, and other aberrant behavior that admittedly persisted in the Soviet Union to some limited extent were merely the malignant remnants of capitalism." This was, in part, an explanation for the presence of *zeks*—Russian political prisoners—in Viktor's hometown. And as a result of this indoctrination, "Viktor still pitied the *zeks* but now understood them for what they were—unfortunate victims of the lingering influence of decaying capitalism" (pp. 28–29).

Later, Viktor Belenko went to work in a tank factory whose educational section employed eleven artists full-time to paint posters proclaiming communist ideology. He learned that "true communism" would arrive in the 1980s, bringing with it the "new communist man," who would be "unflawed by any of the imperfections that had afflicted man through ages past" (p. 56). When he had passed the ideological, educational, and physical exams for air cadet training, he began 15 months of preflight academic studies in science of communism, history of the Party, Marxist-Leninist philosophy, mathematics, physics, electronics, tactics, navigation, topography, military regulations, and aerodynamics (p. 63).

Barron gives detailed descriptions of the ideological instruction that cadet Belenko received from the ever-present political officers of the Soviet Air Force in 1969–1970 (pp. 66–71). They mentioned persecution of the American Communist Party (which made Belenko question why there was no Capitalist Party in the USSR), and described the hunger, poverty, and unemployment in the U.S. (which made Belenko wonder who owned all the autos he saw in the educational films). They spoke, too, of the steady deterioration of American power under decadent capitalism:

> . . . no week passed without warnings of the dreadful threat posed by the encircling Dark Forces of the West and their plots to "kidnap our Mother Country." This ubiquitous threat justified every sacrifice of material and human resources necessary to build Soviet armed forces into the mightiest in the world. [p. 68]

This ideological indoctrination continued at the same brisk pace after Belenko completed training and became a pilot and an instructor. Each Soviet squadron had its own Lenin Room, where the pilots were required to watch Brezhnev's televised speeches and read *Pravda*.

Because such intensive ideological saturation is alien to the

Western experience, many Americans are more comfortable with the belief that ideology is essentially irrelevant, no more than a figleaf to disguise naked aggression and thirst for power. There are those who claim that "traditional Russian expansionism" is a more serious threat to the West than is Marxist ideology. A "tsarist mentality" is said to spring from Russia's historic insecurity as a nation. But in his 1980 book, *The Mortal Danger,* Alexander Solzhenitsyn effectively destroyed that theory:

> In recent years American scholarship has been noticeably dominated by a most facile, one-dimensional approach, which consists in explaining the unique events of the twentieth century, first in Russia and then in other lands, not as something peculiar to communism, not as a phenomenon new to human history, but as if they derived from primordial Russian national characteristics established in some distant century. This is nothing less than a racist view. The events of the twentieth century are explained by flimsy and superficial analogies drawn from the past. While communism was still the object of Western infatuation, it was hailed as the indisputable dawning of a new era. But ever since communism has had to be condemned, it has been ingeniously ascribed to the age-old Russian slave mentality. [pp. 8–9]

The theme of *The Mortal Danger* is that communist ideology, rather than so-called Russian characteristics, is the enemy:

> No matter what the illusions of détente, no one will ever achieve a stable peace with communism, which is capable only of voracious expansion. Whatever the latest act in the charade of détente, communism continues to wage an incessant ideological war in which the West is unfailingly referred to as the enemy. [p. 46]

The tsarist mentality theory received a big boost from the Soviet Air Force when it shot down a defenseless Korean Air Lines Boeing 747 jetliner on September 1, 1983. The Soviets' callous disregard for human life, their paranoid defense of their borders, and their outrageous conduct during the ensuing coverup attempt, all coincided with the most devastating caricatures of the barbaric Russian. It was a performance worthy of Tsar Nicholas II, whose Cossack troops shot down hundreds of unarmed Russian workers gathered in the square in front of the Winter Palace on "Bloody Sunday" in 1905. Yet President Ronald Reagan accurately ascribed the barbarism of the Korean Air Lines massacre to the communist regime rather than to the Russian mentality:

> From every corner of the globe, the word is defiance in the face of this unspeakable act and defiance of the system which excuses it and tries to cover it up. . . . We know it will be hard to make a nation that rules its own people through force to cease using force against the rest of the world, but we must try.

In the end, the shooting down of Korean Air Lines Flight 7 must be seen as a Soviet-Kremlin-communist performance, born of the paranoia that is inherent in the Kremlin's reliance on Marxist-Leninist ideology, rather than an act springing inevitably from Russian character.

Indeed, if we accept the tsarist mentality theory, there is no hope for an end to the nuclear nightmare, because there is no way we can change such a mindset. But even if Russian "expansionism" is viewed as the problem, Marxist-Leninist ideology remains the bedrock of Soviet foreign policy. Thus, we cannot hope to deal with Soviet expansionism peacefully until we have first solved the problem of the Marxist-Leninist commitment to world communist revolution.

Even those on the right who see in communism nothing but a tyrannical perversion of Marx's good intentions, perceive that Marxist ideology is still a key part of this process. As *Time* magazine diplomatic correspondent Strobe Talbot noted in his long feature article in the January 4, 1982 edition:

> . . . the Soviet Union's challenge to the West and the Communist challenge to capitalism and democratic socialism are one and the same. Lenin, Stalin and their successors have set out to alter the world in Marx's name but in the Soviet Union's national interests. Their objective has been not just to proselytize on behalf of their ideology but to enhance the prestige and influence—the security, as they would define it—of their own country. To this end, their ideology has helped greatly . . .

Syndicated commentator Patrick J. Buchanan put the matter even more bluntly in his column of November 19, 1982, written just after Andropov succeeded Brezhnev:

> If the Soviet Politburo should abandon the idea that the United States is its mortal, permanent enemy, what, then, is the raison d'être of the Soviet Politburo? To ask Andropov for an armistice, true peace in the war called peace, is to ask Andropov to surrender his faith and commit political suicide.

Here we have the very crux of the problem: the Kremlin leaders *cannot* seek peace with capitalism in its present form if they wish to maintain their power, because that power is based squarely on an antagonistic relationship with capitalism. For the Soviets, ideology *must* take precedence over all other considerations. Is it any wonder, then, that American negotiators, who systematically ignore the ideological issues, are unable to make progress toward arms limitations or disarmament? For no matter how American negotiators address the Soviets—whether in diplomatic, political, or military terms—they will be answered in Marxist rhetoric.

This inherent obstacle to disarmament is one of the key points in Arthur Macy Cox's 1982 book, *Russian Roulette: The Superpower Game*. In it, Cox points out that all disarmament negotiations between the U.S. and the USSR are fruitless as long as there exists a key difference in each nation's definition of détente. Because Americans view it as a cessation of hostilities, a relaxation of tensions, they find it difficult to understand how the Soviets could claim détente existed when Russian troops (or their Cuban surrogates) were shooting up Afghanistan, Angola, and Ethiopia. To the Soviets, however, détente is, by definition, a means of class struggle; thus, they see no contradiction between détente and the continuing war between capitalism and communism. Cox makes this point by quoting from a speech Soviet Foreign Minister Andrei Gromyko made in Moscow in 1981:

> Proletarian internationalism as a fundamental principle of Soviet foreign policy means that this policy consistently upholds the basic interests of world socialism, of the forces of the international communist working class and national liberation movements. As for peaceful coexistence [the Soviet term for détente] it represents a specific form of class struggle, a peaceful competition, precluding any use of military strength, between two opposite socio-economic systems—socialism and capitalism. [p. 152]

Even more telling is the Soviet response to Cox's suggestion about defining and renegotiating détente, which is included in the book in the form of a commentary by Georgy Arbatov, the Kremlin's leading expert on U.S. affairs. Not surprisingly, Arbatov's rejoinder is couched in Marxist rhetoric, even though Cox's suggestion was intended solely as a tool in diplomatic negotiations:

> All arguments advanced by Mr. Cox lack one essential element: He does not address the question of what forms of assistance to national liberation movements abroad are justifiable, according to our

political theory. . . . The heart of the matter is that the Marxist-Leninist theory rejects the idea of "exporting revolutions"—i.e., promoting them through military intervention. . . .

By the same token, we oppose the "export of counterrevolution"—i.e., attempts to do away with social and national liberation movements with the help of military interventions from abroad. . . . in practically all cases cited by Mr. Cox such attempts at intervention did take place, prompting us, along with a number of other socialist states, to provide assistance to respective movements and governments. [p. 189]

This enlightening Cox-Arbatov exchange underscores once again the vital importance of ideology in virtually every arena of Soviet-American relations. Even if American negotiators were to follow Cox's sensible advice about redefining détente, they would be met with the Soviet position that détente does not preclude continuing Soviet support (military and otherwise) of worldwide revolutionary movements in the cause of "proletarian internationalism," as defined by Marx and Lenin. Clearly, ideology will continue to be a focal point of all détente/disarmament negotiations, no matter how much Americans or Russians may belittle its relevance or vitality. Moreover, as long as the Kremlin can use the international class struggle as a basis (or pretext) for global intervention, there seems little hope of avoiding the kind of Soviet (or Cuban) military adventures that could lead to a nuclear exchange between the superpowers.

Assume for a moment that you are an American diplomat assigned to negotiate an arms control treaty with the Soviets. Assume, too, that you don't believe Marxist ideology actually motivates or controls the actions of the Kremlin or the views of Russian citizens. How would you handle these negotiations? Would you say: *"Look, Ivan, we both know Marxist ideology is as passé as the Cossack cavalry. Sure, you use it for your own purposes—to maintain dictatorial control over your people and to justify your armed aggression in other countries. But everyone knows this is just a ruse, so please put aside the Marxist rhetoric."* How far would you expect to get with that line of negotiation? Probably about as far as a Soviet negotiator might get were he to try a similar tack: *"Look, Sam, we're tired of hearing about America's fight to preserve human rights, freedom, and democracy. Everyone knows that millions of Americans are denied basic human rights, and that preserving freedom is just a convenient pretext for America to justify its capitalist expansion and continued oppression of the underclasses. So let's please put a lid on the 'freedom' rhetoric."*

The point, of course, is that ideology is a two-edged sword, as important to Americans as it is to the Soviets. Our commitment to our way of life under capitalism is as strong as the Soviet commitment to Marxism, and as long as these rival ideologies are pointed at each other as weapons, an end to our mutual hostility—and therefore a solution to the nuclear crisis—is impossible.

Ideology American-style: "Better Dead than Red"

Ideology is probably more important to Americans than to the people of any other nation. The United States was founded on the principles of freedom and democracy and, like the Soviet Union, came into being in an ideological war against monarchist tyranny. Our identity as "land of the free, home of the brave" is firmly imbedded in our national consciousness, providing the impetus for both our foreign policy and the zeal with which we pursue that policy. Indeed, many European politicians and journalists consider the United States almost naïve in its insistence on ideological justification for its foreign policy, fearing, with good reason, that Americans are more likely to go to war over ideology than are Europeans. Certainly, since 1776 we have engaged in many costly wars in the name of freedom and democracy—from the War of 1812 and the Civil War, through the Spanish-American War and World Wars I and II, to the more recent military ventures in Korea and Vietnam.

While many will question whether the preservation of freedom was really at stake in some or all of these conflicts, that was the official rationale for going to war. Without such ideological justification, the American people would be likely to withdraw their support from a government committed to a war in which they no longer believed (e.g., Vietnam and Lyndon Johnson). Although sloganism may be the most visible aspect of ideology—particularly in times of conflict—that in no way diminishes the relevance of ideology as an accurate mirror of public sentiment. To the average American, preservation of freedom may be an abstract concept, but preservation of the American way of life is more tangible; and the tangible part of our ideology is based as much on economic freedom (capitalism) as it is on political freedom (democracy). Whenever that way of life seems threatened, we have been willing to fight to protect it, although we have always portrayed our wars as struggles to preserve "freedom," without mentioning capitalism.

Many observers consider the United States to be almost paranoid in its fear of the Red Menace, precisely because as the leading capitalist nation in the world, it has the most to lose from the spread of communism. That fear—and the "better dead than red" principle it spawned—has not only guided our actions at home and abroad for much of this century, but has also prompted our continuing development of new and deadlier nuclear weapons. As Robert Jay Lifton and Richard Falk point out in *Indefensible Weapons:*

> The Soviet menace is generally perceived as real and must be addressed. In this regard most Americans continue to associate the security of their nation with a sufficiency of military prowess. For centuries such an image of security has been imprinted upon human consciousness. In relation to the Soviet Union it is specifically interconnected with the ideological legacy of more than sixty years of anti-Communist, anti-Marxist, anti-revolutionary encounters and propaganda. [pp. 210–211]

American Reaction to the Virus of Marxism: To the United States and its Western allies, the Red Menace became real almost as soon as there was a Soviet Union. As the first Marxist state, the Soviet Union provided Western Marxists a living organism from which they could draw inspiration for their own revolutionary plans. The existence of the Marxist state in Russia, coupled with the undeniable emotional appeal of Marxism, was to the West clear evidence of the dangerously infectious nature of the Marxist virus. And indeed, from the very first moments of the Bolshevik takeover, American Marxists looked upon it as an international revolution that would eventually extend to the United States, especially through the labor unions. In Harvard University's Houghton Library there is preserved a famous cablegram sent on October 31, 1917 by American journalist John Reed (the character played by Warren Beatty in *Reds*) to the socialist newspaper for which he worked, *The New York Call.* It reads:

> KALEDINE AND COSSACKS HAVE PROCLAIMED MILITARY DICTATORSHIP. GOOD TO BE ALIVE. TROTSKY AND LENIN THROUGH *CALL* SEND TO AMERICAN REVOLUTIONARY INTERNATIONAL SOCIALISTS GREETINGS FROM FIRST PROLETARIAN REPUBLIC OF THE WORLD AND CALL TO ARMS FOR INTERNATIONAL SOCIAL REVOLUTION. SEND ME MONEY.

But if Reed and his compatriots were jubilant at the start of the international socialist revolution, capitalist nations were terrified, immediately perceiving Marxism as a serious threat to their survival. Of this reaction, George Kennan writes in *The Nuclear Delusion:*

... what American statesmen now saw themselves faced with, in the person of the new Russian Communist regime, was ... a governing faction, installed in the seats of power in another great country, which had not even dreamed of declaring war formally on the United States but which was nevertheless committed, by its deepest beliefs and by its very view of its place in history, to a program aimed at the overthrow of the entire political and social system traditional to American society ... a program calculated to inflict ... a damage more monstrous in the eyes of most Americans than any they might expect to suffer from even the worst of purely military defeats at the hands of the traditional sort of adversary. [p. 18]

But although the Marxist enemy was not a traditional one, in that it posed no direct military threat to the West, capitalist nations responded in time-honored fashion—launching in 1918 an abortive military expedition to stop the Bolshevik revolution in its tracks. The rationale for this move was Allied military security: with Russia effectively out of the war against Germany as a result of the Treaty of Brest-Litovsk (March, 1918), the Allies immediately began landing troops in northern Russia for the announced purpose of preventing military supplies from falling into German hands. In point of fact, the Allied forces, whose troops were British, French, and American, actively supported the White Russian armies fighting the Bolsheviks; and although World War I ended on November 11, 1918, the Allied troops fought on in Russia into 1920, long after there could have been any legitimate concern about the safety of military supplies.

The principal architect of this Allied intervention was Winston Churchill, then serving as secretary of war. Although he publicly defended the move on the grounds of protecting supplies, his primary objective was to disrupt—if not derail—the Bolshevik revolution. For Churchill, as for statesmen of other Western capitalist nations, Marxism was from the start a contagious disease, capable of spreading to other nations if it were not stamped out during its incubation period in Russia. Later, in his 1929 book, *The World Crisis,* Churchill described the positive results of this intervention, pointing to the "breathing space" it gave the nations along Russia's western borders (Poland, Estonia, Latvia, Lithuania, and Finland), which were thus able to "establish the structure of civilised States and to organise the strength of patriotic armies." By 1920, these nations had become, in Western eyes, what Churchill called the "Sanitary Cordon," protecting Europe from the "Bolshevik infection" (Vol. 5, p. 288). By 1983, according to Richard Nixon, the Bolshevik infection had grown into "the ideological bubonic plague."

Thus, from the start, the West viewed Marxism not as a mere facade for Russian expansionism or nationalism, but rather as a potentially infectious virus. At the time of the Churchill-inspired Allied expedition, Russian military forces were crippled and the nation was torn by civil war. Certainly, the West did not fear that Russia would force Bolshevism down their throats; the Soviets were having enough trouble securing their victory on the homefront. True, Lenin announced that the Soviet Union would do its utmost to hasten the global spread of Marxism, but that could only occur if conditions elsewhere were ripe for its incubation. Russia itself was not the threat. (Indeed, at the time their support of international revolution was largely symbolic and verbal.) The threat, even then, was Marxist ideology, with its enormous emotional appeal to the hordes of workers and noncapitalists who had little or nothing to gain from capitalism.

It was the inherent weaknesses of capitalism—particularly its undemocratic distribution of ownership—that made capitalist nations vulnerable to the Marxist virus. The Western capitalist nations recognized that domestic dissatisfaction was a greater threat to their stability than the Bolshevik revolution. But instead of applying a domestic remedy by curing the illnesses of capitalism, they mounted their own ideological offensive—anti-communism—and channeled their energies into the task of undermining the Soviet Union. Thus was the stage set for the ideological warfare that has kept the world in turmoil since 1917: the seizure of dictatorial powers by Hitler and Mussolini, which led directly to World War II; the struggle to keep communism out of western Europe, which culminated in the Marshall Plan; the cold war; the Korean and Vietnam wars; the failure of détente; and the present nuclear nightmare.

The Global Slugfest

In the first volume of his World War II memoirs, *The Gathering Storm,* Winston Churchill describes fascism as "the shadow or ugly child of Communism." Explaining how Hitler and Mussolini came on the scene in the 1920s, Churchill writes:

> While Corporal Hitler was making himself useful to the German officer class in Munich by arousing soldiers and workers to fierce hatred of Jews and Communists, on whom he laid the blame of Germany's defeat, another adventurer, Benito Mussolini, provided

Italy with a new theme of government which, while it claimed to save the Italian people from Communism, raised himself to dictatorial power. As Fascism sprang from Communism, so Nazism developed from Fascism. [pp. 14–15]

In his 1983 book, *Marxism and Beyond,* Professor Sidney Hook, the dean of American scholars of Marxism, confirms Churchill's historical perspective:

The Bolshevik Revolution and the operation of the Communist International were largely responsible for the rise of Fascism in Italy and Nazism in Germany. They not only weakened the democratic structure of pre-Mussolini Italy and Weimar Germany by splitting the working class, but by their activities, including abortive attempts at insurrection, they enlarged the mass base and support for the demagogic propaganda of the forces of social reaction. It is not unlikely that if there had been no October Revolution and attempts by the Communist International, serving as the instrument of the Kremlin, to organize revolutions in western Europe, there would have been no victory of Fascism in Italy and of Hitlerism in Germany. [pp. 20–21]

These conclusions of Churchill and Hook are amply supported by the historical facts, which are recorded in illuminating detail in John Toland's 1976 two-volume biography, *Adolf Hitler.* In chapters 10 and 11, Toland describes Hitler's use of the Marxist menace to assist his takeover of democratic Germany in five hectic weeks of 1933. The preceding years of declining production and soaring unemployment had led to the escalation of armed clashes between Nazis and Marxists, resulting in thousands of casualties and great unrest. Old newsreels and snapshots of Nazi rallies of the early 1930s are replete with banners proclaiming slogans such as "Rot Front Verrecke!" (Red Front Perish!). The democratic process was virtually paralyzed as the extreme left vied with the extreme right for control of the parliament (Reichstag), government after government falling after only a few weeks in office. Five Reichstag elections in 1932 brought Germany no nearer to consensus, and as 1933 began, the country was close to civil war, a military coup, or both.

Against this violent background, Hitler convinced a reluctant President Hindenburg and other influential Germans that he alone could save Germany from Marxism. Hindenburg appointed Hitler Chancellor on January 30, 1933, and Hitler immediately called for another Reichstag election, to be held on March 5th. Hitler then urged leading capitalist tycoons (including the Krupps and I.G. Farben) to support his efforts to end the Red Menace. They came through handsomely, contributing the then huge sum of three million marks, enough to saturate the German electorate with Nazi propaganda.

On February 27, 1933, the Reichstag building was set afire by a Dutch communist. Hitler used the fire to fan anti-communist hysteria, and a week later he won a majority in the Reichstag election, which enabled him to claim he had come to power democratically. But his real coup in assuming complete dictatorial power came about through his clever use of the communist menace a week before the election. As recounted by William L. Shirer in his book, *The Rise and Fall of the Third Reich*, on February 28, 1933, the day after the Reichstag fire, Hitler convinced Hindenburg to sign an emergency presidential decree which suspended all civil rights, assuring him the measure was necessary to protect Germany from the "grave danger of a Communist revolution." This decree, in Shirer's words, "remained in force throughout the time of the Third Reich, enabling the Fuehrer to rule by a sort of continual martial law" (p. 274). It also gave him the power to put communist and socialist leaders in concentration camps, thereby eliminating effective opposition to his rule.

In Italy, socialism proved to be an equally useful bridge to power for Benito Mussolini who, ironically, had begun his career as editor of an Austrian socialist newspaper. But shortly after the start of World War I, Mussolini had a change of heart and became an ultranationalist, for which he was expelled from the Socialist party. After the war, he organized a group of nationalists and war veterans into the Fascist party, which was based on violent opposition to communism and backed by wealthy industrialists and property owners. He came to power by marching on Rome in 1922, but he did not consolidate his position as dictator until 1924, when he engineered the murder of Giacomo Matteotti, the Italian socialist leader who was the primary opponent of fascism.

Fear of communism not only contributed to the rise of fascism in Germany and Italy, but also helped it to flourish, staying the hands of those in England and France who might have stopped Hitler short of World War II. Quite a few Englishmen and Frenchmen shared the view of Krupp and I.G. Farben that Hitler's virulent anti-communism made him an asset to the capitalist West despite his embarrassing lack of manners. Repelling the threat of international communism was in fact the basis for the "Axis" alliance, as stipulated in the treaties signed by Germany, Japan, and Italy. The 1936 German-Japanese treaty was called the Anti-Comintern Pact. As Oxford historian A.J.P. Taylor notes in his book, *Origins of the Second World War:*

The Anti-Comintern Pact between Germany and Japan together with the vaguer anti-Communist Axis of Rome and Berlin . . . had a strong influence in England and France. . . . They inclined to be neutral in the struggle between Fascism and Communism, or perhaps even on the Fascist side. They feared Hitler as the ruler of a strong aggressive Germany; they welcomed him—or many did—as the protector of European civilization against Communism. [pp. 110–111]

This neutrality had tragic consequences during the Spanish Civil War of 1936–1939, in which the democratically elected government of Spain was crushed by the fascists led by Franco, armed and supported by Hitler and Mussolini and their foreign legions. The Spanish loyalists pleaded for aid from the United States, Great Britain, and France, but the little help they got came only from the Soviet Union, because the Spanish Popular Front government was dominated by communists and socialists. Thus, the Western democracies allowed the Spanish Republic to be taken over by fascists, and handed Hitler and Mussolini an important victory, because the international spread of collective ownership frightened the West more than the specter of dictatorship.

The capitalist/communist struggle was, of course, put on temporary hold when the Western democracies found themselves allied with the Soviet Union during World War II. But shortly after V-E day, the strife flared up again. Everything the Soviets did in Europe contributed to Western fear of the communist menace: military occupation of Eastern Europe that was converted into permanent political control; growth of Soviet-oriented communist parties in Italy and France; revolutionary breakaways from the old colonial system which the West viewed as victories for world communism. This led to the Truman Doctrine of 1947, which initially was used to keep Greece and Turkey from going communist under Soviet pressure. Thus began the cold war.

Soon after proclamation of the Truman Doctrine came the Marshall Plan, under which the United States pumped $12 billion (at that time a huge sum of money) into the war-ravaged economies of Europe. It was designed to undermine Soviet prestige and improve the economic conditions that might otherwise furnish breeding grounds for the virus of communism. The Marshall Plan is credited with keeping France and Italy from electing communist governments during the decade following World War II. It also had the side effect of paving the way for West Germany to become the most prosperous nation in Europe.

Despite the economic improvement fostered by the Marshall

Plan, Western Europe continued to view the Soviet Union as a serious threat to its security, particularly since the Soviets continued to maintain huge occupation forces in East Germany and the other satellite countries. Since the Western nations had already demobilized, the proximity of the Soviet's superior forces left Europe open to attack, and this fear planted the seeds of the North Atlantic alliance. Thus, in 1949, NATO was formed to counter the threat of Soviet military aggression. All the NATO nations pledged that an attack against one was an attack against all, and that all (including the United States) would respond.

Also in 1949 came the first Soviet nuclear explosion, which prompted both the American decision to go ahead with the hydrogen bomb and NATO's policy of basing the defense of Europe on nuclear weapons. Tensions were already running high when the Korean war broke out in 1950, and the West saw it as the start of the long-expected military push for worldwide communism, particularly since China was already squarely in the communist camp. As General Douglas MacArthur put it in his famous 1951 letter to Congressman Joseph Martin (the letter which resulted in MacArthur's dismissal by Truman for publicly advocating an attack on Red China):

> It seems strangely difficult for some to realize that here in Asia is where the Communist conspirators have elected to make their play for global conquest, and that we have joined the issue thus raised on the battlefield; that here we fight Europe's war with arms while the diplomats there still fight it with words; that if we lose the war to Communism in Asia the fall of Europe is inevitable; win it and Europe most probably would avoid war and yet preserve freedom. As you point out, we must win. There is no substitute for victory.

Note that in General MacArthur's view, the contest was between communism and freedom, rather than between communism and capitalism. Although virtually every communist statement about the Korean War portrayed the enemy as capitalism or capitalist imperialism, you will search in vain for any American public declaration that in fighting against communism in Korea, we were in any measure fighting *for* capitalism, the system of economic freedom that is an integral part of the American way of life.

Both before and after the Korean War, American politicians continued to follow the bipartisan policy of depicting communism as a threat to *freedom*, even when Soviet aggression was aimed at other totalitarian regimes. Indeed, when Truman asked Congress in 1947 to appropriate $400 million in aid for Greece and Turkey to protect them from communist incursion, he proclaimed: "Totalitarian regimes, imposed on free peoples by direct or indirect aggression, undermine the foundations of international peace and hence the security of the U.S." The fact that Greece was then ruled by a fascist monarchy and Turkey by a one-party dictatorship apparently did not disqualify them from the circle of "free nations," for the money was duly appropriated and the communist menace to freedom repelled.

This reluctance to acknowledge our ideological commitment to capitalism was equally evident in our second great war against global communism: Vietnam. In his 1982 book, *Planning a Tragedy: The Americanization of the War in Vietnam,* Professor Larry Berman offers a behind-the-scenes look at the Vietnam debacle, focusing on the deliberations of the National Security Council in 1965. In it, Berman quotes from an April 1965 speech given by President Johnson at Johns Hopkins University, in which he explained the reasons for our Vietnam involvement, using such catch phrases as "freedom," "strengthening world order," and "the insatiable appetite of communist aggression." Capitalism, of course, was not mentioned. And so it went throughout the fateful debates at the apex of American government. Berman reports that when George Ball argued in the National Security Council against escalating American involvement in 1965, he was met by this final rebuff from Secretary of State Dean Rusk: "If the communist world found out that the United States would not pursue its commitment to the end, there is no telling where they would stop their expansionism" (p. 110). While Berman's book clearly indicates that American Vietnam policy was based on anti-communism, pro-capitalism is not mentioned by any of the figures in the book or by Berman himself.

In Vietnam, as in Korea, we were again fighting for freedom, and capitalism was an epithet hurled at us by the communists, rather than a banner that we were defending. Yet how could we justify the spilling of American blood to fight communism if we were not even willing to utter the name of its antithesis—capitalism? The North Vietnamese, like the North Koreans, did not pose any direct threat to American territory, arms, or freedom. But communism itself posed a threat to our way of life based on capitalism. And that threat was the main reason why we were willing to fight these remote and costly wars against what we perceived as revolutionary world communism.

What about the men who actually fought the war? Were they in any way made aware they were fighting for capitalism? For an answer to that question, I turned to one of my law partners, Tim Cook, a Naval Academy graduate who served in Vietnam as a pilot. Tim flew off the carrier USS *Franklin D. Roosevelt* in 1966–1967, and received the Distinguished Flying Cross for heroism. Both at Annapolis (1959–1963) and throughout his service in Vietnam, Tim felt it was understood in the U.S. Navy that America was fighting world communism, but at no time did anyone suggest it was also a fight to preserve capitalism. Communism's threat was its curtailment of freedom—both religious freedom and the freedom to live one's life according to choice. The profit motive was mentioned as something that was missing from the Soviet system, an ingredient needed to get the best performance out of people. Marxist leaders, Tim was told, were megalomaniacs who wanted to control the entire world. "They were of the same cloth as Hitler, but just a different part of the cloth." The famous Khrushchev line, "We will bury you, and your grandchildren will be communists," was often quoted as evidence of the communist intention to take over the world.

Tim formed his own opinion of why we went into Vietnam: "Kitty Genovese." She was the young woman who fought a losing battle for her life on the streets of Queens, New York, in 1964. For more than half an hour, she tried to ward off an attacker who stabbed her repeatedly and finally slashed her to death while 38 of her neighbors watched or listened in silence. Fear of becoming involved kept all of them from phoning the police. In Tim's view, the United States could not afford to become a passive observer, sitting back in silence out of fear of becoming involved in an unpleasant situation. As he puts it: "If we don't come to the aid of small nations that are attacked, nobody else will, and the aggressors will have free rein to take over the world." Emotionally, Tim feels the same way today, but practically, he knows that involvements like Vietnam do not work.

Tim Cook's experience is typical of those who served in Korea and Vietnam. They were fighting against communism because it was alien to everything America stood for, and implicit in their definition of the American way was the economic freedom that capitalism provided. But our politicians were smart enough to realize they would have a hard time recruiting an army of noncapitalists to fight under the banner of capitalism.

It is still American policy to downplay capitalism, even when comparing our economic system to others. In June 1983, political leaders of the capitalist nations formed a new organization called the International Democrat Union (IDU). Launched in London with stirring speeches by British Prime Minister Margaret Thatcher and American Vice President George Bush, it established a right-wing counterbalance to the Socialist International, giving Western conservative political parties a platform from which to respond to socialist and communist propaganda. Although *The Wall Street Journal* called the IDU the "Nonsocialist International" and the *London Times* dubbed it the "Conintern," the word *capitalism* was not mentioned in the IDU's declaration of principles nor in any of the speeches, press releases, or documents attending its founding.

Thus, while leaders in Washington and the Kremlin obscure the issues by talking about freedom and social justice, the real war between capitalism and communism goes on. And we will never end the nuclear nightmare until we face up to this fact and admit that since 1917 we have been fighting hot and cold wars against the threat communism poses to the American way of life based on capitalism. What else is there about the USSR that has threatened the United States for 65 years? Let's consider this question carefully, because our lives may depend on getting the right answer.

I'll give you my answer: As an American capitalist, I feel threatened by the Soviet Union mainly because it is the principal force behind the spread of Marxism. I am afraid that some day Marxism—or some form of state ownership of the means of production—will take hold in the United States, either through the electoral process or by violent means. I fear this will happen, not because Marxism works well in the Soviet Union or elsewhere—it does not—but because capitalism no longer works well enough to hold off the natural tendency of American voters to use their ballots for their own apparent financial benefit whenever possible.

I do not regard the Soviet Union as a threat to American freedom or democracy, unless we are defeated by them in a war—a war which is likely to arise principally because of our ideological differences. For at least the first 40 years following the Bolshevik revolution, Americans had no cause to fear losing a war to the Soviets, and yet our policy then was just as virulently anti-communist as it is today, even to the point of refusing to recognize the Soviet government until 1933.

It is inconceivable to me that the example of the Soviet Union would inspire American voters to abandon our traditional freedom and democracy; indeed, the visible repression of Soviet society is the best assurance that Americans will not voluntarily adopt the Soviet *political* system. But as a capitalist, I have always feared that communist contagion might force us to abandon capitalism. And I believe that since 1917, most American capitalists have been motivated by that fear to take a militant stance against the Soviet Union, even though many of them genuinely believe they are acting out of patriotic rather than selfish motives. American capitalists—and millions of noncapitalists who hope to benefit from the capitalist system—have been able to exercise enough control of the electorate, government, and media to promote anti-communism as the basic American policy. They have done this, of course, by portraying communism as a threat to freedom and democracy, so that the great majority of Americans, who will never have the opportunity to become capitalists, nevertheless will continue to support capitalism lest we lose our freedom and democracy.

I believe that we can no longer afford to delude ourselves about the reasons for our fear of communism. As John Kenneth Galbraith put it in his 1977 article, "The Arms Race and American Politics":

> It would greatly clarify our political discussion if economic interest could be openly recognized and discussed. . . . Supporting economic interest are the two great fears that, in the past, have pervaded our political life. Perhaps they have been as powerful as economic interest or more so. One is the fear of communism; the other is the fear of being thought soft on communism.

The Fallacy of Peaceful Ideological Rivalry

Even during the period of so-called détente in the early to middle 1970s, the ideological warfare continued, as did the uncontrollable arms buildup that is its natural consequence. Indeed, the failure of détente not only confirms the link between ideology and Soviet-American enmity, but also provides a valuable lesson for those who seek to end cold war tensions through "peaceful" economic rivalry. Détente, in American terms, means a relaxation of tensions. Peaceful rivalry suggests a kind of respectful, if intensive, competition. Implicit in both concepts is some degree of cooperation, or at the very least some assurance that competition won't turn into a military confrontation. Is this realistic? Not as long as the Soviets remain committed to a worldwide proletarian revolution, which is, as we've seen, a major tenet of Marxist ideology.

This revolutionary commitment was one of the major reasons why attempts at détente were unsuccessful, and why a "live and let live" philosophy is not likely to take root now or in the future. Remember that the Soviets define détente as a method of class struggle, which makes any Soviet promise of peaceful competition an illusion. Remember, too, that any softening or abandonment of this position on the part of the Kremlin leaders would endanger their power base. Thus, the Kremlin must remain true to the either/or view of economics which is at the heart of Marxist ideology. So it is not surprising that in 1975, in the face of Chinese Communist charges that they were betraying the principles of Marxism-Leninism, the Kremlin felt compelled to reaffirm its commitment to international proletarianism. This was spelled out by Andrei Gromyko in his 1975 statement, "The Foreign Policy of the Soviet Union":

> The Communist Party subordinates all its theoretical and practical activity in the sphere of international relations to the task of strengthening the positions of socialism, and the interests of further developing and deepening the world revolutionary process.

Four years later, Soviet ideologist Viktor Kortunov reconfirmed this policy in an article entitled "The Leninist Policy of Peaceful Co-existence and Class Struggle," published in *International Affairs.* Wrote Kortunov: "No one can put a freeze on the world sociopolitical development on the pretext of détente. International agreements cannot alter the laws of class struggle."

Not surprisingly, the United States did not look favorably upon this abiding commitment to the destruction of capitalism. And to these declarations of continuing ideological enmity, we responded in kind, accelerating both the arms race and the tempo of the rhetorical battle. In the spring of 1982, President Reagan attempted to impose trade sanctions on the Soviet Union in an effort to thwart construction of a 3,500 mile-long natural gas pipeline from Siberia to Western Europe. Reagan hoped that blocking the project would make it more difficult for the Soviets to finance their imports and their own military buildup. At the same time, he attempted to maintain an embargo on grain sales to the USSR. These steps were designed to undermine the Soviet economy and thwart the Kremlin-inspired global communist revolution. In a televised interview with Walter Cronkite on March 2, 1981, Reagan said of the Soviets:

> They have told us that their goal is the Marxian philosophy of world revolution and a single one-world Communist state. And that they're dedicated to that.

In 1983, it was revealed that Reagan's attempt to use economic pressure to influence Soviet internal affairs was the brainchild of Richard Pipes, a Harvard history professor and former member of the National Security Council. This bold move in the so-called peaceful economic competition was codified as official American policy in National Security Decision Directive 75, and was adopted in the hope of reducing the Kremlin's ability to concentrate on military expenditures at the expense of civilian goods. It was viewed in Moscow as nothing less than an attempt to destabilize the Kremlin's control over its citizens and the Soviet satellites. Those critical of this policy questioned whether it was likely to foster a climate of peaceful rivalry, particularly if it lowered the Soviet standard of living. After all, were the Kremlin leaders likely to accept passively what they had to view as economic sabotage, or would they retaliate with all the means at their command?

Then on June 8, 1982, Reagan launched an ideological offensive for capitalism, under the customary cover of freedom and democracy. In a speech before both houses of the British Parliament, which was televised worldwide, he said:

> We invite the Soviet Union to consider with us how the competition of ideas and values, which it is committed to support, can be conducted on a peaceful and reciprocal basis. . . . What I am describing now is a plan and a hope for the long term, the march of freedom and democracy which will *leave Marxism-Leninism on the ash heap of history* as it has left other tyrannies which stifle the freedom and muzzle the self-expression of the people. [Italics mine]

Imagine how these words of peaceful rivalry were received in the Kremlin, and what countermeasures they might inspire if America's punchdrunk economic system were indeed in a position to put Marxism-Leninism on the ash heap of history! In point of fact, neither capitalism nor socialism works well enough to prove which is the better system, and so the attempts to demonstrate economic superiority inevitably escalate to political and military confrontation.

Soviet reaction to Reagan's "ash heap" speech came swiftly. In an interview with *The New York Times* columnist Anthony Lewis, Balentine M. Falin, deputy chief of the Soviet Central Committee's International Information Department, said:

> Attempts to destabilize us are serious. We have to pay attention to them. Richard Pipes, a member of the National Security staff, said there could be no peace with the Soviet Union until it changed its system. Then President Reagan said the same thing in London— the President, not a staff member. It is a precondition.

Criticism of Reagan's message also came from the *London Times* the day after his address, in an editorial that asked these questions:

Is the crusade for freedom to be carried into Latin America, Africa, and the Middle East? If so, there will be some fairly angry friends. Does the crusade involve attempts to penetrate and destabilize the Soviet sphere of influence? If so, other forms of contact are unlikely to flourish.

Consistent with these belligerent policies is the Captive Nations Resolution adopted by Congress in 1959, which remains in effect today. It requests the President to issue a proclamation designating the third week in July as "Captive Nations Week" until such time as all "captive nations" are free of communist control. Every president from Eisenhower through Reagan has done so. The resolution contains the following language:

> Whereas the enslavement of a substantial part of the world's population by Communist imperialism makes a mockery of the idea of peaceful coexistence between nations and constitutes a detriment to the natural bonds of understanding between the people of the United States and other peoples; and

> Whereas since 1918 the imperialistic and aggressive policies of Russian communism have resulted in the creation of a vast empire which poses a dire threat to the security of the United States and of all free peoples of the world; and . . .

> Whereas these submerged nations look to the United States, as the citadel of human freedom, for leadership in bringing about the liberation and independence and in restoring to them . . . religious freedoms, and . . . their individual liberties . . .

Listed in the resolution as captive nations are several of the republics constituting the Soviet Union, as well as all the satellite nations.

How have the Soviets responded to America's 1980s brand of peaceful ideological competition? A typical example of their counteroffensive may be seen in a speech made by Andrei Gromyko before the Supreme Soviet on June 16, 1983, which was reprinted in *The New York Times* on the following day. Said Gromyko:

> The class adversary is placing stress on weakening and, if possible, splitting the socialist community, and although this invariably ends in failure, there is no end to importunate attempts to achieve this aim.
> Hostile actions of a political and economic nature are being taken against the countries of socialism, ideological subversion is being carried out against them, and resort is made to subversive actions and other methods that are impermissible in the practice of intercourse among states.

The thrust of Gromyko's speech was to paint the United States as a warmonger, refusing to negotiate in good faith for arms reduction because it remains committed not only to the destruction of Marxism, but also to the perpetuation and spread, by force if necessary, of imperialistic capitalism.

This charge also appeared in an article by Professor Alexi Arbatov entitled "Strategy of Nuclear Madness," which was published in 1982 in *Social Sciences* (Vol. XIII, No. 1), a journal of the USSR Academy of Sciences. In it, Arbatov declared:

> The very social nature of imperialist policy dictated the choice of the principal methods of countering détente and worldwide progressive change. The accent is now on building up military might, and the threat and use of force. The stockpiling of nuclear weapons has become an inalienable and important element of the policy of accelerating the arms race, aggravating the confrontation of socialism and imperialism at the highest level. [p. 142]

Note that the Soviets see nuclear proliferation as a direct outgrowth of the clash between communism (which the Soviets prefer to call socialism) and imperialism (capitalism). Note, too, that Arbatov links détente with progressive worldwide change. This clearly demonstrates the causal connection between ideology and the nuclear nightmare. To the United States, the Soviet view of détente is tantamount to a call for capitalism's demise. So we accelerate arms production, justifying the move by pointing to Soviet aggression, and reiterate our own pledge to save the world from Marxist tyranny (e.g., Reagan's "ash heap" speech). To which the Soviets respond by matching or topping our arms buildup, accusing us of subversion in seeking the death of Marxism, and justifying their policies in the name of social liberation. And so it goes in the unending game of ideological thrust-and-parry between American capitalism and Soviet Marxism.

These real-world views of the clash between capitalism and communism make it clear that peaceful economic rivalry is not possible; that the competition inexorably leads to political and military confrontations that could too easily bring on a nuclear war. Similarly, attempts to improve relations through trade have foundered on the rocks of the mutual distrust produced by ideological conflicts. As long as the Soviets preach world communism, American voters will not look kindly on trade that strengthens the Soviet economy appreciably, lest we help them to win the supposedly peaceful contest between capitalism and communism. Nor are the Soviets likely to respond favorably to any American overtures of cooperation as long as the United States publicly seeks an end to the spread of Marxism and backs up that policy with efforts to destabilize the Soviet economy.

Under the enormous tensions of the global slugfest between capitalism and communism, it is highly probable that somewhere along the line the nuclear buttons will be pushed and civilization will end. Therefore, the monumental task facing us is to find a way to make American capitalism compatible with Russian Marxism, and thereby pull the launching platforms out from under the nuclear missiles.

Is There Any Way To Disarm This Ideological Time Bomb?

In a 1982 speech, Henry Kissinger summed up the problem with these words: "We face the fact that the Soviet Union is an ideological adversary, and no amount of détente can remove that." What's interesting about this comment is that Kissinger, like many foreign policy experts and Kremlin-watchers, agrees that ideological differences are a major cause of American-Soviet hostility. *Yet this fact, even when conceded, is not generally perceived to be relevant to solving the nuclear arms problem.* Why? Because most people believe that, as Kissinger says, there is no way we can eliminate or reconcile these ideological differences.

But must ideology remain an impassable roadblock? Can we not find some way of eliminating the life-and-death struggle between capitalism and communism, allowing each superpower to pursue its goals without being forced to treat the other as a mortal enemy? I believe we can, but only if we are willing to face some unpleasant truths.

As long as we cling to an economic system that is the very target of Marxism, we will not be able to end the nuclear nightmare. As we've seen, the Kremlin leaders must continue to seek the destruction of capitalism *in its present form;* to ask them to abandon this policy would be tantamount to inviting them to commit political suicide. And as long as American capitalism makes it impossible for the vast majority of people to ever become capitalists, it will stand squarely in the cross hairs of the Marxist gunsight, and it will continue to make Marxism seem attractive even though Marx's glorious vision of a just and classless society has never been realized anywhere.

But is capitalism as we know it really immutable? Might it not be time to suspend our preoccupation with the creation of anti-Soviet rhetoric, and recognize that to a great extent the weaknesses of capitalism have inspired our fear of the Red Menace?

If we hope to erase that fear and end 65 years of ideological warfare, we must ask ourselves this question, never before probed: *Can we modify capitalism—blending its strengths with Marx's vision of economic equality—so that it no longer conflicts with Marxism, without becoming socialists or giving up any of our treasured principles?* Can we, in other words, find an ideological meeting ground between capitalism and Marxism and, at the same time, create in capitalism a system that, because of its fair treatment of all Americans, will have nothing to fear from Marxism?

Please keep this question in mind as we examine in the next chapter the state of American capitalism and the structures within it which might furnish the foundation for the bridge we desperately need to build. And don't be put off by the pessimists who claim that Soviet-American enmity is not about ideology or any manageable issue, but is merely an inevitable consequence of belligerent human nature. If we accept that premise, we're doomed. We must continue to work toward limiting the damage inflicted by human nature, by creating conditions which make it less likely that human belligerence will override our common will to survive. If we don't keep trying, then we simply don't deserve to survive.

Chapter 4

Ownership of the Means of Production Is The Key to Peace

It is seemly . . . that the knight, who rides and does a lord's work, should get his wealth from the things on which his men spend much toil and fatigue.

—Book of the Order of Chivalry

Lack of money is the root of all evil.

—GEORGE BERNARD SHAW,
Man and Superman

Money is like manure. If you spread it around, it does a lot of good. But if you pile it up in one place, it stinks like hell.

—Oil mogul CLINT MURCHISON, JR.

As we have seen, the clash between Marxism and capitalism is the root cause of Soviet-American enmity. Let us now put the rival economic systems under a microscope and try to determine where they diverge and what kind of surgery would be required to knit them together.

Capital Ownership is the Central Point of Marxism

The word "capital" has several meanings. As we use it here, it means all goods that are used in the production of other goods and services—*the means of production*. Today the main forms of capital are the plants and equipment used by businesses, and in the United States the main form of capital ownership is shares of stock in corporations.

If you were to wade through the thousands of pages written by Karl Marx and Friedrich Engels, plus the millions of pages of commentary on their works, you would have to conclude that the central point of Marx's opposition to capitalism was the exploitation of the working class (and the rest of the population) by the owning class— the small group which owns the means of production and which he called "capitalists." The struggle between these two classes is the basic ingredient of Marxism. As Columbia University Professor C. Wright Mills, a leading authority on Marx, points out in his 1963 book, *The Marxists:*

> The work of Marx taken as a whole is a savage sustained indictment of one alleged injustice: that the profit, the comfort, the luxury of one man is paid for by the loss, the misery, the denial of another. [p. 35]

Professor Mills also dramatized the message of Marxism, as directed to the poor and the downtrodden:

> You do not have to be poor. The conditions that make you poor can be changed. They are going to be changed. Inside capitalism itself are the seeds of its own destruction. What will happen, whether you are yet aware of it or not, is that you are going to make a revolution. Those who rule over you and keep you poor will be overthrown. That is the next step forward in human progress. You are going to take that step. By the revolution you can eliminate once and for all the exploitation of man by man; you can enter into a socialist society in which mankind conquers nature. And no man any longer will know poverty and exploitation. [p. 34]

Marx's belief in the inevitable self-destruction of capitalism was based on his claim that capitalists necessarily exploit those who do not own capital, and that these nonowners, being the large majority of the population, will be forced to overthrow capitalism in order to lead decent lives.

Professor Paul Samuelson's famous textbook, *Economics,* gives us Marxism in a nutshell: "Space permits us here to go only to what Marx, Engels, and Lenin thought was the heartland of Marx's theoretical contribution to economics—his belief that he had demonstrated by his new tool of surplus value *the exploitation of labor by capital*" (11th ed., p. 800).

Marx's monumental work, *Das Kapital,* became the foundation of international socialism and communism. It took him more than 15 years to complete the first volume, which was published in 1867. When he died in 1883, the rest of *Das Kapital* was unfinished. The second and third volumes, published in 1885 and 1894, were completed by Engels. Altogether the three volumes cover more than a million words, and I would not recommend them for light summer reading. When *Das Kapital* was translated into Russian, Marx's followers were afraid the tsarist censor would ban the book. But his style was so complex and his ideas so obscure that the censors passed it. Finding it almost impossible to comprehend, and reasoning that few Russians would read it and none would be able to understand it, they did not bother to dignify it by a banning order. Much of it consists of philosophical nitpicking. I have always thought that if Marx and Engels had been maritime lawyers, they would have written a three-volume treatise on the differences between flotsam and jetsam.

Yet, with all its faults, *Das Kapital* remains history's most perceptive analysis of capitalism and capital ownership, even though it emanated from a man who never had a steady job or a bank account and who scarcely participated in any phase of capitalism. Karl Marx's only source of earned income for most of his adult life was the writing of a column on European affairs for the *New York Daily Tribune,* and according to historians, even that column was written mostly by Marx's great benefactor, Friedrich Engels. Marx was heavily subsidized by Engels, who was the son of a wealthy textile manufacturer and a successful businessman himself. Marx's wife, Jenny, came from a wealthy family, and she received a series of inheritances that kept the Marxes from starvation, although they lived in mean circumstances during much of their married life. Jenny also served as Karl's secretary; she even had to copy his manuscripts because his handwriting was illegible.

Marx and Engels were not overly modest about the scope of their work. In his eulogy at Marx's funeral, Engels said: "Just as Darwin discovered the law of development of organic nature, so Marx discovered the law of development of human history." Yet today, a hundred years after Marx's death, it would be difficult to disprove this sweeping statement, for Marx and Engels looked on economics as the locomotive of history, and they were the first to perceive that history was shaped by ownership of the means of production.

Marx took a linear view of history, seeing the development of mankind as a series of progressive steps that lead to predestined scientific conclusions. Marx envisioned an inevitable scientific progression from savagery to feudalism, to capitalism, to socialism, to communism. He regarded each of these steps as a necessary foundation for the following step. The first step in the Marxist revolution against capitalism was socialism, which would be achieved by "social ownership" of the means of production. During this socialist phase, the state would be ruled by the dictatorship of the "proletariat," a term Marx used for the working class, including all those who were not able to accumulate a significant amount of capital. (The earliest use of the term "proletariat" was in ancient Rome, where it denoted the "nonpossessing" class, the lowest class of Roman citizens.) Marx saw the proletariat as slaves exploited by capitalists. He felt it was scientifically inevitable that capitalism would create its own internal crises, which would in turn lead to its demise when the proletariat overthrew the government controlled by the capitalist class.

According to Marxist theory, the USSR, China, and the other "communist" nations are still in the precommunist stage of socialism, characterized by the dictatorship of the proletariat. None of these nations has yet progressed to Marx's ideal of communism—a stateless and classless society. In Marx's own words:

> Between capitalist and communist society lies the period of the revolutionary transformation of one into the other. There corresponds to this also a political transition period in which the state can be nothing but the revolutionary dictatorship of the proletariat.[*Critique of the Gotha Programme* in: *Selected Works in Two Volumes,* Vol. II, p. 30]

During this socialist phase, the distribution of consumer goods is to be made according to performance: from each according to his ability; to each according to his contribution to production. But in the higher stage of communism, society would finally evolve to Marx's ultimate dream: from each according to his ability; to each according to his needs.

At the root of Marxism, then, is the question of who will own the means of production—the MOP, as we shall call it. Lenin and Stalin answered this question by seizing MOP ownership in the name of the Soviet state, thus concentrating all the economic and political power in the leaders of the Communist Party. Article 10 of the 1977 Soviet Constitution confirms the principle of state MOP ownership. In the United States, it has been assumed from time immemorial that the means of production would be owned by those who can barrel their way to the top in a fierce dog-eat-dog contest, known variously as the free market, free enterprise, laissez-faire capitalism, or survival of the fittest. In both nations, however, these divergent approaches to MOP ownership have produced remarkably similar inequities.

MOP Ownership in the Soviet Union and the United States

In the Soviet Union, theoretically the state owns the means of production "in the name of the people." In practice, the Communist Party controls not only the entire state apparatus, but also the benefits flowing from MOP ownership. For that reason, many dedicated Marxists look upon the Soviet system as "state capitalism" rather than "state socialism."

In 1983, there were approximately 18 million members of the Communist Party of the Soviet Union (CPSU), out of a total population of 270 million. Thus, a little over 6 percent of the Russian people control MOP ownership. Even within this group of 18 million, there is a pinnacle class of about one million who are on the *nomenklatura,* the secret roster of those selected by the party bosses for power and privilege. They live much better than the average Russian, who is expected to share the distribution of scarcity. Hedrick Smith, former Moscow correspondent for *The New York Times,* describes in his 1976 book, *The Russians,* how this "communist nobility" bestows upon themselves the finest in food, clothing, housing, education, transportation, and recreation. Therefore, MOP ownership benefits can really be viewed as flowing mainly to only 1 percent of the Soviet population. But since most CPSU members receive benefits that are not available to the other 94 percent of the population, let us be generous and stay with the 6 percent figure.

In the United States, interestingly enough, the percentage of people who receive substantial income from MOP ownership is almost identical. This statistic comes from an authoritative source— our president. In February of 1975, when he was a privately employed radio commentator, Ronald Reagan said on the air:

> Roughly 94 percent of the people in capitalist America make their living from wages or salaries. Only 6 percent are true capitalists in the sense of deriving their income from ownership of the means of production.

It is difficult to obtain exact statistics on how many Americans actually receive substantial income from MOP ownership, but certainly someone as conservative as Ronald Reagan would have no incentive to minimize the diffusion of ownership under our present system. There are, however, a few other sources.

Dr. Robert Hamrin spent four years studying future economic growth as a staff economist for the Joint Economic Committee of Congress. In a 1976 staff study for the JEC based on the latest statistics then available, Hamrin found that half the individually owned corporate stock was owned by the richest 1.04 million Americans (one-half of 1 percent of the population). In his 1980 book, *Managing Growth in the 1980s: Toward a New Economics,* Hamrin analyzed the privately held wealth of the nation and concluded that only about 5 percent of Americans really share in the benefits of capital ownership (pp. 261–2). In this respect, the great egalitarian economy of the United States is on about the same level as the economy of India.

In 1981, the New York Stock Exchange proudly reported that some 32 million Americans (14.4 percent of the population) were individual owners of corporate stock and mutual fund shares. But closer examination reveals that only one-sixth of these shareholders (5.9 million Americans) owned shares worth $25,000 or more; and only 3.1 million owned shares worth $50,000 or more. Given the present state of dividends, the average annual return on portfolios worth $25,000 to $50,000 would be less than $5,000. Therefore, no more than 3 to 5 million Americans receive more than $5,000 of their annual income from stock ownership. Of course, there are other important sources of capitalist income, such as income-producing real estate, savings accounts, and bonds—but the studies indicate that the same pinnacle class owns most of those assets as well.

So there we have it: 6 percent (or less) in the USSR and 6 percent (or less) in the U.S. derive substantial benefits from ownership of the MOP. Thus, at the very moment in history when capitalism and communism are engaged in a death struggle arising from their differing ownership ideologies, it is plain that *neither* system produces substantial socialization of the income derived from MOP ownership. The absurdity of this situation led me to envision the following space-age fantasy:

A small spaceship from another planet is orbiting Earth, which is now a burned-out shell, devoid of life. At the controls of the two-seater is a father who looks something like Leonard Nimoy in his *Star Trek* role as Mr. Spock. He is attempting to explain to his teen-age son the stark scene before them.

SON: How was that planet destroyed, Dad?

FATHER: It was a nuclear war, Son. The two great powers, the United States and Soviet Russia, fired thousands of missiles at each other. The fallout destroyed both nations and killed the rest of Earth's inhabitants as well.

SON: Why did they do that?

FATHER: They were enemies.

SON: What were they fighting about?

FATHER: Well, as far as we know, it was about ideological differences. The United States was the champion of capitalism; the Soviet Union backed a different system: communism.

SON: What was the difference between capitalism and communism?

FATHER: The main difference was the ownership of the means of production. Under capitalism, individual people owned the means of production, while in the communist nations, the state owned the means of production.

SON: I don't understand why that made such a big difference. How many people owned the means of production in the United States?

FATHER: About 6 percent of the population or less.

SON: And in the Soviet Union?

FATHER: There, the state technically owned the means of production, but the state was controlled by the Communist Party, which in turn was controlled by 6 percent of the population or less.

SON: Which system worked better?

FATHER: Neither system worked very well, Son.

SON: I don't think I understand, Dad. You say that in both systems the means of production were controlled by less than 6 percent of the people, and that neither system worked. For *that*, Earth was destroyed?

FATHER: It sounds hard to believe, but that's what our historians tell us.

SON: How could such a ridiculous thing happen?

FATHER: I guess the people of Earth were not very smart.

SON: What about their leaders?

FATHER: Apparently the leaders of both nations feared that the weaknesses in their own economic systems would prove their undoing. The Soviet Union was afraid its people might decide that capitalism had more to offer, so they concentrated on convincing the Soviet people that capitalism was their mortal enemy and that the Soviet leaders had to retain dictatorial powers to continue the worldwide battle against capitalism. The Americans had an equally strong fear of communism, which they considered a contagious disease. They were afraid the disease might spread to the United States because capitalism, which was on the decline, didn't have strong enough antibodies to ward it off. The leaders of both nations found it easier to curse each other than to try to solve their internal economic problems.

SON: But weren't there any great thinkers on Earth who could have prevented such a pointless war?

FATHER: Yes, there were, but they were all mesmerized by the differences between the two systems, instead of trying to build the bridge that would have saved Earth.

To confirm that we have indeed become mesmerized by our differences, note that each nation defines its system by its opposition to the other: the core of Marxism is denunciation of capitalism, and the heart of American policy is anti-communism. As Richard Barnet states in his 1981 book, *Real Security:*

> The U.S.-Soviet rivalry will continue. The identity of each system depends too much on its opposition to the other to permit anything more than antagonistic collaboration between the superpowers for the forseeable future. [p. 107]

As we have seen, this rivalry between the two economic systems cannot be conducted peacefully. As the failures of capitalism and communism multiply, there is increasing danger that one or both sides will, in desperation, resort to military action to compensate for poor economic performance. In *Beyond The Cold War*, Edward Thompson provides a chilling vision of the likely result of continuing economic rivalry:

> Soviet ideologists may suppose that, in the end, Western capitalism will collapse, with conjoint recession and inflation, shortage of energy resources, internal insurrection and revolt throughout the Third World. Western ideologists suppose that the Soviet economy will collapse under the burden of increasing arms allocations, with internal nationalist and dissident movements, and with insurrection or near-insurrection throughout Eastern Europe.
>
> But these theorists need only cross the corridor and knock on the doors of their colleagues in History, Politics or Sociology, to learn that these scenarios might provide, precisely, the moment of the worst case of all. Each of these developments would bring the continent, and ultimately the world itself, into the greatest peril. Each would provide the conditions, not for the peaceful reunification of Europe, but the rise of panic-stricken, authoritarian regimes, tempted to maintain the discipline of their peoples by recourse to military adventures. The break-down of East or West, in a situation of massive military confrontation, would tend to precipitate the resolution of war. [p. 18]

What is particularly frightening about this scenario is that the conditions heralding the collapse of capitalism are already with us.

American Welfare Capitalism: A System At War With Itself

Our present economic system, known as mixed capitalism or welfare capitalism, is supposed to provide enough good jobs to distribute income equitably throughout the population, even though some people will be richer than others. When the system fails to do this, the government intervenes and tries to redistribute some income so everyone can live decently. This is capitalism mixed with some features of welfare state socialism. I think the term welfare capitalism is more descriptive, so let's use it instead of mixed capitalism.

At the heart of welfare capitalism is the concept of redistribution of income through transfer payments. Those of us who are fortunate enough to be productive—who have a good job or own a profitable business—pay taxes to provide the money for transfer payments that keep a lot of less fortunate Americans from starving or revolting, or both. But this system of welfare capitalism is a relatively new idea, and there is no proof that it can sustain itself on a long-term basis. Can we continue taxing the producers to provide a living for the nonproducers without causing permanent inflation and other monumental problems? In fact, mounting evidence both here and abroad indicates that the welfare state based on transfer payments is inherently inflationary, and therefore unworkable.

Today, as we try to sustain economic growth, we face a great many stubborn problems: recurring inflation, huge budget deficits, high interest rates, capital shortages, and massive transfer payments for Social Security and welfare programs that cannot be cut from the budget under the present system. We don't have the money needed to maintain national security in the face of the escalating arms race. We are suffering an erosion of the work ethic because many people find it more profitable not to work. We are also threatened by insolvency of school systems, city and state governments, and the Social Security program. As a result of all these problems, millions of our people feel alienated—cut out of our economic system permanently—and this is one of the causes of our crime epidemic. Respect for law and private property is probably at the lowest level in our history, lower today than it was in the Wild West of the last century.

Peter Passell, who covers economics for the editorial page of *The New York Times,* wrote in its issue of September 12, 1982:

These are not times that breed optimists. After a decade of economic stagnation, the American standard of living has slipped to 11th in the world, well below those of northern Europe. Autos and steel, the industries on which the postwar expansion was based, are in steep decline. Our road, bridge, mass-transit and water systems are literally collapsing. Our banks are loaded with the debts of overdeveloped companies and underdeveloped countries. Our energy supplies are vulnerable to the whims of desert nomads. Our farmers rely on our enemies to buy their surpluses. Millions can't find jobs; millions who have them don't bother paying taxes on their earnings.

And what is the political answer to all these problems? Our major parties are still trying to solve them solely through jobs and transfer payments. Those who are working are taxed more and more in order to transfer money to those whom our system cannot employ. At least, that's what happens when our politicians muster the courage to raise taxes high enough to cover government expenditures. When they cannot, the government simply prints more money, causing the runaway inflation and budget deficits that are threatening the future of all Americans.

It's getting so the only way most of us can tell whether we're in a recession or a recovery phase is to listen to presidential press conferences. Even when things are "good," very high interest rates, unemployment, and inflation persist. It's sadly reminiscent of the struggling stand-up comedian who had to keep telling his audience, "These are the jokes, folks!"

The split society that results from the confrontation between capital and labor, haves and have-nots, owners and nonowners, is a persistent underlying problem of our economy. Stop-gap government measures and welfare have failed to bridge the gulf between the haves and have-nots. These efforts date back to Franklin D. Roosevelt's New Deal, but they have never produced any substantial redistribution of wealth. Indeed, recent studies show that the little redistribution we accomplish comes at the expense of the middle class, while the rich-poor gap continues to widen. On December 11, 1983, *The New York Times* reported on two studies, one conducted by Frank Levy and Richard C. Michel, economists at the Urban Institute, and the other by Stephen J. Rose, a Baltimore economist. Both studies were corroborated by the Census Bureau. They reached these conclusions: In 1978, 55 percent of the U.S. population fell into the middle part of the middle class, with income from $11,500 to $27,400. Adjusting for inflation, in 1983 this class consisted of those households making between $17,000 and $41,000. By 1983, only 42 percent of Americans fell into that class, and of the 13 percent of Americans who left it, three-quarters fell down to *lower* incomes. To make matters worse, the studies showed that in the same five years, average taxes for the *richest* fifth of American households *declined* one-half of 1 percent, while the average taxes for the *poorest* fifth *increased* by more than 2 percent. Little wonder, then, that one of the first signs of "recovery" is the increase in sales of luxury automobiles.

As Senator Russell B. Long said in a May 1981 speech on the Senate Floor:

> The benefits of Government-stimulated economic growth have traditionally trickled down through higher wages, expansion in the number of jobs, and the availability of increased tax revenues to fund expanded social programs.
>
> That approach has produced strains on the economy as the benefits of this growth have resulted in the accumulation of massive amounts of productive capital by a relatively few households while the vast majority have been left with only a meager net worth.
>
> Attention must be given to new ways to distribute the benefits of this growth more widely. Despite all the fine populist oratory and good intentions of great men like Franklin Delano Roosevelt, Harry Truman, Dwight Eisenhower, John Kennedy, and Lyndon Johnson, the distribution of wealth among Americans, in relative terms, is about the same today as it was when Herbert Hoover succeeded Calvin Coolidge.

What Senator Long was pointing to was the failure of the so-called "trickledown" theory of economics, which holds that the profits reaped by the owning class will *trickle down* to the workers and other nonowners—in the form of jobs and increased federal revenues available for transfer payments—and spread throughout society. It sounds good in theory, and until recently, most Americans believed that it actually worked, creating jobs and sustaining the relatively high standard of living that many Americans had achieved. But as that standard of living slips and much of the world moves away from capitalism, the days of trickledown may be numbered. Its success depends largely upon its ability to create jobs, and that ability is rapidly disappearing.

Inflation got us going on the wrong track in the late 1960s, when we tried to finance the Vietnam war without raising taxes high enough to generate the necessary revenue. Now we have come to expect inflation rates of 10 percent or more whenever the government takes steps to increase employment. Yet even a 3 percent inflation rate cuts in half the value of a contribution made to the average worker's pension fund. Indeed, our acceptance of these disastrously high figures is perhaps the most frightening aspect of the economic malaise. Whenever inflation, unemployment, and prime interest rates dip below 10 percent, we hail this dubious achievement as the beginning of "good times" and "recovery." Only yesterday, such figures would have been termed an unmitigated disaster, and would have doomed the incumbent party to failure in the next election.

Meanwhile our poverty rate continues to soar. In 1982, the number of Americans officially classified as being below the poverty line (defined as income of less than $9,862 for a family of four) increased by 2.6 million. This brought more than 34 million Americans—15 percent of the population—officially below the poverty level.

The poor have always been with us, but the most marked change in American society has been in the attitudes of the upwardly mobile middle class—white collar workers, college graduates, intellectuals, and many professionals. Throughout the twentieth century, each generation of Americans reached a standard of real income twice as high as that of their parents, and we came to expect this as part of the American dream. But in the 1970s this performance began to slip badly. Now, at the rate of improvement prevailing during the period 1973–1980, it would take us *300 years* to double our real living standards. At the even lower rate of Ronald Reagan's first two years in office, we won't even be able to sustain our 1979 real income. Little wonder then that many middle-class teenagers feel they will never equal the living standards of their own parents. Yet at the poorer end of our society expectations remain high. Indeed, those expectations have ripened into "entitlements" in the form of transfer payments whose recipients have enough political clout to prevent any serious cuts.

All of these conditions fuel the buildup of crime, which has become our biggest growth industry. I don't have to tell you how many millions of Americans are afraid to walk the streets in their own cities, day or night. Every year more than one million students and well over a hundred thousand *teachers* are attacked in our schools, many of which now require full-time security guards in order to remain open.

Where will all this lead us? Robert Lekachman supplies one answer in his 1981 book, *Capitalism for Beginners:*

> All parties, black and white, male and female, are discovering that capitalism no longer delivers the rising living standards which in time past served as its major justification. Average citizens can no

longer afford the luxury of abstaining from politics or treating contests for office as spectator sports. The self-interest of those who live by their labor requires replacement of capitalism by democratic socialism. [p. 173]

This is not a startling statement for Professor Lekachman to make; he is one of America's leading spokesmen for democratic socialism. More surprising are the forecasts of some of our diehard conservatives. In a 1980 speech at a Florida stockbroker's convention, for example, former Treasury Secretary William Simon said:

My friends, the sad truth is that here in the United States we have a government rolling out of control and careening crazily down its own road to socialism. . . . So many citizens have been trained to see the government as economically omniscient and omnipotent, and to blame all economic ills on "business," that disaster could easily bring popular demand for takeover of the major means of production by the state. Legal precedent and ideological justification exist. It would take little to accomplish this transition.

Journalist Patrick Buchanan, a former speech writer for conservative Republicans, sounded a similar warning in his syndicated column of August 17, 1982. Buchanan observed that the nation faced an economic emergency that the Reagan administration seemed powerless to control. He predicted that unless Congress froze Social Security and all other entitlements through 1984 (which it did not do), the economy would collapse. As to what would follow the failure of Reaganomics, Buchanan adopted the scenario of MIT political scientist Walter Dean Burnham:

Very probably, one of two things: a first-rate political breakdown and regime crisis possibly requiring some form of dictatorship to cope with the debacle, or the rise of a socialist political movement on the ruins of—and extending far beyond—the Democratic Party. The breakdown we shall very probably have before the decade [of the 1980s] is out. The crucial question is what arises from it.

There has never been much of a constituency for socialism in the United States. Labor union pioneer Eugene Debs reached the high water mark in 1912, when he polled 6 percent of the popular vote as the presidential candidate of the Socialist Party. Until recent times, most Americans believed the promises of both major parties that they could keep capitalism working or that they could fix it when it threatened to break down. But that belief is rapidly dissolving, and a reaction could come swiftly in the form of a socialist movement. Although the influence of labor unions has been declining, there are many millions of potential socialists in the ranks of the unemployed, the working poor, and others who have lost faith in American capitalism and have no place else to turn.

If Republicans and Democrats continue to prove equally unable to halt our economic erosion, and are forced to turn to workers' pension funds or the public treasury to bail out troubled businesses, socialism will acquire terrific momentum. All that would be needed to pick up the pieces is a socialist candidate with a suitable television personality. If welfare capitalism is written off as a failure, there is no floodgate to hold back the rush to socialism—for capitalism has no safety valve. When the pie stops growing, why should American voters support a capitalist system that prevents the overwhelming majority of them from ever becoming capitalists? In most of the other Western democracies, noncapitalist majorities have elected socialist governments, and those socialist parties that fall out of power remain the chief contenders. Indeed, in 1983, for the first time in history, all the nations of southern Europe—France, Spain, Italy, Portugal, and Greece—had socialist governments. And since the Bolshevik revolution of 1917, nearly all nations that have undergone revolutions have installed socialist governments, or at least adopted the socialist label.

In the desperate effort to keep American capitalism afloat, many conservative politicians and business leaders are casting longing eyes toward Japan, which has maintained low inflation, high employment, and rapid growth, despite complete dependence on imported oil. For example, in a major article titled "Saving the World Economy" published in *Newsweek* on January 24, 1983, Henry Kissinger concluded:

> The agenda will require a major change in the role of our government. Government, industry and labor must act as partners . . . .
> Of the industrial democracies only Japan has managed this tour de force, and its national strategy is one reason for Japan's competitive edge in world markets. . . . For the stakes are high: whether the economic system as we have known it will hold together—as well as the political relationships that go with it.

But Kissinger and others who envy Japan's success fail to point out that Japan has largely socialized its economy. The Japanese government is the main cog in the economic machine, supplying long-term capital investment funds, short-term working capital, manpower allocation, and economic planning. It provides industry with huge subsidies, including low-interest loans and outright grants; such a grant, in fact (to the tune of a billion dollars a year for machinery research and development), enabled Japanese companies to grab a big chunk of the American machine tool market. Thus, in most of its important aspects, the Japanese economy resembles a socialist or communist model rather than a capitalist one. And although MOP ownership remains largely in private hands, it is nonetheless effectively socialized because Japanese companies are not free to use their assets as they see fit to maximize profits. They must guarantee lifetime employment to their work force, even if this reduces dividends or stock prices. Nor are they free to compete with other Japanese companies without government approval.

If the Japanese-style "partnership" of government, industry, and labor takes root in the United States as Kissinger suggests, it is likely to lead to demand for socialization of MOP ownership, especially since this partnership would have to be financed largely by the workers' pension funds. Would the pinnacle class of American capitalists, numbering less than 6 percent of the population, still be able to dominate MOP ownership when it is being paid for by the public treasury or the pension funds? And regardless of its effect on that pinnacle class, is the Japanese plan the best way for the other 94 percent of Americans to go? As we shall see in Chapter 7 when we examine various worker ownership schemes, this type of socialization is likely to wrest power from one small, special-interest group— wealthy stockholders—only to transfer that power into the hands of an even smaller special-interest group: officials of labor unions. Furthermore, bringing the government into the process of allocating funds for business investment would empower pressure groups to keep moribund companies alive and to gain special favors at the expense of those with less political clout—hardly a formula for reviving the American free enterprise market economy.

Does all this mean that capitalism is doomed to self-destruction, as Marx predicted; must we face up to its obsolescence and prepare to join the worldwide drift toward socialism? For more than 60 years, the United States and other Western democracies have been able to prevent the incursion of communism—and prove Marx wrong about capitalism's demise—by injecting welfare benefits into the otherwise harsh distribution of income inherent in primitive capitalism. As Geoffrey Barraclough points out in *An Introduction to Contemporary History,* the development of welfare capitalism, starting with the New Deal in the United States in the 1930s, has been a direct effect of the Western "fear of communist contagion." The development of economic planning by nonsocialist governments has also been a direct result of the Soviet example. The basis of this movement was, according to Barraclough: ". . . the realization that, if the attractions of Marxism were to be combated, it was necessary to show that liberal society could match its achievements, above all by providing security and a higher standard of living for the workers" (pp. 219–220). In fact, most of the advances that Marx believed would come only through the overthrow of capitalism have long since been peacefully achieved by workers in capitalist nations. These include the eight-hour day, a decent standard of living, social security, welfare, and many other personal benefits that did not exist in Marx's time. But clearly, welfare capitalism has come to the end of its ability to sustain itself without causing ruinous inflation.

Practically all traditional American economists look upon wealth and capital ownership as a permanent part of the social structure, rather than as a potential tool for income distribution. Therefore, you won't find any extensive discussion of the concentration or distribution of wealth in standard economics textbooks. The last few generations of economists have concentrated on keeping the shaky capitalist system afloat through the creation of jobs and distribution of welfare benefits, all the while ignoring MOP ownership.

But the time has come to face up to the ownership question— for in MOP ownership we can find not only the solution to our internal economic crises, but also the bridge to better relations with the Soviet Union. Of course, any solution to our economic problems would ease our fear of creeping socialism and the Red Menace. On a deeper level, however, a change in our system of MOP ownership would strike directly at the deadlock between America and the Soviet Union. By closing the gap between the haves and have-nots— the gap Marx predicted would prove the downfall of capitalism—we can take a major step toward eliminating the differences that lie at the root of Soviet-American enmity.

The importance of focusing on ownership as a means of dealing with both our nuclear and economic problems is underscored by the fact that under accepted wisdom, there are only two choices: private MOP ownership based on savings, or state ownership. Thus, most people believe that if our present system does run out of gas, there is only one option: to adopt a system of state ownership. We have no plan in place for any alternative system, nor do we have economists, legislators, or financiers trained in the design or operation of alternative systems. Yet such plans and skills are needed today to save our domestic economy—and also, I am convinced, to ward off nuclear war.

If we figured out a way to open the ownership of the means of production to all Americans, we could remove Marx's only meaningful objection to capitalism: the overconcentration of capital ownership. Once everyone is an owner, who would be left to be exploited? If workers are also owners, they can hardly be thought of as an exploited class. The entire concept of the class struggle disappears, since Marx's two classes were the owners and the nonowners.

What must we do to make American MOP ownership compatible with Marxism? For the answer let us look first to what Marx and his disciples wrote about MOP ownership.

Marx Left No Blueprint for Socialism or Communism

Even though the writing of the first three volumes of *Das Kapital* stretched over 27 years (1867–1894), there is nothing in the Marx-Engels works that clearly explains how to organize and operate a socialist or communist system. They were preoccupied with ending the evils of capitalism, and they believed that a natural state of social equality would inevitably take its place. Thus, as Paul Samuelson points out in *Economics*, when the Bolsheviks seized power in 1917, they found little practical guidance in the writings of Marx:

> The Soviet leaders had no blueprint to guide them. Marx had confined himself largely to the *faults* of capitalism and had revealed very little of what the promised land was to be like. [11th ed., p. 818]

To apply Marxist ideology to the mature industrial capitalism of the twentieth century, we must look beyond the blurred writings of Marx and Engels, who were addressing the problems of England's primitive factory system in the nineteenth century. We must look to the works of their most important disciple: Karl Johann Kautsky.

Kautsky, who lived from 1854 to 1938, was saddled with the job of applying the morass of *Das Kapital* to industrialized society as it was developing into the form we know today. He published the Marxist newspaper *Neue Zeit (New Times)* throughout Europe from 1883 to 1917, and became a leader of the German Social Democratic Party. He was highly regarded by Marx and Engels, and when Engels died before he could begin writing the fourth volume of *Das Kapital,* that task fell to Kautsky. Drawing on the notes of Marx and Engels, he wrote the fourth volume alone. It was published in 1905 under the title, *Theories of Surplus Value.*

Kautsky was the principal author of the Erfurt program, which established the German Social Democratic Party on a platform of orthodox Marxism. This made him the leading spokesman for the

Second International, which promoted worldwide Marxism from 1889 to 1914. Kautsky spent the rest of his long life interpreting the gospel of Marx in the context of twentieth-century capitalism, which earned him the title, "the Pope of Marxism."

What, then, did the Pope of Marxism have to say about ownership of the means of production? How did he interpret the vague statement of Marx and Engels that MOP ownership must be "socialized"? The clearest answer will be found in these excerpts from his 1932 essay, *"Is Soviet Russia a Socialist State?,"* published as part of a 1946 book entitled *Social Democracy vs. Communism:*

> Certainly, it is the aim of Socialists to deprive the capitalists of the means of production. But that in itself is not enough. We must also determine who is to control these means of production. When another minority takes the place of the capitalists and controls the means of production, independently of the people and frequently against their will, the change in property relations thus accomplished signifies least of all Socialism. . . . In Russia, it is the government, not the people, who controls the means of production. The government is thus the master of the people. . . . Our duty is not merely to abolish the capitalist order but to set up a higher order in its place. But we must oppose those forces aiming to destroy capitalism only to replace it with a barbarous mode of production. . . . What we see in Russia is, therefore, not Socialism but its antithesis. It can become Socialism only when the people expropriate the expropriators now in power, to use a Marxian expression. Thus, the socialist masses of Russia find themselves with respect to the problem of control of the means of production in the same situation which confronts the workers in capitalist countries. The fact that in Russia the expropriating expropriators call themselves Communists makes not the slightest difference. [pp. 89–90]

Thus Karl Kautsky condemned the Leninist concept that the state must own the MOP. Kautsky's authoritative writings supply a firm foundation for distributing MOP ownership directly to the people, rather than concentrating both economic and political power in the state, the bureaucracy, or a political party. Convinced that the Leninist seizure of the MOP was a grave error, Kautsky always carefully distinguished "social ownership" from "state ownership."

Kautsky's views on MOP ownership brought him condemnation by Lenin, who called him a renegade from Marxism. But we do not have to decide whether Kautsky was correct in labeling the Russian revolution non-Marxist and non-socialist. Perhaps both the Lenin and the Kautsky interpretations of MOP ownership are compatible with broad Marxist theory. What is important to us is this: a Marxist of the legendary stature of Karl Kautsky has opened the way for fulfillment of Marxism by "social" ownership of the MOP rather than government ownership. And in this respect, Kautsky was supported by leading Marxists of his time. Included among them were Rosa Luxemburg (1871–1919), who pioneered Marxism in Russia, Poland, and Germany, as well as two other German pioneers, August Bebel (1840–1913), and Eduard Bernstein (1850–1932).

Kautsky himself did not spell out a specific method of MOP ownership that would fulfill the Marxist edict of socialized ownership. But he put his reputation and even his personal safety on the line by insisting that ownership and control of the means of production by all the people was the essence of Marxism. He thereby opened a window of opportunity for us in our quest to end the nuclear nightmare. He taught us that to make American capitalism compatible with Marxism, we do not have to turn MOP ownership over to the government.

What can we make of this opportunity? We can try to build a bridge between capitalism and communism on the foundation that Marx, Engels, and Kautsky left for us—the foundation of MOP ownership by *all* the people. As we start to sketch the design of that bridge, let us consider the U.S. economy in its simplest form: the way in which it furnishes support to the American people.

The Four Means of Support

Americans obtain their financial support in four ways: by working for it (wages); by receiving government checks (welfare); by cheating (crime, tax evasion, welfare fraud, etc.); and by receiving the return on invested capital (capitalist income). The first three methods have been used throughout the world for centuries and have often been fostered by government policies. The fourth, return on invested capital, has never been used as a method of creating an equitable distribution of income. It has remained the sole province of the rich—the "capitalists" who have the savings to buy corporate stock and other forms of income-producing capital.

Wages are obviously the ideal method of supporting people, and as long as our traditional capitalism was able to create enough decent jobs for those who wanted them, it was acceptable to most Americans. But in an increasingly automated era, it has become apparent that no government—conservative or liberal—can create enough jobs to support everyone through wages. The quest to create equitable income distribution through jobs, while the machines and computers produced by industrialization actually destroy jobs, causes a basic contradiction in industrial societies.

If you are a business manager seeking a loan to buy equipment that will reduce your payroll, your bank will be very receptive—but try borrowing money to increase employment! Do you know any business executives who are trying to increase employment in their companies? The medals for excellence in management are bestowed on those who destroy jobs and thus make their companies more "efficient." The managers of our multinational companies have become adept at exporting jobs by shutting down American plants and shifting production to places like South Korea, Taiwan, and Mexico, where labor costs are much lower.

At the 1983 meeting of the Business Council, the chief executive officers of more than 100 of the nation's largest corporations discussed unemployment. Despite their high hopes for the economic recovery under way, they saw little chance of rehiring many of the workers laid off during the recession. In *The New York Times* of May 16, 1983, James H. Evans, chairman of Union Pacific, whose company had laid off 6,000 of its 44,000 employees, explained why few of the 6,000 would be called back:

> We're running 40 percent more freight tonnage than we did 20 years ago—with half as many employees. If we had the same number of employees we had then, we would have priced ourselves out of the market. How have we done it? Automation.

The Business Council members said they had to choose between protecting jobs and protecting their basic businesses, most of which are subject to both domestic and foreign competition. As Chase Manattan Bank chairman Willard Butcher put it, "If we don't modernize and raise our productivity, then we'll have no employment at all."

Earlier in this century, despite our growing population and foreign demand for American food products, millions of agricultural jobs were permanently eliminated by farm mechanization and advancing technology. The displaced farm workers moved to the cities and most found jobs. But there is nowhere for the displaced city workers to move to. As factory after factory shuts down, the service sector cannot expand fast enough to absorb manufacturing workers who are no longer needed. Already our civilization appears to be sinking under a tidal wave of grease from fast-food restaurants, and the service sector itself is rapidly becoming automated and computerized.

Some retail stores are now using computerized displays that are programmed to answer customer's questions and thus eliminate sales personnel. Electronic bank tellers are in wide use. The coming of robotics will make the job situation even more desperate. The robot—the steel collar worker—can work twenty-four hours a day, seven days a week, without making a mistake or getting bored. In 1983, American manufacturers could rent assembly-line robots at a total cost of six dollars an hour—robots that could do the work of humans who are paid three or four times as much for doing the job less efficiently. The Japanese are already using robots in large numbers, and we'll have to follow suit if we hope to remain competitive. Studies by the Congressional Budget Office and other groups estimate that automation and robotics will eliminate three million manufacturing jobs by 1990 and another four million between 1990 and 2000. The age of robotics is nearly upon us, but we are still relying mainly on wages to make capitalism work, and our great thinkers seem to be unaware of a monumental question: *Who will own the robots?*

Many of our leading traditional economists are starting to realize that welfare capitalism cannot create enough jobs any more, but when they search for solutions they are stymied. Thus New York University Professor Wassily Leontief, winner of the Nobel Prize for Economics in 1973, expressed deep misgivings in a February 1983 interview with *New York Times* columnist Charlotte Curtis:

> Labor will become less and less important. More and more workers will be replaced by machines. I do not see that the new industries can employ everyone who wants a job. Think what would happen if all unemployed steel and auto workers were retrained to operate computers. There aren't enough computers to go around. We'd have created a worse problem.

In their search for solutions, presidential hopefuls Walter Mondale and Gary Hart turned to the writings of Harvard professor Robert B. Reich, whose 1983 book, *The Next American Frontier*, urges us to give up heavy industrial production in favor of specialty orders and high technology. But neither Professor Reich nor any of the other high-technology advocates offer any reliable method of determining how many of the millions of lost production jobs such a switch could salvage. (Very few, according to labor economists who have studied the problem.) And while high-technology businesses create a few jobs that pay well for high skills, most of their employees do routine work that brings much lower pay than American factory workers are accustomed to.

Those who rely on the job approach have known for a long time that it cannot keep pace with automation. Back in 1945, Congress tried to shape a new economic policy around the "Full Employment

Act of 1945." But even in those starry-eyed days, Congress soon came to realize it could not produce full employment either by legislation or by any other government action. A year later the bill was passed simply as the "Employment Act of 1946." Even Hubert Humphrey, one of the great champions of full employment, failed in his lifelong quest to make it work. When he was chairman of the Joint Economic Committee in 1976, he castigated the Ford administration for its failure to create jobs through government expenditures. What he later learned through testimony presented to his committee is perhaps the most telling evidence of the impracticality of this approach: even back in 1976, it required $50,000 of federal money to create one job paying $8,000 a year. What's more, after three years only one or two new jobs remained, out of ten supposedly created.

Many of those who try to live on wages are not as well off as those on welfare. Currently, most of the people falling below the poverty line are employed in some way; in contrast, those on welfare and Social Security have their benefits indexed to inflation and so are usually maintained above the poverty level. Therefore, it has become a maxim of welfare capitalism that if you want to avoid poverty, stay out of work!

Another drawback of reliance on wages is that it tempts the government to increase military expenditures in order to create jobs. Many economists and government officials remember well how the U.S. did not recover from the Depression of the 1930s until military preparations began for World War II. In our desperate attempt to create jobs, we have turned our backs on the fact that we have become the world's largest arms peddler. As Senator Mark Hatfield said in a 1982 speech, "We are selling tanks to countries that don't even have a subsistence agriculture." Thus our dependence on wages has accelerated the arms race, made us warmongers, and may lead us into the confrontation that ultimately causes a nuclear holocaust.

The second method of support, welfare, has been the favorite governmental substitute for jobs for the past half-century, but it too has proved unworkable, whether it is used in a democracy or in a dictatorship. Government simply cannot generate enough tax money from the producers to support all those left by the wayside without decent jobs. Recurring worldwide inflation is the inevitable result. Welfare has become a permanent way of life in stagnating industrial nations such as Great Britain, and it is taking firm hold in the United States as well. In Detroit, there are thousands of young people who have never worked, have given up looking for work, and don't even know anyone who has a steady job.

Cheating, the third method of supporting people, includes

criminal and dishonest behavior of individuals and corporations. This third method is fast catching up with wages and welfare. In many places today, the new American Dream is to make it big as a drug dealer. The inability of wages and welfare to sustain our population without bringing on deadly inflation has demoralized our people to the extent that tax cheating and crime have become major growth industries.

So, what is left that has not been tried and found wanting? Only the fourth method of support, capitalist income—the return on invested capital. The first three methods—wages, welfare, and cheating—are used by virtually all economic systems. Only the fourth method is unique to capitalism.

Now, picture the new horizons that would open up if, instead of limiting capitalist income to the present pinnacle class of 6 percent of the population, we made the return on invested capital work for everyone.

Let's Use Capitalism to Save Capitalism

Despite its defects, American capitalism has produced some unique economic and cultural achievements. Marx himself marveled at the productive accomplishments of capitalism, even in its primitive form. In the 1848 *Communist Manifesto,* he said:

> It has been the first to show what man's activity can bring about. It has accomplished wonders far surpassing Egyptian pyramids, Roman aqueducts, and Gothic cathedrals; it has conducted expeditions that put in the shade all former migrations of nations and crusades.

***

> The bourgeoisie, during its rule of scarce one hundred years has created more massive and more colossal productive forces than have all preceding generations together. Subjection of nature's forces to man, machinery, application of chemistry to industry and agriculture, steam-navigation, railways, electric telegraphs, clearing of whole continents for cultivation, canalisation of rivers, whole populations conjured out of the ground—what earlier century had even a presentiment that such productive forces slumbered in the lap of social labour? [International Publishers, New York, 1948, pp. 11, 15]

Over the past 100 years, America's real per capita income, adjusted for inflation, has increased more than tenfold. Under capitalism, we have provided a high standard of living to more millions of people than any nation in history, and in the opinion of many qualified observers, American welfare capitalism has produced the closest thing to a just society that the world has ever seen. Compared to Marxist countries, capitalist nations are more democratic, have more religious and personal freedom, and generally enjoy higher living standards. Indeed, socialism has been around so long that if it really worked, there would be practically no capitalism left today, since capitalism has been retained mainly by democratic nations, where the owners of capital could be outvoted by at least 15 to 1. As John Kenneth Galbraith put it in his 1978 book, *Almost Everyone's Guide to Economics:*

> If economic performance in a socialist society had come as easily and with prospects as brilliant intellectually and otherwise as Marx took for granted (and Lenin also, before it became, for him, a matter of practical experience), there would be no capitalism left. No power or propaganda would have held people to capitalism. [p. 22]

Capitalism has survived in the United States and other democracies because it can change. It is an evolutionary system, flexible enough to keep up with the great sea changes of history. When it started to come apart during the Great Depression, Franklin Roosevelt injected enough welfare socialism into it to stave off a revolution. But the anesthetic effect of the welfare injection is wearing off, and there is nothing left to save capitalism but capitalism itself. We've tried everything else. Now at last we must repair the weakness that Marx focused on: *ownership and exploitation.* The only game plan left is to transform capitalism into a system that works for everyone, so every American can become an owner of the means of production and thus share the main bounty of capitalism: the return on capital investment.

There is such a plan. I call it SuperStock, because it uses corporate stock to perform economic functions heretofore assigned to wages, welfare, and prayer. SuperStock, however, is merely a working title. You may prefer a more conventional name, such as *universal capitalism, democratic capitalism,* or *social capitalism.*

I present the SuperStock plan as nothing more than a starting point for discussion—a means of stimulating debate. I propose it as a potential means of solving many of our major economic problems in a way that will not intensify the global conflict between capitalism and communism. Indeed, if it works, it can serve as the bridge that will open the way for Soviet-American friendship and disarmament.

SuperStock is certainly not the best plan that can be devised. But it is not something brand new, out of the blue. It has been analyzed by enough knowledgeable people to reveal any obvious economic and political flaws, and none has been found. With your help, we can use this plan as a sounding board to engage the interest of the world's great thinkers, those who can produce the ideal plan but are now busily looking off in the wrong directions.

Is there a way to do this? Are there any inherent obstacles in American capitalism that would prevent us from spreading MOP ownership to all of our people? You will search in vain for any such restriction in the Constitution or laws of the United States. Yet most economists, even the liberals, have not opened their minds to such a concept. Professor Robert Lekachman, for example, one of the leading liberal economists, wrote in his 1981 handbook, *Capitalism for Beginners:*

> Under capitalism, a society's capital equipment, its means of production, is owned by a minority of individuals who have the legal right to use this property for private gain. [p. 3]

Professor Lekachman's statement is a perfectly accurate description of American capitalism, but it need not be the ultimate definition of capitalism. There is no reason why capitalism cannot function when the means of production are owned by a majority of individuals rather than a minority. In fact, common sense and experience tell us that capitalism would probably work much better (especially in a democracy) if MOP ownership were in the hands of the largest possible group.

Indeed, if we could possibly find a way to open MOP ownership to all Americans, we would make our economic system consistent with our political democracy and with our concept of fairness, whether you call it social justice, the Golden Rule, the good old American way, or the product of Judeo-Christian heritage.

And that is exactly what SuperStock is designed to do.

Chapter 5

SuperStock: *MOP Ownership for Every American Household*

I conceive . . . that a somewhat comprehensive socialisation of investment will prove the only means of securing an approximation of full employment.

—JOHN MAYNARD KEYNES

Whatever the means used, a basic objective should be to distribute newly created capital broadly among the population. Such a policy would redress a major imbalance in our society and has the potential for strengthening future business growth.

—1976 Report of the Joint Economic Committee of Congress

If you're an average American with faith in capitalism and hope for the good life, you're probably making about $27,000 per year, with a family of three or four to support. You may have a wealthy brother-in-law who just made a killing in the stock market, and a rich neighbor who bought an interest in a lucrative local business. There are capitalists all around you, but on your salary, you're lucky to own the 50 shares of IBM you received as a wedding gift. Like the millions of other noncapitalists who make up 94 percent of our population, you have been taught that it takes money to make money, so you are waiting for the big break—probably a promotion to a much higher-paying job—before you can save up enough money or muster enough credit to become a capitalist yourself.

Of course, all Americans can become capitalists, and millions do own some stock. But as we have seen, no more than 6 percent of Americans receive significant income from ownership of stock or other income-producing capital.

Yet there is a vast hidden reservoir of unowned wealth in this country, in the form of the *new capital* created each year by American business, which could provide a substantial amount of income-producing stock for those Americans who presently own little or no capital. (Capital, in this context, does not refer to money, but rather to the plant and equipment that corporations build or buy every year in order to increase production and generate more income.) The key aspect of this capital is that it is *self-liquidating*, meaning that it is designed to pay for itself out of the increased profits flowing from expanded production. So, for example, the cost of constructing a new automobile factory will, over time, be covered by the sale of new cars rolling off the factory's assembly line. This capital is designed to pay for itself regardless of who owns it—a wealthy investor, a struggling janitor, or a wooden Indian. In theory, then, anyone could become an owner of this new capital, *if* he or she were extended the necessary credit with which to purchase shares of stock in the corporations creating the capital. (See Figure 1.)

In practice, however, credit for the purchase of stock or other income-producing capital is available only to those who already have savings or other holdings—those who can provide good collateral for loans. That's why your brother-in-law keeps getting richer while you hang on to those same 50 shares of IBM. That also explains why he was bragging about how his net worth increased when his golfing buddy, Irving Peerless, chief executive officer of the Peerless Pizza Parlors Corporation, decided to build a new plant to turn out ovens and other pizza-making machinery for his expanding franchise network. Your brother-in-law had been a stockholder of Peerless Pizza Parlors since its first public offering back in the 1960s, and when the new plant was built, the credit power of the corporation went to work for him again, even though he made no further investment.

The Present System—Why the Rich Get Richer

In 1982, even at a time of crippling recession, American business invested over $300 billion in the construction and purchase of new plant and equipment. How is this new capital financed? Under our present system, 95 percent of these new capital expenditures are

Capital investment pays for itself...

...no matter who owns it.

Long-term credit is the key.

Figure 1.

paid for by a combination of debt (loans or bonds) and internal funds (including retained earnings and investment tax credits). Only 5 percent is financed through the issuance of new common stock, and as we've seen, that 5 percent can only be purchased by those wealthy enough to secure credit or risk a cash investment. Essentially then, this yearly pool of new capital is financed through devices that operate like a corporate plumbing system, ensuring that ownership of this new capital flows exclusively to the pinnacle class which already holds most of the nation's privately-owned stock. (See Figure 2.) Here's how it works:

When Irving Peerless decided to build the new pizza-making machinery plant, he calculated the cost at $10 million. One million dollars of the cost was provided by the U.S. Treasury in the form of an investment tax credit equal to 10 percent of the new plant's cost—a gift from the taxpayers. Another $1 million came from state and local tax credits and grants, in gratitude for the jobs the new plant would create. The corporation itself put up $1 million, drawn from its retained earnings—monies set aside from past profits on pizza sales, which remained bottled up in the corporation for reinvestment purposes instead of being paid out to stockholders as dividends. An additional $6.5 million was obtained from banks and institutional lenders, through long-term loans that would be repaid out of the future earnings accruing to the corporation from increased pizza sales. Thus, the corporation's use of credit and tax breaks to pay for newly-formed capital out of future earnings gives its present stockholders an automatic increase in their capital holdings. Without any additional investment on their part, Peerless's current shareholders will reap the benefits of $9.5 million worth of new capital.

Will there be any new stockholders? Yes. As we saw in Figure 2, about 5 percent of new capital is paid for by issuance of new equity. So Peerless Pizza paid the remaining 5 percent of the new plant's cost by issuing $500,000 worth of new common stock. And when it came on the market, it was immediately bought up by people who had the necessary savings or collateral to secure credit. Your brother-in-law chose not to buy any of the new stock, but had he so desired, he could easily have borrowed the money to buy $25,000 to $50,000 worth of it, and he could have let it pay for itself over the years as the machines poured out of the new Peerless plant and inundated America with millions of pizza pies, increasing Peerless's profits, raising its dividends, and making the value of its shares climb. Your brother-in-law was content to let the financial power of Peerless Pizza work for him without any further investment, and so

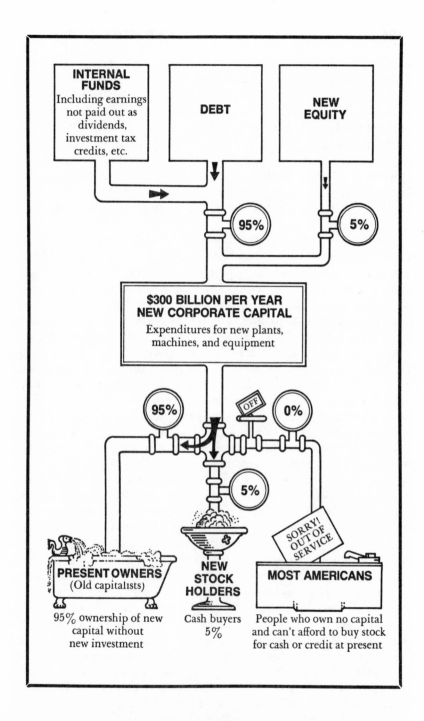

Figure 2. How capital expenditures (additions to the means of production) are financed under American capitalism.

he took a free ride on the long-term credit, tax breaks, and public subsidies available to our large corporations. Had he chosen to buy some of the $500,000 worth of new stock issued by Peerless, the overall ownership picture would not have changed, since he is a member of the elite class that already owns the other $9.5 million worth of new capital Peerless added when it built the new plant.

This use of credit to pay for new capital was particularly irritating to Karl Marx. Refuting the capitalist's claim that capital ownership was based on savings, Marx wrote in the third volume of *Das Kapital:* "What he demands is that *others* should save for him" (Vintage Books edition, p. 570).

As long as this corporate plumbing system remains intact, so too will the process of overconcentrating MOP ownership in the hands of a mere 6 percent of the population. And the remaining 94 percent will continue to be denied any real access to significant capital ownership, thus widening the gap between the haves and the have-nots. This process, according to Marx, is precisely what will lead to capitalism's demise. With the majority of the population lacking real purchasing power, particularly during inflationary times, there simply won't be enough customers for the goods and services produced by American business. And the thousands of automobile dealers, home builders, and other American businessmen who had to shut their doors in the 1980s for want of customers, will probably tell you that Marx was right on this count.

The corporate finance system pictured in Figure 2 is rigged to *absorb* most of the newly created capital into the corporation, providing automatic ownership for its present stockholders. Yet nobody questions this system. Obviously, the major stockholders who control corporate voting power have a vested interest in its maintenance. But what about the millions of Americans who don't own any stock—the noncapitalists? It would seem that they, too, view the system as immutable, accepting without question the notion that they cannot become stockholders if they don't have the necessary savings.

In addition to widening the wealth gap between owners and nonowners, this rigid system keeps billions of dollars bottled up in the corporations for capital expenditures, thereby reducing the income available for mass consumption of the corporations' products. Wealthy stockholders believe this practice serves their interests, for they would otherwise have to pay large income taxes on their substantial dividend income. They prefer to have this money remain in corporate coffers, where the value of their holdings can increase untaxed and without any additional investment on their part.

There is, however, nothing sacred or immutable about this

plumbing system. No American Congress ever approved it; the Constitutional Convention did not even consider it. It is simply one method—and not necessarily the best method—of financing an industrial economy. In prosperous times, while our economy was able to produce enough jobs and income to satisfy the expectations of most Americans, there was no reason to question the system. But with our economy eroding, our whole society in crisis, and our civilization headed for nuclear disaster, we cannot cling to an outmoded financial plumbing system that perpetuates some of the principal inequities of laissez-faire capitalism. If we are to build a bridge between capitalism and communism, we must focus on the plumbing system that produces our MOP ownership and consider how we can modify it to save our economy, our society—and our civilization.

The SuperStock Plan

The purpose of SuperStock is to spread ownership of newly-formed capital throughout society, enabling the noncapitalist 94 percent of our population to derive income from *direct participation* in American capitalism. Remember that business requires over $300 billion a year for new capital, which is not owned by anyone now and which is projected to pay for itself regardless of who owns it. Over the next generation (roughly 20 years), according to the Brookings Institution, *Business Week,* and other authoritative sources, new capital expenditures are expected to total at least *$5 trillion.* (Interestingly enough, that happens to be the total amount of private wealth, i.e., ownership of productive capital, in this country today.)

Imagine then the result if this $5 trillion worth of new plant and equipment could be owned solely by those who presently own no capital: *in one generation, ownership of the productive wealth of the nation could be equalized.* Not only would the SuperStock plan create a more equitable distribution of income throughout society, but it would do so without disturbing present holdings. Because SuperStock is based on ownership of *new* capital, there is no confiscation of wealth involved in the plan.

Can you imagine a better way of ensuring the survival of capitalism than by spreading the benefits of capital ownership to all Americans? Is there any surer way to head off the thrust toward socialism than by making capitalism work for everyone? Appropriately enough, it was Karl Marx himself who first envisioned the role credit and stock ownership might play in socializing capital ownership.

An Important Discovery: Marx's Unheralded Writings

In our search for a method of modifying American MOP ownership in order to build a bridge between capitalism and Marxism, we must start with Marxist dogma itself. To cure the malignancies they perceived in capitalism, Marx and Engels prescribed a simple remedy: socialization of MOP ownership. Remember, however, that they never precisely defined what they meant by socialization. Lenin interpreted their writings as a call for government ownership and control of the means of production—nationalization. To Karl Kautsky, on the other hand, Lenin's brand of state ownership did not rise to the level of social ownership. Taking our cue from Kautsky, let us focus on social ownership, using the word *socialize* in its broad definition: to convert to the needs of the entire society. Certainly, if MOP ownership is made available equitably to the entire society, it is socialized.

Here we shall consider some Marxist writings that, to my knowledge, have never before been examined in light of the possibility of making capitalism compatible with Marxism. Volume Three of *Das Kapital*, completed by Engels and published in 1894, represents the last word of Marx and Engels on socialization of MOP ownership. The following excerpts from Chapter 27, "The Role of Credit in Capitalist Production," (Vintage Books edition, Random House, 1981) have a direct bearing on our search. In this excerpt, Marx and Engels perceive the great potential of the "joint-stock company," England's nineteenth-century equivalent of today's publicly traded corporations:

III. Formation of joint-stock companies. This involves:

1. Tremendous expansion in the scale of production, and enterprises which would be impossible for individual capitals. At the same time, enterprises that were previously government ones become social.

2. Capital, which is inherently based on a social mode of production and presupposes a social concentration of means of production and labour-power, now receives the form of social capital (capital of directly associated individuals) in contrast to private capital, and its enterprises appear as social enterprises as opposed to private ones. This is the abolition of capital as private property within the confines of the capitalist mode of production itself.

***

This result of capitalist production in its highest development is a necessary point of transition towards the transformation of capital back into the property of the producers, though no longer as the private property of individual producers, but rather as their property as associated producers, as directly social property. It is furthermore a point-of transition towards the transformation of all functions formerly bound up with capital ownership in the reproduction process into simple functions of the associated producers, into social functions.

***

This is the abolition of the capitalist mode of production within the capitalist mode of production itself, and hence a self-abolishing contradiction, which presents itself prima facie as a mere point of transition to a new form of production. [pp. 567–9]

Then they went on to describe how the credit system can play a role in socializing MOP ownership through joint-stock companies (corporations):

This credit system, since it forms the principal basis for the gradual transformation of capitalist private enterprises into capitalist joint-stock companies, presents in the same way the means for the gradual extension of cooperative enterprises on a more or less national scale. Capitalist joint-stock companies as much as cooperative factories should be viewed as transition forms from the capitalist mode of production to the associated one, simply that in the one case the opposition is abolished in a negative way, and in the other in a positive way.

Up till now, we have considered the development of credit—and the latent abolition of capital ownership contained within it—principally in relation to industrial capital. [pp. 571–2]

In these passages, Marx and Engels recognized that the modern corporation could be used to socialize capital ownership since it could divide ownership (in the form of readily-transferable stock certificates) among an unlimited number of people. This was in contrast to earlier stages of capitalism, when ownership of an enterprise was solely in the hands of an individual or family. They also foresaw the role that credit could play in this transformation, by fueling the development and expansion of numerous large stock corporations, which would in turn spread capital ownership to a much broader group of people than had been the case in the more primitive stages of industrialization.

Thus, with remarkable insight, Marx and Engels perceived the potential socialization of MOP ownership through the early joint-stock company and the primitive credit system of their time. They found in these two elements, even in such crude forms, a way to overcome their basic objections to capitalism by *the latent abolition of capitalist property*. And in their vision we have a theoretical foundation for the use of corporate stock and credit—the two basic elements of the SuperStock plan—to socialize MOP ownership in a way that does *not* require nationalization.

Although Marx and Engels appreciated the potential of widespread stock ownership and broad use of credit, they could not envision any constructive or "social" use of these elements under capitalism. They assumed both would be used to further overconcentrate capital ownership and perpetuate class divisiveness, and thus they did not lay out any plan for use of these elements in socializing capital ownership. But what Marx and Engels failed to realize is that the credit system could be harnessed on behalf of non-capitalists as well as capitalists.

That this great socializing force was beyond their vision isn't surprising because it has eluded practically all of our twentieth century economists as well. But don't let it elude you. By delivering MOP ownership directly to the people through corporate stock and the credit system, which is the essence of SuperStock, we can fulfill the central goal of Marxism—ending the exploitation of the nonowning class. And bear in mind that the foundation for this method of socializing MOP ownership springs directly from the works of Marx, Engels, and Kautsky.

The New Plumbing System: Using Stock and Credit To Make Everyone A Capitalist

SuperStock is designed to make stock ownership in America's 2,000 leading corporations available to everyone through a plumbing system that would funnel ownership of new capital directly to the 50 million households who now own little or no capital. To understand how it would work, let's go through it step by step, utilizing as a case in point the Peerless Pizza Parlors Corporation, which we shall imagine as one of the nation's 2,000 leading corporations. Remember that in building its new plant, Peerless is creating $10 million worth of new capital *that is not presently owned by anyone* and that will *pay for itself* over time through the increased production and sale of pizza pies.

Under our present corporate plumbing system (Figure 2), Peerless financed this capital primarily through internal funds and debt, which funneled ownership of 95 percent of the new capital into the bathtub of the current Peerless stockholders. There were some new stockholders, of course, but they were members of the elite class that had the savings or the credit needed to buy shares— the same group that owns the other 95 percent of this new capital.

At the heart of the present system, then, is a mechanism for producing capital ownership that has been employed for centuries by wealthy individuals and businesses: *long-term credit.* At the heart of the new SuperStock plumbing system is this same mechanism, but with one key difference: now long-term credit will be extended to the noncapitalists—to *you* and not to your brother-in-law. Here's how it works:

(1) *Financing New Capital:* Under the new federal legislation establishing SuperStock, Peerless will not be allowed to pay for its plants through internal funds or debt. Rather, it will be required to finance its capital growth by issuing $10 million worth of a special type of stock, to be called SuperStock. This stock will not be available to people like your brother-in-law, who already owns a substantial amount of stock. Instead, you and the others who make up the 94 percent of the population who owns little or no capital will be able to acquire a given number of SuperStock shares. Now we come to the heart of the system: how do you pay for the stock? You don't. A loan will be arranged to provide the money needed to pay Peerless for the stock, and eventually the stock will pay for itself out of its own earnings.

(2) *Credit:* The SuperStock legislation will establish a government-guaranteed long-term loan program. In effect, *you* will be using the credit power of Peerless to acquire shares of its stock, just as Peerless now uses its credit power to acquire further capital ownership for its present stockholders. A bank loan of $10 million will be arranged, to provide Peerless with the entire cost of the new plant; Peerless will then issue $10 million worth of its stock (at market value) when it receives the proceeds of the loan. But the loan will not be owed by you or by Peerless—it will be owed by the Super-Stock fund. Until the loan has been repaid, the Peerless shares earmarked for your account will be held in escrow by the bank that made the $10 million loan.

(3) *Repayment:* The SuperStock legislation requires Peerless and the rest of the 2,000 participating corporations to pay out all their earnings as dividends, except those reserves actually needed to run the company. Thus, as Peerless begins to realize higher profits from the output of the pizza machines made in the new factory, these profits will be turned into higher dividends which are used to pay for the shares of SuperStock issued to you. For a number of years, these dividends will be paid directly to the bank, until such time as it has recouped its $10 million loan, plus interest. At that time, you own your shares of SuperStock outright, receiving all future dividends directly.

This new plumbing system, therefore, ensures that Peerless's $10 million worth of new capital is owned by millions of new capitalists—individuals who previously had no real access to capital ownership. (See Figure 3). At the same time, it has no effect on the holdings of "old" capitalists like your brother-in-law. Nor is Peerless itself affected in any adverse way.

I have over-simplified SuperStock to give you a bird's-eye view of it from the standpoint of a single company, Peerless Pizza. Actually, it is designed as a group plan, involving at the start America's 2,000 leading corporations, such as General Motors, IBM, AT&T, Xerox, and Exxon. These are the corporations that every year create most of America's $300 billion of new capital. To pay for this capital, each corporation would issue shares of stock at market value. These shares would be pooled in a sort of mutual fund, with each corporation contributing to the pool the number of shares needed to pay for its new capital expenditures. Shares would be parceled out in bundles to those households eligible for the SuperStock program, with each SuperStockholder receiving shares in all 2,000 companies. So, for example, in a given year a SuperStockholder might receive a certificate of ownership for 9 shares of IBM, 12 shares of General Motors, 6 shares of Exxon, and so on, depending on how much each of these companies spent for new capital additions, the market value of each company's stock, and the number of households participating in the SuperStock plan. Earnings on these shares would be paid out as dividends, and the stock would be held in escrow until the loans had been repaid. Thereafter, ownership and dividends would be put directly into the hands of the participating households—the SuperStockholders. The program, which would be established through federal legislation and administered by a government agency, would continue for at least 20 years, producing in all about $5 trillion worth of new capital ownership for SuperStockholders.

Now let's zero in on the bottom-line questions: How might SuperStock be implemented? What kinds of specific changes would be required?

The Corporations

Participation in the SuperStock program would be open to our 2,000 major "blue-chip" corporations, those that can justify large capital expenditures by projecting sufficient future profits to make these expenditures pay for themselves. We're not going to be turning to start-up ventures, small companies, or financially unstable operations, but to the profitable giants like IBM in whose corporate

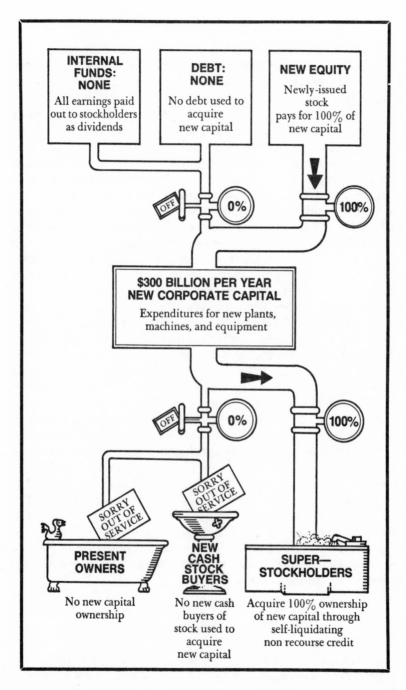

INTERNAL FUNDS: NONE

All earnings paid out to stockholders as dividends

DEBT: NONE

No debt used to acquire new capital

NEW EQUITY

Newly-issued stock pays for 100% of new capital

OFF · 0% · 100%

$300 BILLION PER YEAR NEW CORPORATE CAPITAL

Expenditures for new plants, machines, and equipment

OFF · 0% · 100%

SORRY OUT OF SERVICE · SORRY OUT OF SERVICE

PRESENT OWNERS

No new capital ownership

NEW CASH STOCK BUYERS

No new cash buyers of stock used to acquire new capital

SUPER— STOCKHOLDERS

Acquire 100% ownership of new capital through self-liquidating non recourse credit

Figure 3. The SuperStock plan: Financing capital expenditures through SuperStock, to spread MOP ownership throughout American society and make income distribution equitable.

assets most of the nation's productive capital is concentrated.

It would be up to Congress to establish guidelines for selection of specific corporations. In general, eligibility should be limited to corporations with a solid track record of good returns on invested capital. We might, for example, begin the program with corporations that have annual sales of $100 million or more and have shown a net profit for two of the three preceding years. We might also want to design safeguards; participating corporations could be required to document proposed expenditures by submitting projections to the Securities and Exchange Commission, in much the same way they now have to justify capital additions to their bankers. But there is no need to get the government involved in regulating capital investment or allocating funds. If the new plant does not work out for Peerless Pizza, its shareholders will suffer the same financial losses as under the present system. This puts the burden on Irving Peerless and the other officers and directors of Peerless Pizza to make the same thorough studies and projections for the new plant that they would if they were borrowing the whole $10 million cost.

Pooling of the shares of 2,000 corporations would create a sort of mutual fund or unit trust, and would prevent any inequities in parceling out the shares. Every SuperStockholder would receive a piece of every participating company; there would be no big losers if one of the 2,000 participating corporations did poorly. By the same token, there would be no big winners getting richer than others from the earnings of a particularly hot company. The key is equitable distribution of both stock ownership and dividend income. Pooling also simplifies administration of the program. If individual SuperStockholders were allowed to select specific companies in which to own shares, the system would become chaotic. It would be almost impossible to sort out priorities and parcel out shares. The object is to give *all* Americans the chance to become capitalists, and the fastest and most effective way to meet this goal is to provide them with a diversified stock portfolio that produces a share of the profits of our leading corporations.

The Government

Implementation of SuperStock would, of course, require federal legislation and administration. Although Congress might choose to create a new government agency to run the program, it could be administered by the Treasury Department, the Department of Commerce, the Social Security Administration, or the Securities and Exchange Commission (SEC). The SEC probably would prove the wisest choice since it now regulates issuance of corporate stocks and bonds and would probably be involved anyway under existing laws.

Apart from administrative functions, the government's primary involvement in the SuperStock program would be to act as loan guarantor. Remember that SuperStockholders cannot and will not actually pay for the stock, nor will they even have to sign notes for it. Under the SuperStock system, the government would step in, not with welfare handouts or grants, but with government guarantees of the loans the banks will make to pay for SuperStock. These guarantees could be financed by loan insurance fees in a manner similar to the way the FHA and FDIC operate now.

The risks involved in this plan, for both the banks and the government, are actually quite minimal because SuperStock will be secured by the assets and earning power of our corporate giants. And because SuperStock is essentially a portfolio of diversified stock, if any of the participating corporations failed, the earnings of the remainder would be available to offset the losses. This is one of Super-Stock's great innovations: creating a system of equitable income distribution based on the *strength* of capitalism—the ability of productive capital to pay for itself—rather than on the weaknesses inherent in government welfare handouts.

If you're wondering whether Congress has the power to order our 2,000 leading corporations to issue stock in payment for their new capital additions, the answer is yes. Back in 1937, the U.S. Supreme Court decided that Congress, by virtue of its power to provide for the general welfare, could require corporations to make Social Security contributions for their employees. Thus, if Congress decided that a national policy of capital ownership would promote the general welfare of the American people, it would have the constitutional power to enact the necessary legislation.

There are also precedents for government guarantees of long-term credit. World War II veterans were able to secure government-guaranteed, low-interest home mortgages under the G.I. Bill of Rights. Most of these veterans did not have the savings or income to qualify for mortgages without this government subsidy. This program not only enabled millions of Americans to buy homes with no down payment, but it also helped to usher in one of our most prosperous economic periods. And even today the FHA guarantees banks against losses on loans made for the construction or purchase of homes. Certainly, if the government can guarantee loans for non-productive items like homes, it should be able to guarantee loans for capital outlays that are both productive and self-liquidating.

Repayment: How Would It Work?

At present, corporations pay out only about 30 percent of their earnings as dividends; the other 70 percent is pumped back into the corporation in the form of retained earnings. Obviously, if Super-Stock is to pay for itself in a reasonable amount of time, the share of earnings paid out as dividends would have to be much greater than 30 percent. In fact, under SuperStock, shareholders would receive the *full return* on invested capital. Participating corporations would be required by law to pay out *all* of their earnings as dividends, except for the reserves actually needed to run the company. This would return corporations to their original purpose: serving as instruments for distribution of profits to their shareholders. Indeed, under the new system, corporations would have no use for retained earnings anyway, since they would not be allowed to use them for capital outlays. Paying out of these earnings as dividends would provide additional benefits as well. By pumping more income into the economy, we would be creating more customers, more taxpayers, and more production, all of which should be counter-inflationary.

How long might it take for SuperStock to pay for itself? Anywhere from seven to fifteen years, depending on corporate performance (their rate of return on invested capital), interest rates, and the way the dividends are used. Let's take a closer look at these key factors.

Corporate Performance: Currently, most of our major corporations realize annual pre-tax profits of about 20 percent on their invested capital. If this entire 20 percent were paid out as dividends, SuperStock would repay its entire principal in five years; allowing for a reasonable interest charge, repayment would take seven or eight years. But under our present system, a chunk of these profits ends up in government coffers in the form of corporate income tax payments. Clearly, if SuperStockholders are to receive the full pre-tax 20 percent earnings on their shares, major changes in the corporate income tax structure would be required, at least in regard to the SuperStock program. How might this be handled?

The simplest method would be to eliminate the corporate income tax entirely for those companies participating in the Super-Stock program. Such an exemption would cost the Treasury some revenue, but the loss would be more than balanced by *increases* in personal income tax payments, since all shareholders, including SuperStockholders, would have to pay personal income tax on the dividends they receive. Currently, corporate taxes bring in less than 10 percent of federal revenues. Thanks to tax credits and loopholes, the average tax rate of our large corporations is only about 20 percent, and many of the giants with profits in the $100 million range pay no federal taxes at all. It's quite likely, therefore, that the Treasury would collect more income tax revenue on dividends than it presently does through corporate taxes. For under SuperStock, what the corporations don't pay, the shareholders will.

Bear in mind as well that SuperStock would, in time, replace government transfer payments, such as Social Security and welfare. At present, with capital ownership concentrated in the hands of a small elite class, the government is forced to redistribute income, taxing the producers to provide income for the nonproducers (the unemployed, the disabled, the elderly). SuperStock would change this by putting capital ownership into the hands of those who now receive transfer payments. The dividends on SuperStock would replace the transfer payments, and government (federal, state, and local) would no longer need massive tax revenues.

Elimination of the corporate income tax is not a new idea, but it has never gained popular support because it has always been viewed as a benefit for the already-rich. Under SuperStock, the benefits would go to the entire population. But we need not remove all corporate income taxes in order to implement SuperStock. We could, instead, simply allow the participating corporations a tax deduction for their SuperStock dividend payments, in much the same way they now receive a tax deduction for interest payments. In that way, we could accomplish the objective of getting SuperStock paid for as quickly as possible by capturing the full pre-tax earnings on the new capital, while continuing to collect income taxes on the portion of corporate earnings not related to SuperStock.

One of the reasons corporations currently pay only 30 percent of their earnings as dividends is the double tax penalty. Before dividends can be paid out today, a corporation must pay taxes of up to 46 percent on its profits; then the stockholders must pay an additional personal income tax of up to 50 percent on dividends received. This tax structure encourages corporations to hold back most of their earnings and use them for capital outlays. But if corporations are no longer allowed to use accumulated earnings to pay for new capital, and if they are not taxed on earnings paid out as dividends, there will be no reason to hold back dividend payments.

Thus, if corporate return on invested capital remained at the current 20 percent level, SuperStock would pay for itself in roughly seven years. Indeed, under SuperStock, earnings would be even higher since corporations wouldn't be deducting from profits the interest charges they formerly had to pay on loans made for new capital outlays. If actual returns are less than 20 percent, repayment would of course have to be stretched over a longer period of time. Then, too, the repayment period would depend to an important degree on the amount of interest banks charged for SuperStock loans.

Interest Rates: If interest rates remain at the present oppressively high level (above 10 percent for home mortgages), that seven-year repayment goal isn't likely to be met. But there are several alternatives. The government could arrange for a lower interest rate on the financing of SuperStock shares; numerous similar government programs exist today. For example, sales of large airplanes to overseas customers by companies such as Boeing and McDonnell Douglas are subsidized by low-interest loans from the U.S. Export-Import Bank. This agency, which finances and promotes foreign trade, arranges for interest rates well below the prime market rate in order to spur trade and improve our balance of payments. Such low-interest loans have even been used for trade with communist nations. Other current federal loan guarantee programs, designed to spur the creation of jobs, have interest rates as low as 2 percent. Why not utilize this same sort of interest subsidy for a program designed to strengthen our economy and make all Americans capitalists?

Alternatively, we could simply accept current high rates and finance SuperStock anyway, stretching repayment over a longer period of time, perhaps as much as 30 years, as is done now with many home mortgages.

Dividends: Repayment will also depend on the way dividends are allocated. The SuperStock shares will be held in escrow by the banks until the loans have been repaid, and we could require that all dividends be paid directly to the banks during that period. While this would speed up repayment of the loans, it would also leave the SuperStockholders without any dividend income for at least seven years. If we found it desirable to start the flow of income to the SuperStockholders earlier, we might stretch out the repayment period to about 15 years and split the dividends in half. Fifty percent could go to the banks for repayment of loans and interest; the remainder could be paid directly to SuperStockholders as income.

The SuperStockholders: Who Would They Be?

During the nineteenth century, when land was our chief form of productive capital, the government allocated ownership of this capital to Americans through the Homestead Act, literally handing out 160 acres of land to anyone willing to settle it and cultivate it for five years. Obviously, when it comes to ownership of $5 trillion worth of productive capital in the form of corporate stock, we could not use the Homestead Act method of distribution.

There are a lot of tough decisions for Congress to make in establishing the priorities for access to SuperStock—but they aren't nearly as tough as trying to make welfare capitalism work in a democracy where people have high expectations. Congress could establish some priorities and then have its Joint Economic Committee or other committees review them regularly. The priorities could be adjusted before any great damage was done, since SuperStock must be phased in over a period of at least seven years. But I suggest that Congress retain this function and not delegate it to an administrative agency. It's too important for that. It should remain under direct control of our most sensitive instrument of democracy.

We might start by excluding all households whose current net worth equals $100,000 or more. Or we could establish a point system for eligibility. Points could be awarded for low wages, lack of savings or capital ownership, willingness to work, physical disability, compliance with the law, and public service work. Points could be deducted for criminal violations, unwillingness to work, high wages, capital ownership above a certain level, and so on. Some weight would have to be given to the number of people in the household, and (as under the present system) there would have to be provisions for divorce or breakup of the household. First priority might be given to the working poor—the 20 million or more Americans whose income is below the poverty line even though they work. We might also consider giving special priority to the armed forces, the police and fire departments, nurses, and perhaps even politicians—people engaged in dangerous or demanding public service, which leaves them little opportunity to accumulate capital honestly. The idea is to make participation in SuperStock more attractive to public servants than bribery or featherbedding.

We would have to keep our Social Security and welfare programs alive, at least temporarily, to cover those who did not become eligible for SuperStock. But we should make the SuperStock route much more attractive, to encourage everyone to work out of the welfare system by becoming owners of the means of production.

There is no reason to make SuperStock available to those who commit crimes. Moreover, any SuperStockholders convicted of a crime should have to forfeit their holdings or turn them over to their victims. We need not repeat the fiasco of our Social Security system, where convicts who claimed physical or mental impairment resulting from their own criminal activities received disability benefits while in jail. Congress will also have to face the problem of those who have been convicted of crimes but have demonstrated that they deserve another chance.

The Homestead Act provides a useful precedent for confining ownership privileges to those who comply with the law. When Abraham Lincoln signed the act in 1862, it made land available only to American citizens who had "never borne arms against the United States government or given aid and comfort to its enemies." Another precedent for awarding government benefits on the basis of valuable service and law-abiding conduct is the package of veterans' benefits made available under the G.I. Bill of Rights to those who served in the armed forces. The point is to use SuperStock to encourage compliance with the law; to bring citizens into the mainstream of society by convincing them they have more to gain by honest labor than criminal activities. At present, our system sends out a very different sort of message: by excluding millions of Americans from the benefits of mainstream capitalism, by rigging our laws to shut them out of the system, we are virtually inviting them to break the law and attack private property.

Once eligibility has been determined, how much can Super-Stockholders actually expect to receive in stock and income? Remember that according to reliable projections, American business will create at least $5 trillion worth of new capital over the next 20 or so years. If that figure is divided among the 50 million households who presently own little or no capital, each household would receive $100,000 worth of SuperStock. To express it more graphically:

$$\textbf{\$5 trillion divided by 50 million households} =$$

$$\frac{\textbf{\$5,000,000,000,000}}{\textbf{50,000,000}} = \textbf{\$100,000 per household}$$

And at the current pre-tax return rate of 20 percent on invested capital, each household could expect to receive about $20,000 in dividends after their SuperStock has paid for itself. Would a guaranteed yearly income of $20,000 impair the incentive to work? Perhaps. If so, we might build rewards into the system for those continuing to work.

Remember too, that a lack of incentive to work is built into the present Social Security and welfare systems. If we can get Super-

Stock working to the point where it *does* threaten the work incentive, we will have the time and brains to solve that problem. Some of the potential solutions are discussed later in Chapter 8, under "Super-Stock and Employment."

In any event, we have to face the fact that we are entering the age of true automation, and there will not be work for everyone in the way we now think of work. If we develop a truly affluent society, many people will be able to work in research, the arts, the improvement of our public facilities and environment, or in occupations no one has dreamed of yet—the work of humanity.

Adoption of SuperStock will force us to examine some basic questions: What kind of nation do we want to be? What kind of society can we afford? America was founded on the principle of political democracy, but we've never had economic democracy, nor have we ever dealt directly with the issue of wealth or ownership, either in the Constitution or in congressional legislation. There may be no easy answers, but surely the quest itself is worthwhile. And we can move slowly, particularly since SuperStock must be phased in over a period of at least seven years.

When SuperStock becomes the focus of political discussion, liberals will want to give welfare recipients first crack at SuperStock benefits. Conservatives will probably want the benefits to be divided evenly among all registered voters, regardless of present wealth. Such a plan has been suggested by wealthy Florida industrialist John Perry. His National Dividend Plan would take the entire corporate income tax and distribute it equally among all registered voters, so that multimillionaires and paupers would get an equal share, provided only that they registered to vote. Perry's plan would give each voter only a few hundred dollars, and so it would not correct any of our major economic inequities. He thinks of it as a national profit-sharing scheme that would give all voters a stake in the success of America business. In that sense, it is more of a symbolic change than a structural one, and it could not be regarded as a socialization of MOP ownership that makes American capitalism compatible with Marxism—nor was it so intended.

The Stock: Nonvoting, Nontransferable

I believe the SuperStockholders should not be permitted to vote their shares, or transfer them except by inheritance. While these restrictions would deny the holders of SuperStock some of the advantages of earned or inherited wealth, the immediate reason for the plan is to save our civilization from the nuclear nightmare and to heal our split society by using stock ownership to make *income distribution* more equitable. No doubt the SuperStockholders would have a stronger feeling of participation in capitalism if they could vote and sell their shares or borrow against them, but I'm afraid the plan wouldn't work if we started out that way. If we can get it going to the point where it provides everyone a chance to reap the fruits of capital ownership through healthy dividend payments, that will be enough of a revolution to start off with.

SuperStock is not intended to change the control of corporations or to destroy the business skills it took us generations to develop. The SuperStockholders are not receiving stock from their employers as compensation, and they have no right to demand voting power simply because they are allowed to participate in capital ownership through long-term financing arranged by the government. I see no reason to attempt two simultaneous revolutions by changing the management of our major corporations as well as the ownership. Also, if SuperStock were voting stock, proxies could be accumulated by unions or other organizations who might thereby take control of our major corporations.

There is no reason why SuperStock must be voting stock. Indeed, it does not necessarily have to be stock at all. It could be something like a "capital ownership certificate" which would make the owner a capitalist but not a stockholder. It does not necessarily follow that the people who need more income are the ones whose votes should select and control corporate management.

If we want to make sure we're giving the SuperStockholders something valuable—securities that yield about 20 percent annual return on invested capital—we should not start out by endangering the position of the existing corporate management which makes such a return possible. Depriving SuperStockholders of the vote is not anti-democratic, because we are trying to establish democratic *ownership* of capital. We haven't reached the point of allowing the whole nation to vote in the election of corporate directors. That's another revolution, espoused by groups that are dedicated to changing the social responsibility and other functions of our business corporations.

In his 1973 classic, *Small is Beautiful,* E. F. Schumacher recognized the importance of leaving corporate management free to conduct the company's business as in the past, even when the stock ownership structure is changed for social purposes. He proposed that large corporations be required to issue 50 percent of their stock to "the public hand," but went on to say:

I am convinced that . . . nothing would be gained and a great deal lost if a "public hand" were to interfere with or restrict the freedom of action and the fullness of responsibility of the existing business managements. The "private" managers of the enterprises should therefore remain fully in charge . . . That is to say, the publicly-held shares would normally carry no voting rights but only the right to information and observation. [p. 287]

Having stated my views on voting rights, I must add that some knowledgeable supporters of the SuperStock concept disagree. For example, Ward Morehouse, president of the Council on International and Public Affairs, believes the dangers of giving Super-Stockholders voting rights could be mitigated by allowing them to elect a minor percentage of the corporate directors. This would give them some voting participation without endangering the position of corporate management.

As to nontransferability, SuperStock is designed to provide income which eventually would perform the functions of Social Security, welfare, and other transfer payments. Since shares of SuperStock would be issued to a lot of people who have no experience in ownership of capital, we would have to put restrictions on the right to borrow against it or sell it, so that the recipients can neither squander it nor be cheated out of it. Here we can learn a lesson from the Homestead Act, under which the government gave out ownership of over 250 million acres of public land, only to see most of it bought up by commercial interests after the five-year cultivation requirement had been met.

Some Background on the SuperStock Plan

As noted in Chapter 1, SuperStock represents my modification of the long-standing ideas of other writers. And although it still is probably no more than a Wright brothers' model of universal capitalism, it is not making its premiere appearance in this book. It has been discussed and examined by knowledgeable people during the last seven years, and to date, no one has found any obvious flaws in it.

In 1976, for example, I brought a less refined version of the plan to the attention of the Joint Economic Committee of Congress (JEC). At the time, it was conducting hearings on Employee Stock Ownership Plans (ESOPs) and other similar programs, and I suggested that the inquiry be broadened to include plans that were not based on the employment relationship. The JEC, which is our government's main forum for new economic ideas, found the concept promising, and unanimously approved these recommendations in its 1976 Joint Economic Report:

> To begin to diffuse the ownership of capital and to provide for an opportunity for citizens of moderate income to become owners of capital rather than relying solely on their labor as a source of income and security, the Committee recommends the adoption of a national policy to foster the goal of broadened ownership. The spirit of this goal and what it purports to accomplish was endorsed by many of the witnesses at our regional hearings. [p. 99]

Although the JEC did not recommend any specific method of broadening capital ownership, it concluded:

> Whatever the means used, a basic objective should be to distribute *newly created capital* broadly among the population. Such a policy would redress a major imbalance in our society and has the potential for strengthening future business growth.
> To provide a realistic opportunity for more U.S. citizens to become owners of capital, and to provide an expanded source of equity financing for corporations, it should be made national policy to pursue the goal of broadened capital ownership. Congress also should request from the Administration a quadrennial report on the ownership of wealth in this country which would assist in evaluating how successfully the base of wealth was being broadened over time. [Italics mine; pp. 99–100]

I was particularly gratified that the JEC used the words "distribute newly created capital broadly among the population," since it was the first governmental recognition of SuperStock's essence: the use of *new* capital to distribute income where it was needed most, rather than through employment channels. (The historical background of the plan, and the ways in which I modified it in conjunction with the JEC staff, are covered in my earlier book, *A Piece of The Action,* published in 1977 by Van Nostrand Rheinhold.)

In 1977, the concept was discussed at the Brookings Institution at an all-day seminar attended by about 35 economists, financial experts, and government officials. Numerous questions were raised, but most of those present agreed that the plan was worth a test, and no one pointed out any reason why it could not be made to work. The seminar at Brookings was arranged by Senator Mike Gravel of Alaska, who was a member of the Senate Finance Committee. Senator Gravel had picked up the SuperStock idea from the 1976 Joint Economic Report and had done considerable work on the concept. He had devised his own scheme, which he named the "Full-Return

Stock Plan" because of the requirement that all earnings must be distributed to the shareholders as dividends. He proposed a small-scale test of the plan, selecting 40,000 test stockholders a year for five years, for a total of 200,000 stockholders in the test group. The stockholders were to be chosen at random from all 50 states, and from four groups: the blind and disabled, the low-income working poor, middle-income taxpayers, and Social Security recipients. At the end of the five-year period, each stockholder would own $20,000 worth of stock.

Unfortunately, before Senator Gravel could get his Full-Return Stock Plan into legislation, he was defeated in the 1980 Democratic primary. In proposing such a radical plan, he was a little ahead of his time, for in the 1970s many still had faith in welfare capitalism. Today that faith is waning, and, as we've seen, many observers believe the failures of capitalism—particularly its inequitable distribution of income—will propel us toward socialism.

Our time to save capitalism—and the freedom that goes with it—is running out. We must now face up to the flaws of capitalism and try to correct them, so that our national policy will no longer have to be focused on the flaws of Soviet communism.

SuperStock and "Socialization"

"Socialization" is a word not much favored by Americans. It is suspect in our eyes, associated vaguely with communism, Marxism, and things un-American. But we must not allow such superstitions to interfere with our quest for a method of spreading the benefits of capitalism throughout our society, even though some people will see in any form of socialization evidence of a Marxist plot. This occurred when Franklin Roosevelt proposed the Social Security program, although it is now considered an integral part of welfare capitalism. Indeed, capitalism itself probably wouldn't be around any more if its harsh "survival of the fittest" philosophy had not been tempered by the adoption of Social Security and other social welfare programs.

Fortunately, major dictionaries do not limit their definitions of "socialize" to nationalization of MOP or capital ownership. *American Heritage* defines it broadly as "to convert or adapt to the needs of society." *Webster's* includes this definition: "to adapt to social needs or uses." And as we shall see in Chapter 9, Pope John Paul II, in his

1981 encyclical, *On Human Work,* defined socialization as making *each person* a part owner of the means of production.

Marx believed that capitalism would sow the seeds of its own revolutionary downfall because it was anti-social. He could not visualize that in a democracy, capitalism could be *socialized* by the voting majority. And for the most part, we have failed to grasp this concept, too. Our attempts to achieve social justice through welfare legislation have been weak half-measures at best, creating a disease often more fatal than Marxism—inflation. Over the past 50 years, we have attempted socialization in a crude, primitive way, grafting a social welfare apparatus on top of the sagging foundation of laissez-faire capitalism, until the entire jerry-built structure is about to fall of its own weight. The remedy is to recognize that capitalism itself must be socialized; that capital *ownership* must be shared by everyone. The remedy, in other words, is a plan like SuperStock.

John Maynard Keynes foresaw this as early as 1936. He was a very successful investor and an enthusiastic supporter of capitalism, but this did not blind him to its deficiencies. His master work, *The General Theory of Employment, Interest, and Money,* is certainly the most influential economics book of the twentieth century. I am indebted to Rutgers University economics professor Paul Davidson, a leading Keynesian scholar and the editor of the *Journal of Post Keynesian Economics,* for pointing out to me that Keynes's *General Theory* supplies a strong theoretical and philosophical foundation for the SuperStock solution. In the final chapter, "Concluding Notes on the Social Philosophy Towards Which the General Theory Might Lead," Keynes prescribes the socialization of capital ownership as a step needed to assure the equivalent of full employment and to retain the great benefits of capitalism:

> The outstanding faults of the economic society in which we live are its failure to provide for full employment and its arbitrary and inequitable distribution of wealth and incomes. . . . I conceive, therefore, that a somewhat comprehensive socialisation of investment will prove the only means of securing an approximation to full employment; though this need not exclude all manner of compromises and of devices by which public authority will co-operate with private initiative. But beyond this no obvious case is made out for a system of State Socialism which would embrace most of the economic life of the community. It is not the ownership of the instruments of production which it is important for the State to assume. If the State is able to determine the aggregate amount of resources devoted to augmenting the instruments and the basic rate of reward to those who own them, it will have accomplished all that is necessary. [pp. 372–78]

Thus, Keynes recognized that the Western democracies would need some form of socialization of capital ownership other than state socialism—one that would retain the individualism he saw as "the best safeguard of personal liberty." He also predicted that this socialization would be more favorable to world peace than the old system had been (p. 381).

When Great Britain entered World War II, Keynes perceived the buildup of inflationary pressures and decided that the way to check them was to give workers a share of capital profits. In his 1940 essay, "How to Pay for the War," he proposed a radical plan of forced savings to bring about the broadening of capital ownership. It was based on conditions of wartime Britain, and it had limited purposes, but it contained the following prophetic language:

> We cannot reward the worker [by raising wages] and an attempt to do so would merely set in motion the inflationary process. But we can reward him by giving him a share in claims on the future which would belong otherwise to the entrepreneurs.

Thus, at a time when income distribution through wages alone was threatening to cause inflation, Keynes's mind flashed to a new solution: income distribution through worker ownership of capital, or as he called it, "the accumulation of working-class wealth under working-class control." In the same essay, Keynes said this plan would bring "an advance toward economic equality greater than any which we have made in recent times."

Unfortunately, Keynes did not live long enough to lay out a concrete plan for socialization of capital ownership that would cure the defects (including inflation) he saw so clearly in twentieth century capitalism. But his great writings live on, and they supply us with the support we need for the concept of socializing American capitalism without turning to nationalization. Building on the Keynes foundation, we have no reason to shy away from the word "socialize." One way or another, we *must* continue the socialization of capitalism that began with the New Deal. It is our only hope of avoiding the kind of socialization we really fear: state ownership, leading to restrictions on freedom and democracy.

By spreading capital ownership to all Americans, SuperStock can provide a method of socialization that safeguards all of our cherished ideals, for SuperStock is the economic counterpart of political democracy. As such, it adds an important dimension to the traditional freedom of American society. As John Adams wrote in 1776, when America was yet to be industrialized and land was the principal form of capital:

> The only possible way, then, of preserving the balance of power on the side of equal liberty and public virtue, is to make the acquisition of land easy to every member of society . . . so that the multitude may be possessed of landed estates. If the multitude is possessed of the balance of real estate, the multitude will have the balance of power, and in that case the multitude will take care of the liberty, virtue and interest of the multitude in all acts of government.

What John Adams said about real estate in 1776 applies to corporate stock today: Our freedom and democracy will best be preserved when all Americans—the multitude—are owners. And as we have seen, this is also the key to removing the root cause of our conflict with the Soviets.

The Myth of "Democratic Capitalism"

If you read such leading conservative spokesmen as Jack Kemp, Irving Kristol, and Michael Novak, you will encounter the term "democratic capitalism" as a description of the American economic system. If this label were accurate, you might then ask why we need a radical change like SuperStock. If our capitalism is already democratic, in the sense that its benefits are available to all Americans, doesn't this eliminate the basis for ideological strife with Marxism?

The answer is that if we really had democratic capitalism, we could easily move from there to a position of compatibility with Marxism. Yet this possibility is rarely discussed, least of all by the conservative writers who are trying to plant the "democratic capitalism" label in our national consciousness. Therefore, let us examine their claims carefully and see what they really mean by democratic capitalism.

The leading apostle of democratic capitalism is Michael Novak, a distinguished author and theologian, whose 1982 book, *The Spirit of Democratic Capitalism,* is the last word on the concept as well as the first book-length attempt to define it. Here is the heart of Novak's case:

> What do I mean by "democratic capitalism"? I mean three systems in one: a predominantly market economy; a polity respectful of the rights of the individual to life, liberty, and the pursuit of happiness; and a system of cultural institutions moved by ideals of liberty and justice for all. In short, three dynamic and converging systems functioning as one: a democratic polity, an economy based on markets and incentives, and a moral-cultural system which is

> pluralistic and, in the largest sense, liberal. Social systems like those of the United States, West Germany, and Japan (with perhaps a score of others among the world's nations) illustrate the type. [p. 14]

Under this definition, it seems to me, any substantial factor in American society could be labeled "democratic." We have, for example, widespread crime, tax evasion, racial prejudice, and voter apathy. Because they occur in the same society which has a democratic polity, are they then *democratic* crime, *democratic* tax evasion, etc.?

This comment would be unfair if Novak had presented some evidence that the capitalist economic system itself is democratic. But he did not. Indeed, he admits it is *not* democratic and he goes on to say it would be inappropriate for it to be democratic:

> To begin with, "democratic capitalism" is said by some to be a contradiction in terms, since economic institutions are not usually run by democratic methods. The assumption is that democratic methods are universally desirable. But most sectors of the moral-cultural system do not find democratic methods appropriate in every inquiry or action. . . . So democratic methods have an honored place in a democratic society, but their use is by no means intended to be universal. Even within the political system, neither the executive nor the judicial powers are intended to be exercised by democratic majorities. [p. 175]

* * *

> Corporate life is not organized democratically, like a town meeting, although its forms of internal organization are many and varied. To organize industry democratically would be a grave and costly error, since democratic procedures are not designed for productivity and efficiency . . . it is naïve to demand of a system, whose goal is to increase the wealth not only of the United States but of the world, a form of internal organization inappropriate to the task. [pp. 178–9]

Why, then, does Novak use the expression *democratic capitalism?* Perhaps the answer can be found in his discussion of the works of Reinhold Niebuhr:

> At the end, Niebuhr referred to the U.S. system as a whole in the phrase, "'capitalistic-democratic' culture." The quotation marks and the clumsiness of the expression testify to the complexity of the concept. [p. 328]

Capitalistic-democratic may not roll off the tongue as smoothly as *democratic capitalism,* but it is a more accurate description of the

American system, since a capitalistic market economy and a democratic electoral organization do not necessarily infuse each other with their basic characteristics. For instance, the capitalistic market economy that now exists in the United States has also existed in nondemocratic nations such as Hitler's Germany and Mussolini's Italy. Thus, it appears to me that *democratic capitalism* is a mere play on words which does not provide a suitable foundation for a moral, cultural, philosophical, economic, or religious theory.

Novak goes on to describe this system as "self-correcting democratic capitalism" (p. 336). But he recognizes that the corrections come mostly from social welfare legislation:

> . . . poverty is a threat both to the economy and to the polity of democratic capitalism. It also supplies a moral stimulus. For this reason, democratic capitalism, however grudgingly, adopts social welfare programs, often initially sponsored by socialists. Social welfare programs fit the logic of democratic capitalism and have a legitimate claim on it. [p. 218]

Again, the term *self-correcting democratic capitalism* appears to be a play on words, because the deficiencies in the capitalistic market economy do not correct themselves. Careful reading of Novak's own text shows that they are corrected by the democratic polity under the influence of the pluralistic, liberal, moral-cultural system—in the same way we seek to correct the harmful effects of crime, tax evasion, racial prejudice, and voter apathy.

I believe Novak has done an excellent job of cataloging the desirable qualities of the capitalistic market economy, and I happen to agree that we should do everything possible to preserve them. But I do not believe that *democratic capitalism* or any other play on words is an appropriate or helpful tool for that task. In any event, I see nothing in Novak's book that would interfere with adoption of a plan such as SuperStock which would really make capitalism democratic. As he says:

> [American capitalism] is a system designed to be constantly reformed and transformed, and it alone of all known systems has within it resources for transformation through peaceful means. [p. 359]

So, if anyone tells you that we already have democratic capitalism in the United States, ask him or her what is democratic about a corporate finance system that perpetuates the ownership of capital by a pinnacle class of barely 6 percent of the population and shuts all others out of the long-term credit needed to become capitalists. And who ever voted such a system into existence?

As a lawyer, I have been involved in the creation and management of stock corporations. I would know if there were supposed to be any nexus between capitalism and democracy in the stock corporation. Nobody ever asked me to make a corporation democratic—the law does not require it, nor is it mentioned in any handbook or courses for lawyers. Voting of corporate stock is governed by ownership, and ownership is open only to those who have or can raise cash. Democracy is simply not part of the game and was never intended to be.

If our capitalism is democratic, why doesn't our president ever use the word *capitalism* in his speeches, as the Soviet leaders constantly use *socialism*? Why does capitalism have no flag, no song, no slogan, not even a bumper sticker or a T-shirt? I think it's because the "democracy" of American capitalism bears a chilling resemblance to the nineteenth century concept of equality described by Anatole France, "The law, in its majestic equality, forbids the rich as well as the poor to sleep under bridges, to beg in the streets, and to steal bread."

Since we have never voted on our economic system, we should not be surprised that it is inconsistent with our main goals: social justice, effective democracy, full employment, world peace. You name it, and you'll find the plumbing system shown in Figure 2 working against it. American capitalism splits our society between capital and labor, haves and have-nots, owners and nonowners. Therefore it cannot possibly serve as the basis for ideological rapprochement with the Soviets, unless we make it truly democratic through SuperStock.

Chapter 6

SuperStock and The Soviets:
What's In It For Them?

I do not believe that Soviet Russia desires war. What they desire is the fruits of war and the indefinite expansion of their power and doctrines.

What is needed is a settlement, and the longer this is delayed, the more difficult it will be and the greater our dangers will become.

—WINSTON S. CHURCHILL
"Iron Curtain" speech,
Fulton, Missouri, March 5, 1946

For all their historical and ideological differences, these two peoples—the Russians and the Americans—complement each other: they need each other; they can enrich each other; together, granted the requisite insight and restraint, they can do more than any other two powers to assure world peace. The rest of the world needs their forbearance with each other and their peaceful collaboration.

—GEORGE KENNAN
The New Yorker, October 3, 1983

During the darkest days of the American Revolution, Tom Paine wrote, "We have it in our power to begin the world over again." Now, in these perilous days of nuclear confrontation, we have been given another such chance, and I believe that in capitalism we can find that great power to begin again. But this time, instead of creating a split society that ignores the basic human drive for ownership, we can create a world of true justice and equality.

Through SuperStock, we can harness the positive forces of both capitalism and Marxism, and in so doing, bring an end to the long-running conflict between rival economic systems.

Sounds great in theory, you say, but what about the real world? Suppose we do adopt SuperStock as our national economic policy and begin to make it work on the home front. How could we then use it to bring about the miracle of nuclear disarmament? How could we convince the Soviets that it is in their interest to accept the American move toward SuperStock as an opening to peace?

To answer that question, we must understand precisely what we are up against—what the Soviets want and why they want it. We must, in short, take a closer look at the problems and attitudes that shape the Soviet mentality, and recognize that their unique history has generated a chronic sense of insecurity, which is further intensified by their current domestic problems. Remember that in little more than sixty years, the Soviet Union has undergone a rapid metamorphosis from backward agrarian society to world superpower, thanks largely to their development of nuclear weapons. In the eyes of the Kremlin leaders, the Soviet nuclear arsenal is their only real claim to equality with the United States, and they are not going to give up that arsenal unless we can offer them something in its place which will assure them of continuing superpower status.

With that difficult problem in mind, let us briefly scan Russian history and the Soviet mentality in search of a solution—the *settlement* that Winston Churchill urgently called for in his famous 1946 Iron Curtain Speech.

A Look Inside The Soviet Union

Economic problems are found in every industrial society today, but the Soviet Union has been hit particularly hard. During the 1970s, their economy grew rapidly, but it has since bogged down under the weight of stagnating productivity. Its days of rapid growth are over, and the Soviets' rigid bureaucratic system is poorly equipped to stimulate productivity; there are, after all, few incentives for people to work hard. As a result, according to Professor Marshall I. Goldman, director of the Russian Research Center at Harvard University and a severe critic of the Soviet economy, the Soviets are not only finding it difficult to sustain growth in their core industries, but they are also unable to compete with the West in new areas of development. In a November 12, 1983 *New York Times* article, Goldman noted:

Brezhnev is leaving the generals and the citizens an economy that's stagnating, if not receding. It showed negative growth in 1979 and there are some industries, like steel, that are still showing a negative growth. At the same time, they can't get into new technology; they don't know how to innovate; they haven't kept up with computers and with electronics, and they've had four bad harvests in a row.

The Soviet failure is most obvious in agriculture, especially when compared to the United States. In 1950, the USSR produced 0.8 metric tons of grain per hectare (2.471 acres). The U.S. produced exactly twice that much: 1.6 metric tons per hectare. In 1982, despite massive efforts to improve productivity, the Soviets produced only 1.4 metric tons per hectare, while the U.S. increased its output to 4.2 metric tons per hectare—three times as much as the USSR. Paying the price for these failures is the Soviet citizen. According to John Burns, Moscow correspondent for *The New York Times,* many Russians are worse off today than they had been in the 1970s when basic staples like milk and meat were easier to obtain. At the time of Brezhnev's death in 1982, Burns wrote in *The New York Times:* "Even in Moscow, food stores are sometimes nearly bare, or filled with half-rotten produce. Finding such items as automobile tires or a solid pair of winter boots can be a nightmare. In other parts of the country, food rationing has become routine." Of course, food and quality consumer goods have always been in short supply in the Soviet Union, in part because the Soviet people are supporting the most massive military buildup in history. They are in fact subsidizing the satellite nations—even the conquered East Germans—at the expense of their own living standards. And while the average Russian often stands in line for two hours to buy potatoes, the Hungarians, for example, eat better without having to queue up.

But if material goods are scarce, the desire for them is not. Like Americans, young Russians want to buy blue jeans, tape recorders, and stereos; Russian families want comfortable homes, entertainment, travel, automobiles. And their willingness to forego these luxuries is sorely tried by the high living standards of the elite *nachalstavo,* those top Party members who enjoy luxurious homes and apartments, chauffeured limousines, and first-class dining and travel. With the good life in the Soviet Union so dependent on political activity and whom one knows, it's not surprising bribery is rampant. So, too, are black market operations, including "left hand" factories—underground companies that secretly manufacture consumer goods right on the premises of government-owned factories.

If scarcity were not enough of a problem, what is produced is often of third-rate quality. The Saratov refrigerator has become a symbol of shoddy Soviet products; its door handle often gives a substantial electric shock to anyone trying to open it. Soviet electric razors and clothes dryers are also handled with great care by those familiar with their shocking propensities. And this from a nation that has produced some of the most sophisticated military equipment in the world. Commenting on this irony in a *Newsweek* piece on November 29, 1982, Henry Kissinger observed:

> Thus the paradoxes of the Soviet economy; shortages and surpluses exist side by side; and congenitally inferior goods are produced with no relation to the desires of its people. It is an amazing phenomenon—a superpower whose intercontinental missiles terrify the world cannot produce a single industrial commodity competitive with the products of even newly developed market economies like South Korea or Singapore, not to speak of the mature industrial democracies . . .

Contributing to the Soviets' economic woes is the massive problem of drunkenness. A 1982 report by Georgetown University demographer Murray Feshback revealed that Russian urban families spend about the same proportion of their weekly budget on alcohol as American families spend on food. Rapidly rising consumption of alcohol was a major cause of the Soviet Union's unprecedented rise in death rates; between 1960 and 1980, the life expectancy of Russian males dropped by five years. Nor is drinking confined to vodka and wine. According to Feshback's report, it includes airplane de-icing fluid, after-shave lotion, furniture polish, insecticides, and eau de cologne, which is drunk widely by fishermen on the White Sea!

Not surprisingly, this pandemic alcoholism has led to a high level of absenteeism and sloth in the Soviet workplace. In his first major speech after succeeding Brezhnev in 1982, Yuri Andropov declared war on "shoddy work, inactivity, and irresponsibility." But observers in Moscow, who are used to seeing half the workers doing nothing, wondered how he could win that war unless he provided incentives to modify Marxist-Leninist ideology—which would endanger the Kremlin's dictatorial powers.

But everything is relative. Despite these horror stories, it would be a great mistake to assume that the Soviet regime will be overthrown if economic performance does not approach that of the United States. Marc Greenfield worked as an English editor for Moscow's Novosti Press Agency from 1979 to 1981. Writing in *The New York Times Magazine* of October 24, 1982, Greenfield said:

In their talks with me, Russians visualized the outside world as a hostile camp ready to tear them apart. However, they regarded the United States with great respect and curiosity, and were tremendously impressed by what they knew of the American standard of living. On the other hand, Soviet society, with all its faults, seemed to meet their most important needs. This is the first generation of Russians since their revolution that has not known war or starvation, and their living standards, though low by our criteria, are higher than most Russians can remember. As for freedom, they seem to find enough of it in Russia's vast open spaces and in freedom from economic insecurity. With jobs guaranteed by the state, people can spend their last ruble without worrying about the next paycheck. . . .

A first step toward understanding the Russian colossus might be the realization that it is the most developed of the world's underdeveloped nations, and not—as it is usually put—the other way around. The Russians are a tired people hoping for a better future and trying as best they can to live under very difficult circumstances in a world that puzzles them as much as they puzzle it.

Greenfield's observations were confirmed in a 1982 CIA study of the Soviet economy, the gist of which, as summarized in *Newsweek* on January 10, 1983, was:

Between 1950 and 1980 . . . the Soviet gross national product grew at an average rate of 4.8 percent a year, surpassing the 3.4 percent growth of the American economy. . . . More recently, however, Soviet growth has slowed steadily to a rate currently less than 3 percent a year. . . . Housing shortages remain acute, and Soviet living standards still lag far behind those of Western Europe, Japan and the United States. Nevertheless, the report casts doubt both on Moscow's supposed vulnerability to Western trade boycotts and on expectations that Soviet consumer dissatisfaction may be increasing.

While the Soviet economic situation has not materially affected the Kremlin leaders' ability to govern, it has nonetheless increased their sense of vulnerability to what they perceive as the Western threat—much as our economic difficulties have intensified our fear of the Red Menace. But for the Kremlin, this sense of insecurity is heightened by the ethnic diversity and religious leanings of the vast nation they govern.

The Soviet Union spans two continents (Europe to Asia) and eleven time zones. It is composed of more than fifty different nationalities, many of which have their own language and cultural practices. And that's just the Soviet Union itself, without considering the satellite nations. Pure Russians now make up barely half the population. More than one-sixth of Soviet citizens are Muslims.

Religion remains a strong factor in Soviet life, particularly among the non-Russian ethnic groups. Among the pure Russians, the Orthodox Church is enjoying a revival that coincides with the decline of Marxist ideology, which was intended as a substitute for religion.

The Russian people have a history of turning to religion in time of stress, even under communism. Though Stalin had virtually crushed the Church, it rose from the ashes of the Nazi invasion to inspire the nation. It raised large sums of money, reopened many closed churches, and flourished throughout World War II. Now there are more than thirty million regular churchgoers and at least as many sympathizers, even though Soviet law requires all Communist Party members to spread atheistic propaganda.

These religious and ethnic factors limit the Kremlin's power to govern, short of using military force on their own people. Which explains, in part, why the Kremlin can hardly abandon Marxist ideology, since it is supposed to be the cement holding the nation together.

Adding to the Kremlin's sense of insecurity is Russia's military history and geopolitical position. In addition to being landlocked, the USSR is surrounded by unfriendly neighbors, who in the past have seen Russia as fertile ground for expansion. Throughout its early history, invasions from the east were common, and while Russia finally repelled the invasions of Napoleon and Hitler, its people have never forgotten the costs. Even today their neighbors remain hostile, although many bear the communist label.

On the southeast, with a shared border of 4,500 miles, lies China, an unfriendly nuclear power with a billion people. Next to China is Pakistan, an ally of both China and the United States. Sharing Russia's southern border are the unstable Islamic nations whose resurgent Muslim fundamentalism threatens both communism abroad and the Soviet government's relations with its own fifty million Muslims. Then there is Turkey, a staunch NATO ally. And finally there are the East European satellite nations, which would seem to provide at least one secure Soviet zone. But if war came, how many Russian troops would be needed to assure the loyalty of Hungary, East Germany, Poland, Czechoslovakia, Bulgaria, and Romania?

Behind all these menacing neighbors are the declared enemies of communism: the United States, NATO, and Japan. While there are hundreds of communist parties throughout the world, most now refuse to swear allegiance to Moscow. Little wonder then that the Russian mentality has been shaped by the threat—and reality—of war and encirclement, especially since the price they've paid is so high. As Leonid Brezhnev said during an American television appearance on June 24, 1973:

> The Soviet people, perhaps better than any other people, know what war is. In the Second World War we achieved a victory of worldwide historical importance. But more than 20 million Soviet citizens died in that war. 70,000 of our towns and villages were razed. One third of our national wealth was destroyed.

To fully appreciate this Russian attitude toward war, one should visit the huge mounds of earth around Leningrad, each of which contains more than ten thousand bodies—the soldiers and civilians killed defending that city against the Nazis. In all, as Brezhnev noted, the Soviets lost over 20 million people, a death toll greater than that of all the other combatant nations combined.

Since the close of World War II, this historic insecurity, fear of encirclement, and paranoia has been transferred to the United States—and understandably so. Not only do we oppose everything the Kremlin stands for, but we have thousands of nuclear weapons targeted on Russian cities. Indeed, President Truman's decision to bomb Hiroshima and Nagasaki was in part an attempt to show the Soviets our enhanced power to curb worldwide communist revolution. As Thomas B. Larson wrote in *Soviet-American Rivalry:*

> No doubt these bombs were used on President Truman's orders to hasten Japanese acceptance of defeat, perhaps as a means of keeping Russian forces out of Japan proper. But certainly Washington saw them also as a stark demonstration to Moscow of American military muscle. The last act of World War II became the first act of a new struggle for world leadership pitting America against Russia. [p. 1]

Thus, if ideological differences have shaped the superpowers' struggle for world leadership, traditional Russian paranoia has intensified it—paranoia that we've fed by what the Soviets see as our unremitting hostility toward them. It's not surprising, therefore, that from the Kremlin's perspective, Soviet self-interest now lies in global confrontation with capitalist America. But does this mean the Soviets will settle for nothing less than the complete destruction of the United States and other capitalist democracies, or that nuclear war is inevitable and indeed part of a deliberate Soviet plan for world conquest?

There is, of course, no way to provide a sure answer to that question. Herman Kahn's NUTS advocates would say yes; George Kennan and other prominent observers believe the opposite. Indeed, in Kennan's eyes, Kremlin policy is less an aggressive drive for conquest than it is a defensive reaction shaped by the very problems and attitudes we've just examined. In a famous article published in *The New Yorker* on November 2, 1981, Kennan wrote:

> I see a group of troubled men—elderly men, for the most part—whose choices and possibilities are severely constrained. I see these men as prisoners of many circumstances: prisoners of their own past and their country's past; prisoners of the antiquated ideology to which their extreme sense of orthodoxy binds them; prisoners of the rigid system of power that has given them their authority; but prisoners, too, of certain ingrained peculiarities of the Russian statesmanship of earlier ages—the congenital sense of insecurity, the lack of inner self-confidence, the distrust of the foreigner and the neurotic fear of penetration by other powers into areas close to their borders, and a persistent tendency resulting from all these other factors, to overdo the creation of military strength. I see here men deeply preoccupied, as were their Czarist Russian predecessors, with questions of prestige—preoccupied more, in many instances, with the appearances than with the realities. I do not see them as men anxious to expand their power by the direct use of their armed forces, although they could easily be frightened into taking actions that would seem to have this aim.

From all the evidence available, I think it is fair to conclude that Kremlin policy is a matter of trial and error, just as it was in Lenin's day. The Soviets are great opportunists, and they will take advantage of any chance to advance worldwide communism. But they realize they are playing with forces that are difficult to control. On the whole, they just seem to react to each crisis as it comes, without pursuing a deliberate policy of provoking war with the United States.

However, this doesn't mean that war won't occur. There are many danger points that could trigger a war without either side really wanting it, particularly while each nation sees in the other a threat to its basic survival. And as long as we both remain committed to antagonistic ideologies, that threat endures, as do the pressures on both nations to deploy more nuclear weapons. As Milovan Djilas wrote in the *London Times* on June 28, 1983:

> Nuclear weapons have not only the decisive and most important role in the Soviet arsenal, but, even more important, it is only through their possession that the Soviet Union, a second-rate economic power, becomes a military superpower. The Soviet Union will not and cannot therefore abandon its nuclear weapons, or significantly reduce its nuclear arsenal.

Our first step, therefore, must be to eliminate the source of hostility—the ideological barrier that now stands between us. We must, in short, draw the Soviets out of their encirclement paranoia, which now extends to all of their neighbors and even to some of their own republics. And we must convince them that global confrontation is *not* the best way to safeguard their interests. We can't, however, do this by economic or ideological competition, or even by increasing trade. We can accomplish this only by offering them a full and equal partnership in such spheres as energy, space, development of the Third World, and the curbing of terrorism. And with the ideological battle over MOP ownership behind us, we can make such an offer without risk to our own way of life.

The mind-boggling processes of deterrence and ideological warfare do not permit clarity. Each side tries to keep the other off balance by clouding the basic issues, which makes it difficult to discover what our real intentions are. Through SuperStock, however, America can signal its intentions, making it crystal clear to the Soviets that we are not only taking a major step toward ideological accord, but are also offering a partnership that suits their self-interest. While little else is certain today, we can say with a reasonable degree of certainty that: (1) Our offer of world partnership is in the Soviet Union's self-interest; (2) They will always act in their self-interest. As the Harvard Nuclear Study Group said in its 1983 book *Living with Nuclear Weapons:* "We can trust the Soviets in one sense. We can trust them to pursue their interests" (p. 37).

Of course, an appeal to the Soviets' self-interest will not necessarily eliminate their expansionist policies. Both self-interest and lust for power are aspects of human nature that cannot be eliminated by SuperStock or any other plan. But if we make the offer of world partnership attractive enough, they can satisfy their desire for power through partnership rather than through dangerous and expensive nuclear confrontation. We cannot ask the Soviets to throw in the only chips that elevate them from second-rate status to a superpower, unless we give them an effective substitute for their nuclear arsenal—equal status on the world stage. But remember that an offer of partnership will not be credible as long as the ownership barrier stands between capitalism and communism. Thus, removing that barrier through SuperStock increases our chances for peace enormously, replacing enmity with a solid bridge that can join, rather than divide, Soviet and American interests.

Clearly, war is in no one's best interests. Neither is MAD-NUTS deterrence. Given the economic problems plaguing both nations, the expense of maintaining and enlarging nuclear arsenals cannot be said to serve the self-interest of either superpower. SuperStock, in contrast, can serve everyone's self-interest by enabling us to transcend our ideological differences and open the way to peace.

Finally, remember that Russia and America have never opposed each other in war. Thus, if the ideological basis for war were eliminated, I believe there would be no reason strong enough for the Russians to start one, and many reasons why they would be eager to avoid not only war, but also continued nuclear escalation. Now let us explore some specific ways of accomplishing this.

The Opportunity For Disengagement

If we socialized American capitalism through SuperStock, the main source of ideological contention between the U.S. and the USSR—ownership of the means of production—would be eradicated. What, then, would there be to fight over? The Soviets could claim that imperialistic, exploitative capitalism was dead, having succumbed to the irresistible forces of Marxism-Leninism. And the United States could emerge from its seventh decade of fearful reaction to Marxism without any further reason to let that fear shape its policies.

By eliminating the basis for class warfare, we will, in effect, be creating a home-grown antidote to the epidemic of worldwide Marxist revolution. And with the inoculation of SuperStock, we need never again resort to armed conflict to fight the Marxist virus, as we did in 1918 when Winston Churchill spearheaded the dispatch of Western forces to Russia because of his deadly fear of "Bolshevik infection," and as we did in Korea, Vietnam, and Central America. What's more, we can administer the life-saving injection ourselves any time we wish, without waiting for any action on the part of the Soviet Union.

This is in fact one of the great strengths of SuperStock; *it can be put into operation without any agreement or action by the Soviets.* With the exception of unilateral disarmament, which is tantamount to surrender, what other proposed solutions to the nuclear dilemma can be executed by us alone? Indeed, as we saw in Chapter 2, all the others depend on complex agreements between the superpowers, which cannot be negotiated while mistrust and fear hold sway. But with SuperStock, we can disengage ourselves *unilaterally* from the worldwide struggle between capitalism and communism. And by that action, we can remove the basic cause of American-Soviet enmity—our fear of communism, their opposition to exploitative capitalism—and open the way to ending the nuclear nightmare.

This is a breathtaking prospect. Let's examine it carefully, noting first of all that unilateral *disengagement* does not mean unilateral *disarmament*. Worldwide disarmament will, in time, flow from it, but we can take the initial step of unilateral disengagement without disarming ourselves. Indeed, the purpose of this disengagement is to convince the Soviets—and the world—that nuclear weapons are no longer needed because the ideological power struggle which is the root of the nuclear arms race has become irrelevant.

Why irrelevant? Because with MOP ownership in the United States socialized via SuperStock, the two systems will be as close to compatibility as they can get. We will no longer have to fear the end result of Marxism: socialization of MOP ownership. And the Kremlin can use our change to bolster its own image, reminding the Russian people that the Soviet example and half a century of international proletarianism led directly to socialization of American MOP ownership; that without the Soviet commitment to worldwide communist revolution, capitalism would not have been under such great pressure to clean up its act.

That we are not turning to state ownership to clean up our act should not affect our goal of better relations with the Soviets, since even Marx failed to provide a real blueprint for the achievement of a just and classless society. He never imagined the first communist revolution would take place in Russia or any other nonindustrialized nation. His scenario envisaged a rebellion by factory workers who had been ground under the heels of greedy, silk-hatted capitalists. Because he underestimated the strength and flexibility of capitalism, he thought it would self-destruct long ago. That it has adapted to changing times is a tribute to its flexibility and an affirmation of the basic human drive for property ownership. Although Marx claimed that self-interest would wither away, the human experience has demonstrated this is a pipe dream that runs counter to human nature. Clearly, his revolutionary route to social justice is not the only way, and the Soviets could not credibly claim that it was. Nor could they claim that state MOP ownership is essential, since Marx decreed the demise of the state as a prerequisite to the achievement of true communism.

Thus, while our path toward a classless society will not mirror the Soviets', SuperStock is nonetheless an appropriate method of socialization for the United States as well as other advanced industrial democracies whose thousands of large corporations contain within themselves the seeds of mass MOP ownership. For that very reason, SuperStock may not be an appropriate system for the USSR, which has never known democracy and was an underdeveloped agrarian nation when the Bolsheviks took power in 1917. But the method used to socialize MOP ownership is not important. What is important is that socialization occurs, and SuperStock can and will accomplish this task in a way that Marx and Engels themselves recognized, even though they did not realize it could happen within a capitalist system.

Socializing American MOP ownership will also bring us closer to "democracy" and "freedom" as defined by the Soviets. Because the Soviet Union is a totalitarian state, most of us would readily give it a zero on democracy and freedom. But the Soviets have done some creative work on their definitions of these concepts. While we think of democracy as government by the people through elected representatives, the Soviets claim to have adopted Aristotle's definition of democracy as "government in the interest of the poor." Thus, because the Soviet government is dedicated in principle to the interests of the poor masses, Soviet leaders, like the dictators of other "people's democracies," give themselves high marks in democracy without having to put up with the inconvenience of elections, civil liberties, or opposition parties.

The Soviets scoff at the idea that American democracy extends equal rights to all citizens; indeed, they claim most Americans have practically no economic rights—and that real political power is actually concentrated in the hands of the small capitalist ruling class who own and control the means of production. And to prove their claims, they point out that we do not even have the courage to define our economic system in our Constitution, our laws, or any official document.

While I certainly cannot support Soviet claims that their system is democratic, they have correctly identified the large gap in the United States between political democracy and economic democracy. However, by opening MOP ownership to all Americans, we can not only close that gap, but also meet the Soviet-adapted Aristotelian definition of democracy as "government in the interest of the poor." Indeed, we could go a giant step further than Aristotle by redefining American democracy as "government dedicated to *eliminating* the poor." Thus, SuperStock would bring us a lot closer to the Russian view, yet would in no way affect our important traditions: free elections and the other cherished liberties that guarantee political democracy and personal freedom.

A similar dichotomy exists between American and Soviet definitions of freedom. We protect our freedom by prohibiting government interference through the Constitution, which defines and limits the powers of both federal and state government and prohibits actions that obstruct citizens' liberties and human rights. Yet there is no mention of economic rights. Our laws protect the ownership of property once it has been obtained, but when it comes to acquisition of money and property, Americans are left to their own devices.

In contrast to this somewhat negative approach, the Soviet concept, at least on paper, seems more positive. For instead of prohibiting state interference, the Soviet Constitution and economic system purport to establish the state as the instrument by which all Soviet citizens are provided with the material means of achieving liberty, i.e., the economic necessities of life. But through SuperStock, we could ourselves define economic freedom in this way. For the first time, the American government would be able to provide its people with the most important material benefit of all: the right to participate in ownership of the means of production. We would then be in harmony with the Soviet view of freedom as freedom from economic insecurity.

SuperStock would, then, unite the U.S. and the USSR on definitions of democracy and freedom, thereby making it more difficult for either nation to hurl these words as epithets in propaganda battles. Right now, of course, freedom is a favorite denunciation for both sides. We use it to justify capitalism and to condemn Soviet totalitarianism. We even call ourselves "leaders of the free world," using the word to mean freedom from communist rule. They counter with claims of economic freedom through government guarantee of livelihood and argue that America will never be free while its people can only participate in the economic system as "wage-slaves of the capitalist class." In the current climate of bitter enmity, even words become powerful weapons. But once SuperStock is adopted, these weapons, too, will lose their dangerous edge.

In every important respect, therefore, SuperStock can bridge the ideological chasm between American capitalism and Soviet Marxism, while maintaining the incentives of capitalism. Certainly, not all Americans would be equally rich, but neither are all Russians equally well off under the Soviet system, which permits wide divergences in living standards and personal wealth. Indeed, the Soviets' experience teaches us that the desire for self-betterment and acquisition—sometimes called by less flattering names such as greed and avarice—is an immutable part of human nature. While Marx called himself a scientific socialist and scoffed at those he labeled utopian socialists, his dream that human greed would wither away and there would no longer be a need for the state is obviously contrary to human nature, as illustrated by the following story:

A teacher who was trying to explain Marxism asked one of the students, "If you had two Cadillacs, would you give one to somebody else?" The boy answered, "Yes." Then the teacher asked, "If you had two motorboats, would you give one to somebody else?" "Yes," replied the boy. "And if you had two color TV sets, would you give one to somebody else?" "Of course." "And if you had two baseball bats, would you give one to somebody else?" "Hell, no!" replied the boy. "Why not?" asked the teacher. "Because I *have* two baseball bats!"

Unlike Marxism, SuperStock squares with human nature because it gives *everybody* the opportunity for self-betterment through property ownership—and the chance to be that most envied of characters: a capitalist. Unlike Marxism, which has always been associated with terrorism and revolution, SuperStock can be adopted peacefully and gradually. Unlike Marxism, SuperStock would stifle neither creativity, genius, ambition, or great achievement. It is essentially an attempt to combine the best elements of both capitalism and Marxism, and as such, it allows us to preserve and improve the way of life we cherish, while also moving away from ideological strife with the Soviets.

A Marxist proverb states, "There are many roads to socialism," and once we're on our own road, we won't have to fear the other paths. If communism seems the best system (as in the Soviet Union), we can watch it take root without concern. If democratic socialism is the method of choice (as in France), so be it. With MOP ownership effectively socialized here, the development of state ownership in any nation would no longer pose a threat to us.

Since World War II, the United States has dedicated most of its military and foreign policy to fighting the Red Menace. As we saw in Chapter 3, our unprecedented expenditures on the Marshall Plan and the enormous losses suffered in Korea and Vietnam were part of our ongoing attempt to contain communism—to limit its domain to the Soviet Union and its East European satellites. Our motivation was fear, and that fear was justified: capitalism's weaknesses made it vulnerable to the Marxist virus. If Marxism succeeded in destroying private MOP ownership in many parts of the world, what would prevent American noncapitalists from using their huge voting majority to follow the socialist or communist banners? But if we recognized the lack of consistency between our political and economic systems, we tried to ignore it, perhaps because we saw no other solution. Now, with SuperStock, we can finally make our economic system as democratic—and as secure—as our political system.

Once we have innoculated ourselves by spreading MOP ownership throughout American society, it will make no difference to us if other countries nationalize MOP ownership, or vest it in their labor unions, or use a system like SuperStock. We will be immune from overtures to socialize it in other ways—especially ways that would dissipate the great benefits of American capitalism and deprive all Americans of their existing individual MOP ownership.

Thus, SuperStock removes the ownership issue from the field of battle and with it, the element of fear that distorts the actions and attitudes of both superpowers. And in place of the dark cloud of fear appears the door to nuclear disarmament—a door now barricaded on both sides by the antagonistic ownership ideologies of capitalism and communism. Through SuperStock, we can remove those barricades by rectifying the basic fault Marx found in capitalism: the exploitation of the working classes by the pinnacle class of capitalist owners. The other facets of Marxism, such as dialectical materialism and atheism, are not the stuff of which twentieth-century wars are made. The sole bone of contention—the only one that contains the seeds of war—is the age-old controversy over exploitation and ownership.

True, we are left with some non-Marxist problems that might cause a war: Russian nationalism and expansionism; the tsarist complex; the Russian leaders' thirst for dictatorial power. But none of these factors ever threatened us before the Bolshevik revolution of 1917. We have, in fact, never seriously considered going to war against the USSR for any reason other than the threat that international Marxism poses to American society—more precisely, to the American way of life as developed under capitalism.

But what about the Russians? Are they likely to go to war for reasons other than Marxist ideology? Even in the absence of ideological conflict, Soviet leaders might still seek worldwide supremacy and control, but they would have no ideological or ethical basis for doing so. Many of the nations that support the Soviets in the cold war do so from their belief in Marxism and their opposition to exploitative capitalism. The Kremlin would not only lose this support, but would also find it more difficult to elicit continued sacrifices from its citizens in the name of international class struggle. While these factors alone would not be enough to end Soviet-American enmity, they would be strong enough to make the Soviets more receptive to a genuine overture of peace and partnership from the United States.

Knowledgeable observers like George Kennan, John Kenneth Galbraith, and George Ball believe that the USSR is not intent on world conquest, but rather is seeking a face-saving way out of the nuclear nightmare. But under the present conditions of global ideological warfare, the Kremlin cannot demonstrate this peaceful intention *without risking loss of its power base.* We must, therefore, give them the opportunity to respond to a positive program rather than a threat, something that removes the basis for ideological warfare and lets them save face: an offer of peace through partnership. Only in this way can we test the thesis of Kennan, Galbraith, and Ball. Certainly we have nothing to lose and everything to gain by trying.

The Prospects For Peace

There are two ways to evaluate the effects of SuperStock on the chances for peace. If you're an optimist, you may conclude that ideological accord will very probably bring peace and partnership, since both sides have so much to gain. But even if you are a pessimist and the last sentence sounds like Pollyanna to you, consider this question: *How will we ever end the nuclear nightmare if we do not eliminate the ideological conflict?*

SuperStock may not bring peace, but without it—or some other way of removing the ideological basis for the capitalist-communist confrontation—I see no real hope for peace. Viewed in this light, SuperStock is at the very least a prerequisite, a necessary step toward peace—although it may or may not actually produce peace. It is the bridge we have been searching for—a bridge that rises above the old swamps of enmity and joins Soviet self-interest with American self-interest. All other approaches to Soviet-American friendship must grind to a halt at the line now drawn between capitalism and communism.

Once we adopt SuperStock, our relationship with the USSR can take three possible forms: a new era of friendship, cooperation, and partnership; a continuation of the present "peaceful" rivalry; or a triggering of all-out nuclear warfare. Each of these three possibilities requires close analysis.

The Optimist's Viewpoint: A New Era Of Partnership

In light of Russia's historic insecurity and encirclement paranoia, its position as a superpower—as America's equal—is of enormous importance to its leaders. Witness these words from President Brezhnev's report to the 1976 congress of the CPSU:

> As a result of the negotiations with U.S. President Nixon in Moscow and Washington, and later of the meetings with President Ford at Vladivostok and Helsinki, important and fundamental mutual understanding has been reached between the leaders of the Soviet Union and the United States on the necessity of developing peaceful, *equal* relations between the two countries. [Italics mine]

"Equal," of course, is the key word here. But is such equality likely to develop while we are engaged in a battle over which system of MOP ownership should prevail—to the exclusion and destruction of the other? With the ideological warfare ended, however, there can be true equality between our nations, and that is the first and most important message we must convey to the Russians. We cannot, therefore, simply adopt SuperStock or a similar method of socializing MOP ownership. We must also signal our intentions loudly and clearly: "We are modifying MOP ownership as a direct result of your example. We are taking this step not only to improve our internal economy, but also because we want to reach out to you in friendship and dissolve the cause of our long-standing enmity."

We must, in other words, allow the Kremlin leaders to claim a victory, or at least a tie, as the foundation for Soviet-American parity. They must be able to announce that ideological warfare has ceased, not because the Soviet Union is weak, or a less-than-worthy adversary, but because America has seen the error of its ways— through the example of Marxism—and has taken steps to mend those ways by socializing capital ownership. Thus, if we go about it in the right way, SuperStock can give the Kremlin an unprecedented opportunity to save face and to make a lasting peace with the United States on terms that will benefit both.

To make it clear that a partnership between equals would serve the Soviets' self-interest, we must be ready to suggest specific joint projects. We could start with joint procurement of oil, gas, and coal, and then move on to more sophisticated programs: space exploration, seabed mining, worldwide pollution control, nuclear fusion, and—most important of all—Third World development. As Richard Barnet said in *Real Security:*

> There is panic and violence in the world—not, as at other historical moments, because of a fanatic belief that one system or another has a monopoly on truth, but because of widespread feelings that no one in charge knows what to do. The failure of both "so-

cialist" and "capitalist" regimes to bring liberation or dignity to billions of people has unleashed in many parts of the Third World a profound spiritual reaction—a radical rejection of the dominant international culture. [p. 117]

Through Soviet-American partnership, these problems could be turned into huge opportunities for world-wide progress and prosperity. Today, both superpowers are pumping billions into Third World nations as part of the global slugfest between capitalism and communism. Much of this money goes into military equipment and training, while the crying needs of these nations for development of agriculture, education, and health care are largely ignored. This was the theme of *The World Challenge,* an important book published in 1981 by Jean-Jacques Servan-Schreiber, the French author and former cabinet minister. He points out that the industrial nations (including the U.S. and the USSR) can no longer expand production except at the expense of each other, and therefore they *must* develop the Third World as a new market if they are to maintain their own living standards. As Servan-Schreiber puts it:

> It is no longer possible for industrial countries to maintain their expansion by trading among themselves. They are all together on the path of economic chaos. . . . we must invent another cycle of development, one that will pass through and only succeed with the Third World, the last "new frontier" on the planet. [p. 128]

With the ideological roadblock removed, a Soviet-American partnership could end the obscene Third World arms race and turn the inhabitants of those impoverished nations into customers instead of cadavers.

There would also be opportunities for direct collaboration between the Soviet and American economies. For example, the Siberian natural gas pipeline (which the Reagan Administration tried so hard to block that we nearly fell out of bed with our NATO allies) would be a perfect project for a joint venture combining Soviet natural resources and American technology.

Even without these "extras," life would be a lot easier for the Soviets as American allies. They would no longer have to support expensive losers like the Cubans, to whom they give about $3 billion a year (five times the U.S. aid to *all* of Latin America). They would also have fewer problems with the noisy satellite nations, the Arab oil sheiks, their own ethnic and religious groups, and the Russian people themselves, whose demands for meat, milk, and stereos are not likely to diminish. And after all, who could top an offer of entente with an "ideologically correct" American nation? The Cubans? The PLO?

Indeed, the benefits to both nations would be enormous. Money now being appropriated for military expenditures could be devoted instead to solving the internal problems plaguing both superpowers. Then, too, with a united front, the U.S. and USSR could address the problem of protecting the world against terrorists who will soon be equipped with nuclear weapons. We are almost at the point where a gang no larger than Jesse James's can hold mighty nations at ransom with nuclear weapons. Unless the U.S. and the USSR join forces to halt horizontal proliferation of nuclear weapons, instead of nurturing it, the struggle between our economic ideologies may soon become irrelevant anyway. Capitalists and communists alike will be fried in a nuclear holocaust triggered by a terrorist's cruise missile fired for God-knows-what cause.

But, you might say, suppose the USSR signs a treaty of friendship with us and then continues to back Marxist parties in Latin America. Suppose, too, that those parties come to power as a result of Soviet or Cuban military aid. Well, those Marxist armies will not need many Soviet or Cuban weapons because we won't be giving any weapons to their enemies. After all, why should we? Marxist victories, no matter where they occur, will no longer be a threat to the United States. With SuperStock immunizing us from Marxism and fostering Soviet-American accord, we won't have to oppose any nation because of its system of MOP ownership—whether that system is state ownership, union ownership, or individual ownership.

On the other hand, suppose there was a real threat to our national security. Suppose, for example, that despite signing the treaty, the USSR deployed nuclear missiles in Latin America or otherwise caused the Marxist forces there to threaten our security or that of our allies. We would, of course, then have to invoke the Monroe Doctrine and remove those threats. I believe Congress and the American people would support such action vigorously, in contrast with today's agonizing debate over covert measures and military assistance, when the enemy is the shadowy Marxist virus and there is no mention of the word "capitalism" or any positive policy other than the threadbare "democracy and freedom" banner.

Obviously, any new Soviet-American friendship treaty could not supercede or nullify the Monroe Doctrine. But there should be no reason for the Soviets to violate the Monroe Doctrine once ideological warfare has ceased. Self-interest would dictate that the Soviets exploit the opportunity for direct partnership with the U.S., instead of returning to the dangerous, expensive, no-win strategy of arming insurgent Marxist groups.

It must be emphasized, however, that before we approach the USSR, we must tap our best brains and develop detailed programs for worldwide cooperative ventures. We must have a specific plan for launching history's greatest development program: a partnership between the U.S. and the USSR. And an integral part of this plan must be removal of all nuclear weapons from the earth. At the same time, we must make sure the Soviets realize we are lighting flares to illuminate the world, not throwing smoke bombs to disguise duplicity.

Does it all sound too good to be true? I don't believe so, but it is also important to recognize that socializing American MOP ownership would not automatically end our conflict with the Soviet Union—even if we actually bypassed SuperStock and went all the way to socialism or communism. When France elected a socialist government in 1981 and embarked on large-scale nationalization of MOP ownership, their relations with the Soviets did not improve. In fact, Socialist Premier Mitterand moved further away from the USSR than had his capitalist predecessors, and he also vowed to build up France's nuclear deterrent. And certainly, there's no love lost between various communist dictatorships, as evidenced by current relations between Vietnam and Cambodia, and Red China and the Soviet Union. The Chinese-Soviet enmity confirms that adoption of Marxist ideology alone is not enough to assure peace without a further move toward partnership that clearly serves Soviet self-interest, especially when there are non-ideological reasons for friction. By the same token, the fact that Red China once was a Soviet ally and can return to that status at any time, shows the great potential rewards of removing the ideological barrier.

Moreover, these analogies should not discourage us from trying the SuperStock approach, because the case of the United States and the Soviet Union is a unique one. The U.S. is the worldwide symbol of capitalism; the Soviet Union represents worldwide communism. Each nation holds the other's life in its hands to a much greater degree than in any other relationship in history. Each holds the key to the other's survival, peace, and prosperity. Each is now strangling the other's economy by perpetuating an arms race that can only end in disaster. As Father Robert Drinan says in his 1983 book, *Beyond the Nuclear Freeze:*

> Because of the nuclear weapon, the United States and the Soviet Union are in a relationship of mutual hostages. Putting it another way, either the hostility decreases or the likelihood of mutual destruction increases. [p. 121]

No other pair of nations has ever been in this predicament. The U.S. and the USSR *must* strike a deal, and SuperStock can open the way by removing the only ideological obstacle. That rising tensions demand some kind of accord was the theme of a recent article by Columbia University professor Seweryn Bialer, one of our leading Kremlin watchers. In the July 1, 1983 issue of the *International Herald-Tribune*, Bialer wrote:

> In an era of increasingly powerful and accurate nuclear weapons and a continuous arms race, the danger to both East and West has increased dramatically; so has their need for managing and regulating conflict and cooperation. This is probably the first time in history that alliances divided by such sharp differences have shown so much interest in conflict management and cooperation. This change in attitude is one product of the nuclear revolution in international affairs.
>
> In a world of strategic parity and mutual assured destruction, détente between West and East in one form or another is simply unavoidable.

This rationale is our only hope for any progress toward disarmament. And imagine how much stronger it would become if we could eliminate the "sharp differences" mentioned by Professor Bialer.

Now take a moment to dream a bit. Imagine an American President addressing the United Nations and offering to the Soviet Union a full and equal partnership in a new era of world peace and disarmament, accompanied by joint Soviet-American development of space, energy, and the Third World. Or visualize the President inviting the Soviet leader to a meaningful summit meeting, held, appropriately, at Trier, the birthplace of Karl Marx. What better way to announce our goals: That we intend to use the positive elements of Marxism as a path to world peace and that the Soviet Union's patron saint has shown the way to social justice.

The Midway Position: Continuing The "Peaceful" Rivalry Between Capitalism and Communism

Our adoption of SuperStock would leave the Soviets with four basic options:

1. They themselves could adopt SuperStock as the culmination of Marx's dream, and with the main cause of enmity removed, they could enter into a partnership with the United States.

2. The Soviets could avoid adoption of SuperStock, yet neutralize its threat to Kremlin power by entering into a partnership

with the United States. And since such a partnership would achieve our ultimate objective of ending the nuclear nightmare, we would have no reason to try to spread SuperStock to other nations or use it as a foreign policy tool to embarrass the Soviets at home or abroad.

3. The Soviets could try to prolong the international ideological warfare between capitalism and communism, even though they might lose to the new SuperStock form of capitalism and such loss might eventually cause the Russian people to demand individual MOP ownership, democratic elections, and other reforms distasteful to the Kremlin.

4. They could consider use of SuperStock in American foreign policy as sufficient provocation for a nuclear attack on the United States.

The first three options are not mutually exclusive. The Soviets might start out with number three, keeping their guard up while studying the situation. If we convinced them we were offering a genuine partnership, they might move to number two. And eventually they might even move to number one, adopting SuperStock themselves, which would make the partnership even more secure.

Suppose that the Soviets started with option number three, trying to continue the ideological rivalry even though they could no longer credibly brand American capitalism as exploitative. Does this mean we would have to carry on with our end of the dangerous and pointless rivalry as before?

I think not. I believe that even without a partnership, we could substantially disengage ourselves from the rivalry because, as stated earlier in this chapter, we would have nothing to lose from the spread of Marxist ideology.

Nevertheless, there are many possible scenarios. The Soviets' insistence on continuing the ideological rivalry might conceivably force us to respond in some way. Somewhere along the line, a hawkish American administration might lose patience with the Soviets and decide to use SuperStock as an ideological weapon. And the United States might decide to use SuperStock as the basis for a new foreign policy designed to win us friends and markets throughout the world. For the sake of completeness, we shall examine these possibilities briefly, bearing in mind that some of this discussion necessarily will be inconsistent with the idea of unilateral disengagement.

Let us consider first the likely nature of any ideological rivalry that the Soviets might force on us. Would that renewed rivalry between SuperStock and communism be more likely or less likely to cause nuclear war than is the case today without SuperStock?

Even in the narrow context of economic rivalry, SuperStock

towers over Reaganomics and all other conceivable methods of making capitalism work. Indeed, if Reaganomics achieves its goals, it will only intensify ideological warfare. The same is true of the liberal Democratic brand of welfare capitalism, which ignores the vital question of capital ownership. But with SuperStock eliminating contention over MOP ownership, competition with the Soviets on other issues should be calmer and less likely to escalate to warfare. The fear that now characterizes our relations would be less intense, even in the absence of full partnership. Secure in our possession of an antidote to domestic Marxist incursion, we would have no reason to fear the spread of Marxism elsewhere. As our tension relaxes, this should calm Soviet fears and lessen their paranoia. "Live and let live" could indeed become the order of the day, and in time that neutral position might well ripen into real cooperation and partnership. Toward that end, once the ideological barrier has been removed, American foreign policy should be orchestrated to remind the Soviets continually of how much they have to gain by becoming our partners.

In the interim between our adoption of SuperStock and the achievement of partnership with the Soviet Union, we could use SuperStock to improve our relations with other nations. As examples, let us consider the developing nations, our neighbors to the south and north, and Great Britain.

SuperStock is, of course, designed for industrialized nations whose large corporations furnish a ready foundation for broadening MOP ownership through capital expansion, credit power, and ability to make self-liquidating capital additions. But what about the developing nations, a category that includes most countries and most of the earth's population? (These nations are also called nonindustrialized, underdeveloped, Third World, or just plain poor.) What they are trying to develop is a higher standard of living, and almost invariably they see industrialization as the quickest way to that end.

Even now, the industrial countries are deeply involved in helping developing nations to industrialize. These efforts involve three forms of financing: foreign capital in the form of loans or equity investments, foreign-aid handouts, and capital investments made in conjunction with wealthy local financiers or businesses. In all three cases, little or no new capital ownership is created among the local residents, most of whom were poor before such aid and remain poor afterwards. Therefore, this financing, even in the form of handouts, is generally not much appreciated by most local residents. In fact, their resentment often results in the expropriation of foreign investments. Moreover, the few jobs created by these efforts usually do not significantly increase the purchasing power of developing nations. To reach that goal, industrialization combined with the diffusion of capital ownership would appear the best approach. This opens the way for the United States to improve relations with developing nations by helping them to install their own SuperStock system.

Obviously, Third World implementation of SuperStock would not be easy, but there is at least one potentially viable scenario. Suppose that American multinational corporations were able to secure the necessary guarantees of credit through the World Bank. This would enable them to establish industrial enterprises that would eventually be owned by the local citizens once the SuperStock had paid for itself from its own earnings. The multinationals could supply the management and the technology. At the same time, they would be taking advantage of lower costs of raw material and labor, which might result in higher profits and quicker repayment of capital investments. That has, in fact, always been one of the big attractions of the Third World for the multinationals.

This use of SuperStock, if viable, would improve our relations with many foreign countries and make us much more popular in the United Nations General Assembly. It would also create new customers for American business. Local industries would be able to pay American companies for their goods and services, and the local residents, with more cash in their pockets from capital ownership, might become customers for American goods and services. How such a plan could be implemented in specific Third World countries would require detailed study, of course, but it appears to have a much better chance for success than any of the strategies currently employed by the State Department and our multinationals. And it would certainly enable Third World nations to build enterprises that would ultimately be owned directly and individually by needy citizens, rather than corrupt government officials or a few wealthy locals who bank the profits abroad.

If we undertook this policy while the Soviets remained antagonistic, we would have to make certain they did not look upon it as a provocation. One way to avoid that problem is to offer the Soviets a direct partnership in each such project at the outset, thus dramatizing the great advantages they could gain from an overall partnership.

The always troublesome area of Latin America provides a good example of how SuperStock could be used to improve our foreign relations, even if the Soviets insisted on prolonging the rivalry. Frustrating U.S. experience there for decades has demonstrated the futility of backing local political parties, whether they call themselves right, left, or centrist. Many Latin American nations have a dozen or more parties whose leaders and policies change with alarming frequency. President Carter's policy of basing our Latin American relationships on human rights did little to improve matters; in fact, it opened the way for takeover by Marxist guerrillas who often have no greater regard for human rights than the right-wing parties we had supported in the past. Carter's strategy delivered Nicaragua to the Sandinistas, whose eventual domination by Marxist-Leninist factions made them a threat to our security in the Western Hemisphere. However, President Reagan's policy of supporting groups that use military oppression to remain in power is proving equally disastrous. Generally, none of the groups contending for our aid are strong enough or pure enough ideologically to support a clear-cut, logical American foreign policy, and thus function as useful allies.

In the end, when traditional capitalism fails to meet high expectations—as it must in the weak economies of Latin America—the Marxists will be standing in the wings, ready to pick up the pieces. As Robert E. White, former U.S. ambassador to El Salvador, put it in an article in *The New York Times Magazine* on July 18, 1982:

> The workers and peasants will know that all they can now expect is a return to the old system of privilege for the few and misery for the many. Much as they may fear the upheaval and dislocation of a leftist victory, they will increasingly, if grudgingly, give their toleration and support to the guerrillas, feeling that only thus can they put an end to the atrocities routinely committed by the unfettered military . . . When guerrillas have the advantage of exploiting a political status quo that has become unacceptable to most of the population, all they have to do to win in the end is endure.

Right now, we are trapped in a no-win struggle in Latin America. I picture President Reagan as a somewhat rumpled knight on horseback, jousting with a champion of Marxism. Both combatants are in heavy armor and have suitable banners on their horses. Theirs says *Equality and Justice through Socialism.* Ours says *Freedom and Democracy*—but predictably does not mention capitalism. The Marxist knight is armed with a lance, a noble-looking weapon even though it has blood on it. And against the long lance of Marxism, President Reagan is armed with a red rubber suction cup mounted on a short broomstick—a plumber's helper! That's how traditional capitalism shapes up as a tool of American foreign policy in Latin America and most of the world. Little wonder, then, that this policy creates the impression that we fear and oppose progress toward social justice throughout the world.

If we adopted SuperStock, we could throw away the plumber's helper, for SuperStock would be an effective shield against the Marxist lance. And even if a hawkish American president decided to continue the ideological battle against Marxism in Latin America, SuperStock would make a far more effective weapon than the plumber's helper of traditional capitalism. (Again, I believe such a battle can be avoided by unilateral disengagement once the United States installs SuperStock, but here we are trying to anticipate many possible twists in Soviet-American relations.)

While our adoption of SuperStock will free us from any concern about the methods other countries use to socialize MOP ownership, there are special cases where it might be prudent for us to help other countries install their own SuperStock plans. One such special case is Mexico.

Under our present system, the chance that Mexico might some day be taken over by Marxists creates the unacceptable risk of having the archenemy at our southern border. Under SuperStock, of course, a Marxist Mexico would not in itself be a threat to us, unless it became a military base for Cuba or the Soviet Union. But if Mexico went Marxist while we were still trying to achieve a partnership with the Soviet Union, we might have to contend with a cutoff of Mexico's huge oil reserves and the chance of Cuban or Soviet military infiltration. The best way of avoiding that uncomfortable scenario would be to help Mexico spread ownership of its oil, its industry, and its agriculture to its whole population.

Fortunately, the concept of spreading capital ownership is not new to Mexico. Andres Molina Enriquez, a driving force in the 1911 Mexican revolution, proposed wide distribution of capital (in those days it was farmland) through long-term credit many years ago. And today, Dr. Abel Beltran-del-Rio, a leading economic consultant to the Mexican government, is a staunch supporter of the SuperStock plan.

With Mexico, we might even consider joint ownership of Mexican and American companies by citizens of both countries. Such joint ventures would be particularly useful in the energy field. As in other developing nations, oil discoveries have not brought prosperity to the average Mexican; they cause inflation and high expectations, but don't create a lot of jobs. Mexico's oil fields, developed by American companies whose interests were later expropriated, could be turned into an asset that would create income for all of their people, in cooperation with the United States. American participation in Mexican profits would benefit American SuperStockholders, and the arrangement would assure us oil supplies outside of the volatile Arab world. SuperStock would also be a way of reducing the flow of illegal immigration, since it would enable the Mexican people to raise their standard of living without total dependence on jobs and welfare.

In line with this philosophy, we would probably feel more comfortable if our huge neighbor to the north were also a SuperStock nation. Fortunately, Canada is already a few steps ahead of us in the march toward SuperStock. In the early 1970s, the socialist government of British Columbia took over ownership of important forestry, coal, oil, and gas companies. In 1978, a new provincial administration reversed that course, but instead of returning the companies to old-style private ownership, they placed ownership in the hands of the newly-formed British Columbia Resources Corporation and gave five free shares of its stock to every adult resident of that province.

With its vast natural resources and huge capital requirements, Canada is an outstanding prospect for SuperStock. The combination of plentiful resources and a small population would make it possible to spread MOP ownership to the entire populace with relative ease, giving every Canadian a relatively large income. We could also consider various joint ventures; for example, providing Canadian citizens with an opportunity to own stock in American companies, in exchange for cheaper and more plentiful supplies of oil and other resources that would benefit shareholders of many American corporations.

As in the case of Canada, our relations with nations that adopt SuperStock are likely to improve through common interests. On the other hand, an all-out drive to enlist the whole world in a SuperStock crusade would put us back into ideological contention with the Soviet Union. Therefore, our proselytizing efforts should be limited to nations that are already firmly allied with us and are not likely to become targets of Soviet international proletarianism in the near future. One such candidate, obviously, is Great Britain, the nation that virtually invented the industrial revolution and capitalism itself. SuperStock would be especially therapeutic there because Britain is a badly split society, with every election the focus of the continuing class warfare that Marx used as his model a century ago. The rioting and looting in London, Liverpool, and Manchester during the early 1980s show the degree to which class divisiveness still exists in the United Kingdom.

Despite broad welfare legislation and nationalization of such major industries as coal, steel, autos, and aircraft, Britain's class structure has survived. Indeed, nationalization favored the bought-out owners, who received huge sums for their moribund industries while everyone's taxes were increased to foot the bill. By and large, the nationalized industries have done poorly under British government management. But they would offer a perfect starting place for the British version of SuperStock. Nobody has any feeling of ownership about the nationalized companies now—not the workers, the managers, nor the British public. The British coal mines, railways, and automobile factories have seen more than their share of strikes, even though they are owned by a government that is frequently controlled by the Labour party.

Instead of returning the nationalized companies to private ownership, they could be owned by everyone in Britain. This would supply the missing link for British industry: the healing factor, the team spirit needed to create incentive for increased productivity. Sharing the bounties of industry merely by creating jobs has never been enough to make British capitalism work in the twentieth century. Indeed, by the 1983 elections, most of Britain was resigned to accepting 13 percent unemployment, the highest rate in British history. Fewer than half the young people leaving school in 1983 will find jobs. Although Margaret Thatcher had presided over the doubling of unemployment during her preceding four years, and bankruptcies of companies, partnerships, and individuals reached all-time highs in 1982, her Conservative party was reelected by a landslide because the voters concluded that neither Labour nor any of the other parties could create jobs without bringing back ruinous inflation.

To solve the endemic problems of the British economy, Nicholas Davenport, an English financier-journalist who worked closely with Keynes for many years, suggested the use of a plan like Super-Stock. In his 1964 book, *The Split Society*, Davenport wrote:

> How to make people who possess no capital feel that they have a stake in the country is an awkward political problem. As long as they suspect that the nation is being run in the interests of the finance-capitalists—the 2 percent of the population who own half the wealth of the nation—they will always feel alienated and at times incensed.
>
> The Labour attempt to bring about a wider distribution of capital through nationalisation was futile. Their whole socialisation programme tended to make the rich richer. And it brought no uplift in the worker's status. It was merely a change, as I have said, in

management—and that of a peculiarly bureaucratic type. . . .

Labour should realise that a wider distribution of capital cannot be secured by nationalisation (which makes the rich more liquid) or by heavy discriminating taxation (which would merely drive the rich abroad) or by confiscation (which is rightly impossible in a democratic state). It can only be done by making poor people less poor and giving the mass of wage and salary earners a better chance to acquire some capital. [p. 169]

In Britain today, the effort to broaden capitalism is being spearheaded by the Wider Share Ownership Council, led by the highly-regarded and energetic Harry Ball-Wilson, a World War II RAF pilot. Ball-Wilson has been able to convince leaders of the Conservative, Liberal, and Social Democratic parties to adopt the principles of broadening stock ownership, at least to the extent of supporting profit sharing and employee stock ownership plans.

SuperStock might even provide a solution to the desperate situation in Northern Ireland. Although many people consider this a purely religious matter—a war between Catholics and Protestants— there is a very strong economic factor involved which could be the key to this seemingly insoluble dilemma. The Protestants dominate economic life in Northern Ireland, thanks largely to England's King James I, who forced the Irish Catholics to deed their land over to English and Scottish Protestants in 1603. Today, the Protestants of Ulster have a much higher standard of living than their Catholic neighbors. The struggle for economic survival and self-respect permeates every level of Ulster life. And the high rate of unemployment among the Catholics, which they attribute to Protestant repression, breeds continuing violence. But there aren't enough jobs to go around.

Whether or not SuperStock can solve this awful problem is anyone's guess, but economic teamwork in the form of shared ownership in leading Ulster industries is a promising antidote. It is certainly more promising—and in the long run much cheaper— than keeping the British Army there.

These examples illustrate the many possible uses of SuperStock to improve our foreign relations. I believe the SuperStock principle could be adapted for use in most of Europe, in China and Japan, and eventually in much of the world. But we would not be able to help many nations install SuperStock at first; for overriding the great global potential of SuperStock is the need to use it first to end the nuclear nightmare. For that purpose, it must be handled carefully, so the Soviets see it as a means of disengagement, not as another ploy in the ideological power struggle between capitalism and communism.

Properly planned, a new American foreign policy built around SuperStock would give the Kremlin rulers many chances to perceive that partnership with the United States would be in their self-interest. But if it appears to them to be a capitalist weapon designed to destabilize the Kremlin, it can also lead to disaster.

The Worst Case Scenario: Triggering Nuclear War

One would think that SuperStock would be less of a provocation to the Kremlin than our direct attempts to sabotage the Soviet economy. Witness our 1982 campaign to kill the Soviet natural gas pipeline to Western Europe, when we ordered American contractors to renege on delivery of equipment and tried to pressure our NATO allies into boycotting the project. And what about our military and financial aid to many foreign armies who are shooting at Soviet-backed Marxist armies?

Yet, if SuperStock is not handled properly, it could prove even more dangerous than our present stumbling deterrence policies, primarily because it has a much better chance of working. If it succeeded in America and was copied abroad, it might show up the Kremlin in the macho game of world power politics. It might create a demand for individual MOP ownership in the USSR—and with it, movements toward pluralism and democracy, two dirty words in the Kremlin lexicon.

Despite this hazard, I think we *must* take the chance. Given the unique potential of SuperStock to end the nuclear nightmare, we cannot discard it without trying to shape it into a package that will clearly appeal to the Soviets' self-interest.

We can only guess at what it will take to make the Soviets open their minds to such a proposal. But we can find hope in an experience Bertrand Russell described in an interview published in the March 1963 issue of *Playboy:*

> Last summer I sent a message to Moscow in which I expressed the wish that in all negotiations between East and West, the negotiator for the Communists should begin by saying that the universal victory of capitalism would be less disastrous than nuclear war. At the same time, the Western spokesman should start by admitting that the universal victory of communism would be preferable to the destruction of mankind. In a speech last July, Khrushchev singled out this suggestion and said that he entirely agreed.

If Khrushchev could publicly accept the idea that a universal victory of capitalism was preferable to nuclear war, there is cause for hope that his successors would open their minds to a plan that gives humanity the power to win a universal victory over the defects of both capitalism and communism.

Chapter 7

SuperStock Compared To Other Economic Remedies

The purpose of studying economics is not to acquire a set of ready-made answers to economic questions, but to learn how to avoid being deceived by economists.

—JOAN ROBINSON
Professor of Economics, Cambridge University

The ideas which are here expressed [in *The General Theory of Employment, Interest and Money*] are extremely simple and should be obvious. The difficulty lies, not in the new ideas, but in escaping from the old ones, which ramify, for those brought up as most of us have been, into every corner of our minds.

—JOHN MAYNARD KEYNES

By now you may be wondering, "Why us?" If eliminating ideological conflict is the key to peace, why must we be the ones to make such a sweeping change in our economic ideology? Why not the Soviets, particularly since in the view of most Americans, they opened hostilities in the first place by declaring war on capitalism? We have, of course, already touched on the answer: asking the Kremlin leaders to abandon international proletarianism would mean asking them to relinquish their main source of power and legitimacy. It would, in other words, mean inviting them to commit political suicide.

Our economic system, in contrast, is much more flexible. Unlike Soviet communism, American capitalism is not defined or even mentioned in our Constitution or laws. We Americans, moreover, have greater power to influence our government. We are free to take a fresh look at capitalism and determine whether it can be made more compatible with communism. It is, therefore, up to us to take that first step toward ideological accord.

The two systems are converging anyway, if only because the repeated failures of both have produced a natural flow toward accommodation. We used to think of capitalism as a system based on private ownership and initiative, with independent decisions by producers and consumers determining prices and policies. Yet here in the United States, we find extensive government participation in economic decision-making, large social welfare programs, and massive redistribution of income, all key elements of a socialist system. Similarly, although the essence of socialism is government ownership and operation of the means of production, the problems inherent in nationalization have prompted many socialist parties to abandon the idea. The Socialist International, for example, which is a descendant of Marx's First International, and which numbers among its members the strong labor parties of Sweden, West Germany, Holland, and Denmark, no longer advocates government MOP ownership.

Communism, too, is changing, adapting itself to the requirements of the post-industrial age. Defined as an advanced form of socialism, it is, according to Marxists, the last stage in the historical sequence of slavery, feudalism, capitalism, and socialism. In its ultimate form, government itself would become unnecessary and would wither away; in the meantime, dictatorship of the proletariat would prevail. Yet numerous communist parties claim to have given up the idea of dictatorship or one-party rule. And some communist countries are beginning to experiment on a small scale with private ownership and profit systems, in an attempt to create incentives for increased productivity. Even in the Soviet Union, there is a great deal of income inequality, with three-quarters of the industrial workers paid at piece rates.

Today, none of these systems exist in pure form anywhere, and in most nations the three are combined in hybrid forms that almost defy definition. In many ways, therefore, SuperStock represents a natural culmination of this trend toward accommodation, particularly in that it brings together the best elements of capitalism, socialism, and Marxism.

If accommodation is vital in the international field, it is no less so here at home. For more than fifty years, we've managed to keep capitalism alive by tempering its harsh "survival of the fittest" philosophy with various social welfare programs. But our Band-Aid remedies are no longer working, precisely because they are not sweeping enough; they provide only temporary relief from symptoms while ignoring the disease itself—the widening gap between capitalists and noncapitalists. And as long as the disease remains untreated, capitalism remains in danger, vulnerable not only to the Soviets, but to internal pressure as well.

As far back as 1975, the eminent conservative economist, Arthur F. Burns, then chairman of the Board of Governors of the Federal Reserve System, stated publicly that he did not believe capitalism could survive without basic structural changes. But what kinds of structural changes could be made without endangering the productivity, freedom, and high standard of living that characterized American capitalism in the past? Neither Burns nor anyone else has been able to answer that question. Instead, since the 1960s, our economists, politicians, and think-tanks have focused solely on conventional remedies and stopgap measures, none of which have been successful. It would seem, therefore, that SuperStock is indeed an idea whose time has come, not only for the sake of our relations with the Soviets, but also as our best—and perhaps last—chance to save capitalism. It also represents the realization of our long quest for real equality, economically and socially as well as politically. And in marked contrast to other proposed "cures" for our economic malaise, it represents our only real hope for treating the disease itself.

If we don't embrace a program like SuperStock, what other choices are open to us—Milton Friedman on the right, Gore Vidal on the left, and the picked-over carcass of New Deal welfare capitalism in-between? And what kind of future are these choices likely to provide? Indeed, we need only look closely at current remedies to realize they are not only ineffective, but also likely to further divide our split society, to aggravate the very disease they are intended to cure.

The Current Cures Are Worse Than The Disease

My deep concern about the fate of capitalism and the need for structural changes began in the late 1960s, when in the course of my legal work, I began to study economic projections extending to the year 2000. The picture was bleak, but even more discouraging was the fact that none of our so-called experts seemed willing or able to face up to the real problems of American capitalism and seek effective solutions. Then, in 1972, I was greatly cheered to learn that

Lewis Lehrman had created the Lehrman Institute for that very purpose. This was part of his intensive preparation for a new career in politics, in which he later ran a close but losing race as the 1982 Republican candidate for governor of New York.

In my view, Lew Lehrman was an ideal candidate for the job of masterminding the rescue of capitalism: brilliant, inquisitive, young, business-trained, politically oriented, and possessed of a large fortune that he was willing to tap for the public good. He established his institute in a Manhattan townhouse and staffed it with top-flight economists and public policy experts. He orchestrated their efforts himself, bringing in scores of reputable scholars and experienced policy-makers who represented every established school of thought on capitalism. And what did this ten-year effort bring forth? The one structural change that Lehrman recommended was . . . a return to the gold standard!

I still admire Lew Lehrman's patriotism and his willingness to propose radical change. But I did not sleep easier after learning that the gold idea was the best suggestion he could make, given his unique access to our greatest minds. I was further chilled when the Carter administration showed its desperation by establishing a presidential commission to consider the proposal. Indeed, in its lead story on the commission's deliberations, *The New York Times* used the headline, "GOLD STANDARD: SERIOUS TOPIC" in order to reassure readers that they had not mistakenly turned to the entertainment section.

In 1982, after two years of study, the Gold Commission decided it was not a good idea to go back to the gold standard, for reasons that would occur to most high school history students. While a return to the gold standard would stop inflation in its tracks, it would also be likely to unleash a 1930s-style depression, and it would put our economic growth in the hands of the world's two largest gold producers: South Africa and the Soviet Union. Commenting on this proposal, Herbert Stein, the prominent conservative economist who served as adviser to several Republican presidents, noted: "There are about 15,000 professional economists who say, 'We are absolutely sure that this is a crazy idea,' and about six people who think they are absolutely sure that it's a wonderful idea." But among those six "gold bugs" were Congressman Jack Kemp, Professor Arthur B. Laffer, and Jude Wanniski, all prominent members of the team who shaped the economic policies of the Reagan administration.

The gold standard story and Reaganomics are but two illustrations of the desperate condition of American capitalism. Like the "crazy idea" of returning to the gold standard, the mere fact that

Reaganomics got a serious hearing at the White House should have shaken our confidence. That it was actually put into legislation and enacted by Congress as the best available solution to our economic crisis should absolutely petrify us. For what, after all, is the essence of Reaganomics, but a joining of two conflicting policies—large tax cuts (creating unprecedented 12-digit budget deficits) and tight money. And if there is any logic at all to the "science" of economics, how could such a policy possibly be expected to work?

During the first televised debate of the 1980 presidential campaign, journalist Jane Bryant Quinn asked candidate Ronald Reagan whether he really thought he could simultaneously cut income taxes, increase military expenditures, and balance the budget. Reagan's reply? The reduction of nonmilitary expenditures and the increased savings and investment spurred by tax cuts would rejuvenate the economy and enable him to deliver on his promises. I don't know any knowledgeable person who believed this was possible—and, of course, it wasn't. Not surprisingly, Reagan was unable to reduce nonmilitary expenditures significantly. The tax cuts and military boosts produced a record $200 billion budget deficit, and investment actually fell. The only surprise was that such a hare-brained scheme survived Jane Bryant Quinn's first public questioning and went on to win a comfortable majority in Congress.

As Hodding Carter III put it in his *Wall Street Journal* column of August 12, 1983, "The best way to think about Reaganomics is to consider the effect of malaria. Extremes grip its victims, with severely high fever followed by chills." The real tragedy of Reaganomics is that we didn't have malaria until Dr. Reagan administered his cure. And who is paying the price for the extremes of inflation and recession that Reaganomics has inflicted on us? Certainly not the capitalists, but the struggling middle class, the working poor, the elderly, the disabled—in short, those most in need of economic security. A perfect example is the Reagan administration's efforts to reduce inflation, the one area in which they can claim economic progress. How have they managed this feat? By using the same technique employed by many of their predecessors, both Democratic and Republican—creating a recession. It is the only known way to reduce inflation. But it exacts a fearful toll.

Tightening credit and increasing interest rates cuts business investment and deliberately creates unemployment. It forces many small and weak companies out of business because they depend on borrowed money to survive. When credit is tightened, loans are not forthcoming, or come at too high a cost for weak companies, whose profit margins can't support double-digit interest rates. Nevertheless, past Democratic and Republican administrations have used the brutal weapon of recession because nothing else was able to halt runaway inflation. In so doing, they destroyed businesses, farms, and jobs that represented the life work of millions of Americans. They also destroyed many people and families. But the Reagan administration was the first that showed the will to halt inflation regardless of the human costs. In a 1976 study of the human cost of unemployment, the Joint Economic Committee of Congress found that a mere 1 percent increase in unemployment produced a sharp rise in the suicide rate, in heart attacks, liver disease, mental illness, imprisonment, and the number of wives and children battered by men who had been thrown out of work, deprived of their self-respect, and dumped onto the garbage heap of our society. No wonder then that Professor John Kenneth Galbraith describes this method of fighting inflation as "crucifixion."

What Reagan hoped to create by reducing inflation and taxes was a rising tide of prosperity that would, in theory, lift all boats. And indeed, the lowering of inflation and temporary "recovery" produced a stock market rally in 1983 that lifted the yachts to a new high-water mark. But the ferry boats of the middle class, the leaky rowboats of the working poor, and the millions of desperate swimmers seeking to board anything that floats, were not likely to be lifted by Reaganomics or any other version of the trickledown theory.

The lethal effects of Reaganomics and the serious attention devoted to the "crazy idea" of the gold standard, should make us wonder: What are our safeguards against economic remedies that are worse than the disease? I'm afraid the answer is that we haven't any real safeguards, because the "rules" of welfare capitalism are largely myth.

This problem is the subject of a 1983 book written by Massachusetts Institute of Technology economics professor Lester C. Thurow, entitled *Dangerous Currents: The State of Economics.* Thurow argues that the economics profession is largely ruled by the "equilibrium price-auction model," which views the world as controlled by supply and demand. He describes the model as follows:

> The equilibrium price-auction view of the world is a traditional view with a history as old as that of economics itself: the individual is asserted to be a maximizing consumer or producer within free supply-demand markets that establish an equilibrium price for any kind of goods or service. This is an economics blessed with an intellectual consistency, and one having implications that extend far beyond the realm of conventional economic theory. It is, in short,

also a political philosophy, often becoming something approaching a religion.

Price-auction economics is further blessed because it can assume mathematical form—it can work hand in glove with calculus. Expression in mathematics imparts to the theory a seeming rigor and internal strength. But that rigor easily degenerates into scholarly rigor mortis, as mathematical facility becomes more important to the profession than a substantive understanding of the economy itself. [pp. xviii–xix]

Thurow calls Reaganomics a set of "punk beliefs" that nevertheless captured the central economic-policy-making apparatus of the United States, largely because the price-auction model prevents American economists from formulating any alternative theories that will hold water (pp. 125, 137). In the dream world of price-auction theory, unemployment is impossible because the jobless would force themselves on employers at wages so low, employers couldn't resist hiring; factors such as inflation and employee motivation are irrelevant; and after something like the 1973 OPEC oil price increases, prices for other items should drop because of reduced purchasing power! Little wonder, then, that proposals like the gold standard and Reaganomics can gain political support without effective screening by the economics profession.

Nor is it surprising, given the number of economists who accept these myths at face value, that viable solutions to our economic crisis are not forthcoming. Although most members of Congress, most economists, most members of the New York Stock Exchange, and even many Reagan administration officials perceived from the start that Reaganomics was a hoax, many jumped on the bandwagon anyway—because they had no better ideas of their own. Even Hodding Carter III, who so eloquently debunked Reaganomics, was unable to provide any better answers when he worked in Jimmy Carter's administration. And when the disastrous effects of Reaganomics became apparent, the Democratic Party was still unable to regain control of the Senate in the 1982 mid-term elections. Why? Because they could not come up with any economic plan that seemed more workable than Reaganomics or a return to the gold standard.

Personally, I am glad Reaganomics was tried. In some ways it can be considered an attempted structural change, since its real objective was to reverse the course of welfare capitalism (which began with Franklin Roosevelt's New Deal) and take us back as far as possible to laissez-faire capitalism, which to some Reagan advisers is what made America a great nation. Reaganomics was tried and found to be an error, but at least that has advanced us one step, since the only tool we have to work with in the "science" of economics is trial and error.

Of course, knowing what doesn't work is only a small step in the right direction. We also have to find out what will work, and here too, we must rely on trial and error. We'll never find out whether SuperStock is a workable solution if it is dismissed at the outset as too good to be true, or too radical. Certainly, it is innovative, but the basic concept of broadening capital ownership is not a new idea. It has flourished for a number of years in this country in the form of worker-ownership plans which provide company employees with an opportunity to own company stock or otherwise share in the company's profits. And in recent years, with economic conditions growing ever bleaker, these plans have gained momentum because many people view them as a possible solution to the problems inherent in capitalism.

But are such plans likely to prove any more effective in the long run than the conventional remedies embraced by politicians and economists? I fear not, and a closer examination simply affirms once again that SuperStock remains the only solution broad enough to address the major weakness of capitalism: the inequitable distribution of income and wealth caused by overconcentration of capital ownership.

Worker Ownership Is Not The Answer

The idea of workers owning shares in the enterprise that employs them is even older than Marxism. In 1826, German economist Johannn Heinrich von Thunen wrote a book on this subject called *The Isolated State.* Von Thunen, however, did not confine himself to theoretical speculation. He owned large agricultural estates, and he applied his theories to his own farm workers, paying them the prevailing wages, and in addition, agreeing to share his profits with them. But instead of paying these profit-sharing bonuses in cash, he reinvested this money in equipment that would improve his farms' productivity. Each employee had an individual account to which his share of the profit was credited each year. The interest on this share was paid out annually in cash to the worker, and when the worker retired or left von Thunen's employment, he received his share of ownership in cash.

During the nineteenth and twentieth centuries, von Thunen's idea was carried on through many types of profit-sharing and ownership-sharing schemes within individual companies throughout Europe and the United States. There are many individual success stories, notably the Sears Roebuck and Eastman Kodak profit-sharing plans, which invested their funds mainly in stock of the employer company; this made the employees, at least indirectly, owners of substantial shares in the company for which they worked.

Worker ownership is an attractive idea: it seems to provide a logical incentive for increasing productivity, and it dampens the fires of class struggle by giving workers a stake in maximizing company profits. The concept of broadening worker ownership of the employer company is something like motherhood and apple pie, and therefore regularly finds its way into the platform statements of both the Democratic and Republican parties. But these boilerplate political endorsements don't say much about how worker ownership is to be created. Therefore, let's look at the specific plans that have been used for this purpose.

ESOP and Other Worker Ownership Plans

Government-subsidized worker ownership in the United States began in 1928, when Congress enacted special tax benefits designed to encourage the use of profit-sharing and stock bonus plans to provide workers with retirement income. These tax laws allowed companies a business tax deduction for their contributions to such a plan; at the same time, the plan's income was sheltered from federal taxes until workers received the cash value of their vested benefits upon retiring or otherwise leaving the company's employ. With a few notable exceptions, such as Sears and Eastman Kodak, these profit-sharing plans diversified their portfolios, rather than investing solely in shares of the employer company. And while profit-sharing plans were adopted by numerous companies, the stock bonus plan, which was enacted as a means of issuing employer stock to employees, was rarely used until 1973. Since then it has provided the foundation for Senator Russell B. Long's crusade for stock ownership plans (SOPs).

Convinced that broadening stock ownership was the best way to ward off the threat of socialism, Senator Long, then chairman of the Senate Finance Committee, used his great influence to enact legislation authorizing a series of stock ownership plans. By 1982, plans of this type had been installed by about 5,000 corporations. The most important SOPs are the ESOP (Employee Stock Ownership Plan), the TRASOP (Tax Reduction Act Stock Ownership Plan), and the PAYSOP (Payroll-Based Stock Ownership Plan).

ESOP is the most widely used of these plans, and is financed by employer contributions, which are used to buy stock of the employer company. The stock is then held in trust for employees. Generally, shares are allocated on the basis of each employee's relative wage, but some companies do make equal contributions for all employees, regardless of their compensation. Employees receive this stock only after their employment has been terminated. As with other employee benefit plans that qualify for tax benefits under the Internal Revenue Code, ESOPs must be established and operated for the benefit of the employee participants.

Lawyers and corporate financiers have developed some sophisticated uses of ESOPs, the most prominent of which is the "leveraged" ESOP, so called because it involves use of bank loans to buy employer stock. This enables ESOPs to buy large blocks of stock on the installment plan—something that trustees of other employee benefit plans cannot do. Also, it provides the biggest advantage of ESOPs from the corporate standpoint: It enables the employer to take a tax deduction for payment of both the principal and the interest on the money borrowed by the ESOP to buy the corporation's stock. Interest is always a tax-deductible expense for corporations, just as it is on your personal income tax return. But repayment of the loan *principal* is never a tax-deductible expense, for individuals or corporations, unless a corporation has a leveraged ESOP.

The ESOP doesn't actually give the corporation a tax deduction for principal payments, but it has the same effect. The corporation makes tax-deductible contributions to the ESOP, and the ESOP uses these contributions to pay off the loan principal and interest. Therefore, the expenditure that is usually called "nondeductible repayment of loan principal" is changed to "deductible contribution to ESOP."

To illustrate the leveraged ESOP, let's assume Peerless Pizza wishes to raise $1 million through that device. First, Peerless would adopt an ESOP, get it approved by the Internal Revenue Service as a qualified employee benefit plan, and then set up a trust as part of the plan. Then Peerless would arrange a loan of $1 million from its bank. The loan is actually made to the ESOP trust rather than to Peerless, but Peerless guarantees that the loan will be repaid. Peerless's employees are not responsible for repaying the loan; only the ESOP trust and Peerless sign the note. Now the Peerless ESOP trust is holding $1 million lent by the bank, which it has to repay, let's say, in five annual installments of $200,000 each, with interest. The ESOP trust then uses the $1 million bank loan to buy $1 million worth of newly issued stock from Peerless at market value. The ESOP holds this stock in trust for the employees of Peerless, who will receive shares in proportion to their salaries when they retire or leave the company. Peerless makes an annual contribution to the ESOP to cover the principal and interest payments on the bank loan. Its maximum tax-deductible contribution to the ESOP would be 15 percent of its payroll. Since Peerless's payroll is over $100 million, it can contribute as much as $15 million per year and get a tax deduction. To repay the bank loan (including interest) for its ESOP, Peerless would have to make contributions of about $300,000 per year for five years, well within the 15 percent of payroll allowed by tax law.

This plan would enable Peerless to repay the entire principal and interest of the $1 million loan with tax-deductible contributions to the ESOP. If Peerless had received a simple $1 million bank loan without using an ESOP, it would have had to repay the principal with after-tax funds, and so would have had to earn a lot more than $1 million in profits to repay $1 million.

However, leveraged ESOPs are not considered advantageous for large, profitable corporations, since the corporation must repay a bank loan in addition to diluting its stock by issuing shares to the ESOP, thereby in effect paying twice for the same $1 million financing. Leveraged ESOPs are used mostly by smaller corporations or those having a special reason for issuing a large block of new stock, such as warding off an unfriendly takeover attempt or getting rid of an unprofitable division by selling it outright to employees.

In principle, ESOPs should help capitalism to work better by giving workers a real stake in the system, but they have had a controversial history. Proponents can point to some very successful plans, such as those installed by E-Systems of Dallas, Texas; Lowe's Companies of North Carolina; and the Hallmark Greeting Card Company of Kansas City, Missouri. ESOPs have also kept failing businesses in operation by enabling workers to buy their companies, thereby salvaging their jobs. Such rescue actions saved the South Bend Lathe Company of Indiana; the Okonite Company in New Jersey; the General Motors ball-bearing plant at Clark, New Jersey (which was reorganized as Hyatt-Clark Industries, Inc. and purchased from General Motors in 1981); and the National Steel Corporation's Weirton, West Virginia, steel works, purchased by employees through an ESOP in 1983.

However, opponents of ESOPs can point to many adverse results. Both South Bend Lathe and Okonite had labor troubles even after their workers became 100 percent owners, as did Hyatt-Clark, whose workers had to reduce their wages by 25 percent to keep their jobs. The Weirton steel-workers also took a substantial pay cut.

ESOPs have generally been used in small closely held corporations, but even in the larger ones (including South Bend Lathe), there has been a fairly general pattern of using the ESOPs as a substitute for a pension or profit-sharing plan whose funds had been invested in a diversified portfolio. This puts all the workers' security eggs in one basket—the basket of the employer. On retirement, the workers will wind up with little or nothing if the employer's business has gone bad, since they will have lost fairly secure pension benefits that were eliminated when the ESOP was installed.

Nor are these the only problems associated with ESOPs. My impression, based on attending seminars for lawyers interested in establishing ESOPs, is that they are generally designed to benefit owners of closely held corporations who can use the tax concessions provided by ESOPs to improve their own financial positions. This was, in fact, the conclusion reached in a 1980 report entitled "Employee Stock Ownership Plans: Who Benefits Most in Closely Held Companies?" presented to the Senate Finance Committee by the comptroller general. The report noted that the tax benefits associated with ESOPs for 1979 cost the public treasury between 1.5 and 2.3 billion dollars. It went on to say:

> An analysis of Plan transactions showed that most were not being operated in the best interest of participants. Specifically, one or more of the following problems were present in each of the closely held plans:
>
> —The company sold or contributed company stock to its Plan at questionable prices. . . .
>
> —Participants were not assured of a market for company stock distributed by the Plan.

In addition, according to the report, the companies involved in the survey had established ESOPs "primarily for reasons other than to improve employee motivation and productivity, and management had not tried to assess the effect on its employees." Generally, the employees interviewed did not feel that ESOPs had any real effect on their own work or the work of their fellow employees. This finding was confirmed in studies done by the University of Michigan and the UCLA Graduate School of Management, which covered several hundred ESOPs and found no conclusive evidence that ESOPs improved employee morale, motivation, or productivity. Seventy-one percent of the companies in the UCLA survey believed their employees' understanding of the ESOP was "fair" or "poor," which may be attributable to the fact that ESOP is a deferred benefit, not payable until retirement, and therefore unlikely to have much impact on an employee's day-to-day needs. Other studies have reached conclusions more favorable to ESOPs, but at best, the claim that they increase productivity and profits must be considered unproven.

Although ESOPs are intended to benefit employees, their use is not always motivated by this concern. Owners of privately held corporations can use ESOPs to reduce estate taxes and to retain control of the business while selling it to employees over a period of years. And since the owners themselves are usually high-salaried employees who will be receiving shares in proportion to their own salaries, they can get back large blocks of stock after selling to the ESOP. Probably the majority of ESOPs involve profitable privately held corporations, and thus represent a use of tax concessions to benefit people who are hardly in need of such breaks: owners of successful businesses.

ESOPs are sometimes used when the federal government steps in to bail out a troubled corporation. For example, under the Chrysler Corporation Loan Guarantee Act of 1979, Chrysler was required to set up an ESOP and contribute approximately $40 million a year until the trust's assets totaled $162.5 million of Chrysler stock, to be divided among the company's 94,000 American and Canadian employees. This stipulation was the work of Senator Long, who believes that whenever the government is called upon to bail out a corporation, the benefit should not all go to its creditors and stockholders but should also make the workers part-owners, even though their ownership does not take effect until they retire or otherwise leave the company.

The occasional misuse of an ESOP to dump over-valued stock into an employee fund or to duck the obligations of a pension plan should not rule out their honest use in other situations. But in my opinion, there are some basic reasons why ESOP cannot be developed into a broad-based ownership plan to solve America's major economic problems. For one thing, billions of dollars in tax revenues are lost in the ESOP process, and ESOPs used to rescue losing companies (such as South Bend Lathe and Okonite) involve further subsidies from the public treasury in the form of long-term, low-interest loans or loan guarantees that are too risky for commercial banks. Using an ESOP to save jobs really involves shackling a losing company's workers to the future of the losing enterprise. Some companies rescued by ESOPs will survive by reducing the payroll, scrapping the pension plan, or cutting other corners. But many others will go down the drain because their businesses have become inherently unprofitable. In any event, the rescue-type ESOP does not plug needy people into the strength of the American economy, i.e., the 2,000 or more large successful companies that account for most of our corporate profits.

Some of ESOP's deficiencies could be remedied by further legislation. Right now, as we have seen, ESOPs are not attractive to large successful companies because they represent an expensive method of financing—issuing stock in addition to paying interest and repaying loans. But even with modifications, ESOP would not be an ideal method of broadening capital ownership. Indeed, wide use of ESOPs would create many new inequities because they mainly benefit workers with secure jobs in successful companies whose stock is likely to retain or increase its value over many years. And these people are already better off than the majority of Americans, so they are least in need of tax subsidies and government-sponsored stock distribution programs. Moreover, if these subsidies were increased, everyone would want to work for the few companies whose shares retain their value over the long haul.

ESOP, of course, offers no benefits to the unemployed, the very poor, or the great mass of Americans who cannot look forward to long-term jobs with our strongest companies. Senator Long, to his great credit, sponsored the ESOP program and widened its use, but he does not claim it will lead to universal capitalism. He would like to sponsor a broader plan to make all Americans eligible for ownership, but until he finds one, he is going to keep on pushing the ESOP concept.

One of the offshoots of ESOP was the TRASOP program, which Senator Long pushed through in the Tax Reduction Act (TRA) of 1975. In effect, TRASOP enables a company to take an additional 1 percent investment tax credit, over and above the 10 percent credit allowed for the purchase of new capital items, *provided* that an amount equivalent to this 1 percent tax credit is contributed to a Tax Reduction Act Stock Ownership Plan (TRASOP) and used to buy employer stock.

To illustrate the TRASOP, let's go back to the new factory that Peerless Pizza built at a cost of $10 million. As we saw, the tax laws allowed Peerless an investment tax credit of 10 percent, or $1 million, for building the plant. In addition, if Peerless elected to establish a TRASOP, it could take an additional tax credit of 1 percent of the value of the new plant—$100,000—if the money was contributed to a TRASOP and used to buy Peerless stock. The $100,000 contribution would be made to a trust established under the TRASOP, which would buy $100,000 worth of Peerless stock for its employees. And like an ESOP, that stock would be distributed to employees in proportion to their salaries when they retired or left the company.

From a corporate perspective, TRASOP is more attractive than ESOP because the one percent tax *credit* is more valuable than the tax *deduction* permitted under ESOP. A tax deduction is merely subtracted from gross income, but a tax credit is subtracted directly from the taxes payable by Peerless, and thus amounts to a gift from the treasury to Peerless. In effect, the tax credit means the U.S. Treasury foots the bill for stock presented to employees. And because TRASOPs cost the employer nothing, large successful companies have used TRASOPs to a much greater extent than ESOPs.

Capital-intensive industries such as oil and timber were among the first to take advantage of TRASOP. In fact, the plan's chief weakness is that it favors employees of capital-intensive companies because the tax credits and the amount of stock the employees receive are based on the size of capital outlays. To remove this bias, Senator Long engineered an amendment to the 1981 tax laws, which linked tax credits and employer contributions to a percentage of a company's payroll rather than a percentage of its capital outlays. The amended tax credit plan, known as PAYSOP, went into effect in January of 1983 and allowed a credit equivalent to one-half of 1 percent of the payroll. In 1985, the credit will jump to three-quarters of 1 percent of payroll, and PAYSOP will remain in effect until December 31, 1987. So, right now, Peerless Pizza, with its annual payroll of $100 million, could contribute $500,000 a year to a PAYSOP trust (one-half of 1 percent) and receive a tax credit for the entire amount. Certainly, PAYSOP seems more equitable than TRASOP, but like all employee ownership plans, it simply isn't broad enough to provide a foundation for socialization of MOP ownership.

For similar reasons, pension and profit-sharing plans are equally limited in their ability to broaden capital ownership. Unlike the SOPs, their funds generally are not invested in stock of the employer. Since they are designed to provide old-age security through monthly cash payments to employees upon retirement, their funds are usually invested in a diversified portfolio administered by trustees. Therefore, they are not viable tools for socializing MOP ownership. In various forms they have been around for a hundred years, and while they do temper some of the harsher aspects of capitalism, they do not address the basic issue of Marxism: exploitation through MOP ownership.

In the final analysis, although all forms of government-sponsored worker ownership have some positive aspects, none are broad enough to serve as an instrument for the socialization of MOP ownership. The reason is simple: those employed by our stable, successful companies whose stock is worth holding represent a minority of the work force and an even smaller minority of the total population. Most Americans are self-employed, or work for companies whose stock is not traded publicly, or work for government or nonprofit organizations, or do not work at all. Thus, SOPs and other government programs provide subsidies to an already privileged group, using tax money that inevitably reduces the funds available for the truly needy. These ownership schemes do nothing to help the poor or the great majority of Americans who are not fortunate enough to be employed by blue-chip companies.

Worker ownership plans have been in existence for several generations, but they have never had any appreciable impact on our economy, although they have made a small number of employees much richer than they would have been if they had relied entirely on their salaries. Peter Drucker, the eminent commentator on American business, has made a detailed study of profit-sharing and employee share ownership. In his 1976 book, *The Unseen Revolution— How Pension Fund Socialism Came to America,* he concluded:

> For well over a century, if not for longer, there has been a persistent belief that a change in the "system" which made the workers the "owners" would automatically take care of the problems of industrial society, whether the disease be diagnosed as "alienation," as "subordination of man to the machine," as "the assembly line," "exploitation," or simply the boredom and drudgery of work. But for well over 100 years we have also known that this belief is a delusion. For worker ownership has a much longer history than most people realize. It has been tried many times, and has never had any but the most transitory impact on the work, the worker, or the relationships at work. Even total ownership of a business and full worker control seem to have little effect on industrial and human relations at work. [p. 133]

Drucker goes on to give examples based on his broad knowledge of American and European business. He also points out that the great majority of workers will be employed by corporations whose stocks perform erratically during the average employment period of forty years, and many will see their employers' securities become practically worthless. If there is any motivation involved in that kind of ownership, it is likely to be the reverse of what we are looking for.

In 1975, when I began studying ideas for improving capitalism, I had high hopes that an expansion of worker ownership would do the trick. But to my great disappointment, I found that Peter Drucker was right. Worker ownership does not provide the answer.

The workers themselves can't save enough to buy substantial ownership, and use of government subsidies will only further divide our already split society.

Furthermore, apart from these shortcomings, worker ownership plans also have a potentially dangerous side effect: they create large pools of worker-owned stock that can be exploited by ambitious labor leaders.

The Specter of Pension Fund Socialism

Employee pension funds now own collectively close to half the stock of major American corporations. Even during a recession, millions of dollars pour into pension coffers every day. Because their operating expenses are minuscule, their surplus funds build up faster than in any other unit of our economy. Total pension fund assets are rapidly approaching the *trillion* dollar mark. The value of pension assets in many giant corporations (such as Boeing, U.S. Steel, and United Technologies) exceeds total shareholders' equity. In emergencies, when a real safety net is needed, pension funds are called upon to bail out failing businesses and even governments, as was the case with New York City.

To quote Peter Drucker again:

> Only in the United States do the employees both own and get the profits, in the form of pensions, as part of wage income. Only in the United States are the employees through their pension funds also becoming the legal owners, the suppliers of capital, and the controlling force in the capital markets. . . . The United States alone, in terms of economic structure, has made the final step to a genuine "socialism," in which (to use Marxist terminology) "labor" as the "source of all value" receives the "full fruits of the productive process."
>
> In other words, without consciously trying, the United States has "socialized" the economy but not "nationalized" it. America still sees herself, and is seen elsewhere, as "capitalist"; but if terms like "socialism" or "capitalism" have any meaning at all, the American system has actually become the "decentralized market socialism" which all the Marxist church fathers, saints, and apostles before Lenin had been preaching and promising, from Engels to Bebel and Kautsky, from Viktor Adler to Rosa Luxemburg, Jaures, and Eugene Debs. [p. 4]

In the broadest symbolic sense, Drucker may be right: the growth of pension funds has brought a form of socialized capital to the American economy. However, under present law, the pension funds do not represent employee or social ownership of the MOP. Contrary to Drucker's statements, pension funds do not give employees either legal ownership or control of any capital, nor do they enable employees to share in corporate profits. While pension fund money is parked in the stock of various corporations from time to time, the worker-beneficiaries do not become stockholders, nor do they usually even know in which companies their pension fund has been invested. On retirement, they simply receive monthly cash payments, without ever becoming stockholders in any companies in which the pension fund may have been invested.

Nevertheless, Drucker's perception is important because it portrays what pension funds *might become.* Today they are sleeping giants because they do not exercise their ownership rights as do ordinary stockholders. Their investments are usually administered by trustees (often bank officers) who are constrained by the "prudent man" principle of the Employee Retirement Income Security Act of 1974 (ERISA), the law governing pension plans. ERISA requires trustees to invest the pension funds as would any prudent individual—in a manner which will best promote the financial security of retired employees. But if the law is changed and the sleeping giant awakens to grasp the power inherent in the ownership of most of America's capital, this power is much more likely to be exercised by labor unions than by active or retired workers.

Until recently, the major American labor unions showed no interest in activating a true ownership role through their pension funds. But in 1980, the AFL-CIO adopted a new policy, dedicated to "social investment" of pension funds. In effect, they want to use pension funds to promote unionism and protect the jobs of their members. Although they do not yet have legal clearance around the "prudent man" obstacle, it is difficult to quarrel with their reasoning. Why should auto workers in Detroit have their pension money invested in the Sun Belt and in foreign corporations that are destroying their jobs?

Mark Green, in his 1982 book, *Winning Back America,* argues the unions' case forcefully:

> Why shouldn't workers use their money to promote their economic interests? Lawrence Smedley of the AFL-CIO's Social Security Department recognizes that "The traditional relationship between labor and capital must be re-evaluated, as labor now owns capital." As part of any re-evaluation, state and federal law should relax strict adherence to the "prudent man" test to permit pension fund beneficiaries to make non-reckless, socially desirable, *and* profitable investments. As one possibility, up to 25 percent of a pension fund could be exempted from the strict "prudent" stan-

dards. Then, if a union wants to invest not only in AT&T, or J.P. Stevens, but in firms making environmental equipment, American cars, mass transit, or single-dwelling homes—because the immediate return looks favorable, because it spurs jobs in needed areas, or because the long-run social return seems promising—it would have that option. [p. 54]

Note that Mark Green speaks of the *union* as making the investment, recognizing that these funds would be controlled by labor leaders rather than individual workers.

The political ramifications of union involvement have already created problems in Canada, where pension fund socialism is more advanced. The Caisse de depot et placement du Quebec, known as "the Caisse," is custodian of a group of Quebec pension funds, including the province's counterpart of Social Security. It has become the largest investor in the Canadian stock markets and is viewed as an ally of the Parti Quebecois, which came to power in 1976 on a platform advocating Quebec's separation from the Canadian confederation. Although the Caisse denies that it is a tool of the separatist party, its investment policy is worrying Canadian industrialists. It now owns nearly 10 percent of Canadian Pacific, the largest company in Canada. Canadian Pacific's management is concerned that as the Caisse increases its stock ownership, it might abuse its power by forcing the company to favor operations and employees in Quebec. The Parti Quebecois itself has advocated state ownership of banks and large businesses.

As the American economy continues to stumble and the cash-rich pension funds are called upon again and again to rescue failing enterprises, the idea of pension fund socialism is bound to gain momentum. This would open the way for labor union socialism, concentrating power in the hands of a small group of labor leaders. Certainly, this is not the type of socialization that the majority of Americans want, nor would it necessarily promote ideological accord with the Soviet Union, since the USSR has no labor unions comparable to our own. Nor would pension fund socialism solve our major economic problems or close the gap between haves and have-nots. Pensions, after all, are a privilege accorded only to the elite minority of Americans who manage to maintain long-term employment with financially sound enterprises.

Furthermore, if we allow labor unions to exercise control over large blocks of stock through pension funds, monumental conflicts of interest are bound to occur. On the one hand, the unions would be representing current workers in wage negotiations and could, through voting control of the board of directors, push wages to the highest possible level. On the other hand, pension fund stock would decrease in value if wage increases led to a decrease in profits. And so it would go, around and around in a circle, until the union officials who wear all these hats met themselves coming and going.

The Meidner Plan: Pension fund socialism is gaining momentum in Europe. In Sweden, the Meidner Plan has been under development for a decade and is likely to be implemented during the late 1980s. In its original form, as designed by union economist Rudolf Meidner, it would require Swedish companies to pay 20 percent of their annual pre-tax profits into a special fund for the purchase of stock that would be issued to the labor unions—not to the workers, but to the unions themselves. Individual workers would not receive any share ownership or dividend payments. The stock would remain in the fund in collective form, and would always be controlled by the unions. Under this scheme, all significant businesses in Sweden would be majority-owned and controlled by the labor unions in less than 20 years.

Implementation of the Meidner plan was delayed by the defeat of Olof Palme's Social Democratic Party in the 1976 elections, in which the plan was an important issue. But Palme returned to power in 1982, and one of his first acts was to reactivate the Meidner plan, even though the Social Democrats' leading economist, Professor Assar Lindbeck, resigned in protest because he believed the plan would cause "the collectivization of society." The Meidner label was dropped and the scheme was renamed "wage-earner funds." Popular opposition to the original plan (including complaints from the labor rank and file) forced Palme to reopen the question of union ownership. In November 1982, Palme announced his government's new economic policy, which included payment of the Meidner-inspired 20 percent of pre-tax profits into a special fund for two years, during which Palme hoped to work out details of the wage-earner funds with opposition parties. Thus by 1985, Sweden will probably have some version of the Meidner plan in effect.

Similar plans are now under study in Denmark, the Netherlands, and West Germany, and it is only a matter of time before such plans develop a constituency here. Therefore, unless we adopt SuperStock or a similar method of broadening capital ownership democratically, the insidious growth of pension fund socialism is likely to continue, paving the way for takeover of American industry by the labor unions and the eventual creation of a labor party that could put political as well as economic control in the hands of labor leaders, and thereby create a serious threat to our democracy.

Thus we circle back to the central point of this chapter: Super-Stock is an idea whose time has come. It is the *only* solution broad enough to heal our split society and promote ideological accord with the Soviets, and yet it will enable us to retain the great benefits of capitalism, freedom, and democracy. Unlike Reaganomics and the various SOPs, it can provide economic security for *all* Americans. And unlike expanded use of pension funds, it will not put our future in the hands of powerful labor unions. Indeed, as we shall see in the next chapter, it will benefit all segments of our society.

Chapter 8

The Domestic Effects of SuperStock

The freest government cannot long endure when the tendency of the law is to create a rapid accumulation of property in the hands of a few and to render the masses poor and dependent.

—DANIEL WEBSTER

Throughout this book, I've stressed the importance of self-interest as a primary human motivation. So it now seems appropriate to consider how SuperStock can serve *your* interests—yours and all Americans, rich, poor, and middle-class. The most important way in which it can serve your interests is to end the nuclear nightmare. Obviously, if SuperStock can open the way for Soviet-American peace and nuclear disarmament, it will serve the interests of every person on earth.

But if nuclear confrontation is our most threatening problem, it is certainly not our only problem. Most of us are also seriously concerned about our own future in these unstable times. So you might well wonder: What will SuperStock do for me? What impact will it have on my life and work? How will it affect the economy, my standard of living, and social problems like crime and political unrest? This is what we shall explore in this chapter—the far-reaching effects of SuperStock on all aspects of American society.

A Shot In The Arm For America

The changes required to implement SuperStock would be less radical than the Income Tax Law of 1913 and the Social Security Law of 1934; the benefits to our society, however, would be far more profound. By providing all American households with yearly dividends of up to $20,000 we could create the new customers and provide the massive infusion of purchasing power needed to match our huge productive capacity. Increased production would, in turn, help to reduce inflation, as would the eventual replacement of all social welfare transfer payments with the income earned by investment in productive capital.

Of course, these changes would not occur overnight, but the very prospect of making American capitalism work for everyone would start the juices flowing. In fact, the mere announcement of the SuperStock initiative would provide an enormous psychological boost for our society. Right now, according to many professional economists, fear itself impedes economic recovery. Inflation is accelerated by the expectation that it will continue and by the perception that the government has no plan to stop it except by creating recessions. Many wage and price increases, for example, are based not on present needs, but on the expectation of prolonged inflation. Thus, fear and pessimism feed what amounts to a self-fulfilling prophecy. Leading economists all the way back to Adam Smith, Alfred Marshall, and John Maynard Keynes have recognized the strong influence of emotional and psychological factors on the economy. Marshall, Keynes' mentor, ascribed many economic phenomena to "human nature." Keynes himself wrote in his 1936 classic *General Theory:*

> There is the instability due to the characteristic of human nature that a large proportion of our positive activities depend on spontaneous optimism rather than on a mathematical expectation, whether moral or hedonistic or economic. . . . Thus if the animal spirits are dimmed and the spontaneous optimism falters, leaving us to depend on nothing but a mathematical expectation, enterprise will fade and die—though fears of loss may have a basis no more reasonable than hopes of profit had before. [pp. 161–2]

In 1982, Professor Shlomo Maital expressed a similar theme in his book *Minds, Markets, & Money,* concluding that "minds pervade markets." It would seem, therefore, that SuperStock would provide the vital ingredient missing from the standard remedies for our economic malaise: a credible basis for optimism.

It would be difficult to imagine a policy more suitable for creating national unity and improving the American morale. SuperStock is consistent with America's greatest traditions, both liberal and conservative. It is conservative in that it would reduce taxes, eventually eliminate transfer payments, and check the growth of government bureaucracy, while preserving private ownership and existing financial institutions, and supporting business. It is liberal because it does more for the ordinary individual than all of the government welfare schemes ever dreamed up. And it would enable Americans to achieve economic independence without relying on welfare.

As a new national economic policy, SuperStock would require extensive legislation and therefore broad political backing. But because it meets the objectives of the left, the right, and the center, it should receive overwhelming support from all sectors. And because it addresses everyone's concerns, it is the only solution capable of uniting us emotionally. In fact, like Marxism, SuperStock appeals to our most basic emotion—hope for a better future. Unlike Marxism, SuperStock can deliver on its promises without destroying democracy. It would put all of us on the same side and in the same class. And it would even give us something to be patriotic about: an American form of capitalism that is truly democratic and that can lead the world toward nuclear disarmament.

For the first time, our economic system would mirror our system of political democracy, and we would be affluent enough to deal with problems like poverty, pollution, health care, and crime. We would no longer have to feel guilty about an undemocratic, inequitable capitalist system, so we could begin to enforce the criminal law in good conscience.

The inequities of our capitalist system, in fact, are important causes of crime and social unrest. I am not one of those who would suspend criminal laws until we have created a utopia with equal opportunity and wealth for all. If we let crime proliferate because criminals are poor—or for any other reason—we'll never survive. But there is no doubt that people in the poorest sector of the economy, the sector which breeds most of our criminals, will continue to feel alienated as long as they remain shut out of the economic system. Our jails are already overflowing, and we are drifting dangerously toward accepting unemployment rates of 20 to 40 percent among the people who commit most of our violent crimes. Yet what can we do now but hand out welfare, even though we know that government handouts do not breed greater respect for the law?

Now consider SuperStock's impact on this critical problem. By giving everyone the opportunity to become part of the establishment, we will take a major step toward removing the primary cause of crime. There will be no basis for anyone to feel exploited or left out of the system. There will still be criminals, of course, but few enough to be controlled by reasonable police action. Remember, too, that we can encourage the highest standards of behavior and morality by closing the plan to those who commit crimes. With all households assured of a sizeable income, few people would have logical reasons to take the risks of imprisonment and loss of SuperStock dividends.

Now let's take a look at SuperStock's likely impact on some of our other critical problems.

SuperStock and Inflation

One of the main causes of our recurring inflation is the attempt to support our population through wages and welfare. The false promise of full employment, which cannot be realized in this mechanized age, creates inflationary pressures on our politicians. So they hand out more welfare in place of the nonexistent jobs. As taxes increase to feed the growing appetite of welfare and Social Security programs, cost-of-living salary raises become a necessity. As a result, we pay people more money for doing the same amount of work, which creates strong inflationary pressure. SuperStock, however, would relieve much of this pressure by eventually assuming the functions of Social Security and welfare, thus making our economy less dependent on wage increases. Workers who have an ownership stake in the means of production and are receiving a second income from that ownership will have less need to press for wage increases.

What's more, SuperStock would make it easier to swallow some of the harsh medicine needed to halt inflation, such as raising the Social Security eligibility age to 67 or 68, and implementing government spending limits. SuperStock would eliminate the need for the "us against them" philosophy; policies that do not work under welfare capitalism or socialism, such as public works programs and wage-price controls, should become workable. In the split society of American welfare capitalism, such government policies have two strikes against them before they start, with powerful special interest groups poised to defeat legislation required to make such programs effective. With the nation united by socialization of MOP ownership, we could put the necessary teeth into such legislation. Certainly, wage and price controls would be more palatable if enacted by a united society such as we had during World War II, when the controls worked quite well.

Perhaps we might finally adopt a Tax-Based Incomes Policy (TIP), an idea proposed by the late Professor Sidney Weintraub of the Wharton School which has been endorsed by both political parties but never put into effect. TIP is intended to curb inflation via tax credits—without causing recession. So, for example, if we wanted to hold price increases to 5 percent per year, we could offer producers tax credits for meeting that goal. And workers willing to accept wage increases of 5 percent or less could receive an incentive in the form of similar tax credits. Alternatively, workers or producers exceeding these limits might be subject to tax penalties. Despite the obvious merits of TIP, it has never come close to enactment because the "us against them" factor in our present system makes it virtually impossible to achieve effective legislation.

Now to the bottom-line question: Is SuperStock itself inflationary? The $300 billion worth of credit needed to finance the purchase of SuperStock shares might appear to be inflationary, since creating massive amounts of new credit is virtually the same thing as printing money. However, there is no reason why this credit feature has to be inflationary.

Actually, the loans used to finance SuperStock would not create entirely new credit demands, since our corporations are already borrowing huge sums to finance capital expenditures. Moreover, by doing away with transfer payments, SuperStock eventually will reduce the need for massive government borrowing to finance budget deficits, a process that raises interest rates and fuels inflation. In this respect SuperStock will have a counter-inflationary effect.

When Senator Mike Gravel held a seminar on his Full-Return Stock Plan at the Brookings Institution in 1977, one of the questions raised was the inflationary effect of this credit scheme. According to Professor Lawrence D. Klein, the Nobel Prize-winning Wharton economist who chaired the meeting, the expansion of credit to finance the stock purchase program would not be inflationary if the money was used for investment that raises productivity. That, of course, is precisely where the SuperStock money goes: to pay for new plants and equipment. Klein also noted that wage demands were likely to be more moderate if workers were stockholders, since they would benefit from lower labor costs which would increase profits and dividends to shareholders.

Nevertheless, if the creation of credit for the SuperStockholders does prove inflationary, we can implement the plan gradually. Instead of committing the entire $300 billion in new capital during the first year, we might begin with only a quarter or half of that amount. The important thing is to get started in the right direction. In fact, if we cut the entire plan in half, we'd still wind up with a much stronger economy than we have today.

In the event that implementation of SuperStock strained our credit facilities, we could consider setting priorities for access to credit. The point here is that credit used to pay for SuperStock shares will bring us closer to world peace and economic justice, whereas loans for such transactions as one huge company taking over another are not really productive; these could be given a lower priority or cut off entirely until the credit strain is eased.

In considering the inflationary potential of SuperStock, we should calculate the costs of carrying out the plan, for if it involves large costs to the government, it can be as inflationary as welfare capitalism. But as we have seen, SuperStock differs from welfare capitalism in that it ties benefits to profits—the profits and dividends actually produced by American capitalism, which all of us, working together, can create by tapping the inherent strength of the system. Therefore, SuperStock should prove far less costly than welfare capitalism. It could eventually reduce or eliminate government expenditures for Social Security and welfare, and even more important, it could reduce our huge military expenditures, for if it can lead the way to nuclear disarmament, the massive 12-digit military budgets projected for the future can be cut back substantially.

The administrative costs of SuperStock would be negligible, probably far below the present costs of welfare and Social Security administration. And the risks involved in government loan guarantees would be minuscule. Today the government makes credit guarantees amounting to hundreds of billions of dollars for programs that cannot do half as much good as SuperStock. And what about the many large guarantees our government has made with very high risks of default, such as to Chrysler or New York City? SuperStock loan guarantees would not be nearly as risky. They would be backed by strong security: the shares of our 2,000 leading corporations. Even if some of them went into bankruptcy, the others would back up the loans. Don't forget, SuperStock is based on the strongest segment of our economy.

Thus, SuperStock should, in fact, pay for itself many times over. It can pay its own cost of administration and save us many billions of dollars each year from our present government expenditures, to say nothing of saving our lives. There is no other economic idea for which this claim can be made.

Superstock and the Income Tax System

According to Lionel S. Johns:

An overriding reason for the complexity of the current federal income tax system is that it has been used to implement a broad array of social policy goals. As a result, its efficiency as a tool for raising revenue has declined, and it has become much too complex for most people to understand.

Not only is the tax system too complex for most people (including judges and lawyers) to understand; it is inequitable because it allows the rich to take advantage of loopholes and tax shelters, while it imposes disproportionate burdens on taxpayers at the lower end of the income scale. There is broad agreement among leaders of both political parties that the tax system should be simplified, and that the top rate could be cut to 30 percent or less without decreasing revenue if most deductions were eliminated. But as long as transfer payments are needed to keep capitalism afloat, it will be difficult to muster the Congressional votes for tax reform.

Since SuperStock would do away with the need for transfer payments that come from tax revenues, our social policy goals could be accomplished without having to filter the money through our horrendous tax system. Thus we could simplify the tax system, reducing rates across the board and eliminating the inequitable loopholes.

SuperStock and Employment

In an increasingly automated age, no plan is capable of producing full employment. SuperStock, however, represents our best hope of reducing current unemployment levels. By supplying additional purchasing power and sorely needed funds for new product research and development, it would certainly create new jobs. Even more important, once SuperStock is adopted, unemployment would be less of a problem because people would receive a substantial dividend income whether or not they worked.

This of course raises another key question: Will the work incentive prevail if people can live well without working very hard or perhaps without working at all? I don't believe capital ownership automatically diminishes a person's willingess to work. Many people who own substantial amounts of capital continue to work; indeed, many work harder than those who own no capital. Perhaps the key is the element of participation. Owners enjoy working within a system that offers them full participation, but workers who are shut out of ownership rarely develop the same enthusiasm for their jobs. It's quite possible, therefore, that the prospect of full participation offered by SuperStock will strengthen, rather than weaken, the work incentive.

But even if this doesn't prove to be true, the problem is not insurmountable. We might, for example, make larger blocks of stock available to able-bodied people who continue to work. For most, the opportunity to augment spendable income through working should be incentive enough, especially when inflation cheapens the dollar.

In 1977, the University of Michigan Survey Research Center found that 75 percent of Americans would prefer to continue working even if they could live comfortably without working for the rest of their lives.

But however we decide to solve this problem, SuperStock offers us a unique opportunity to start fresh, avoiding the disincentives that exist in our present welfare programs, and creating new work incentives. Indeed, whatever the problems of administering Super-Stock, they cannot be worse than the problems of welfare capitalism. Moreover, we Americans are renowned for solving management problems. Given a more logical and equitable system like Super-Stock, we can quickly become experts at using its new powers to reward those who contribute as much as they can to our society.

Not everyone enjoys work for its own sake—but just about everyone loves ownership. And if ownership requires work and other socially desirable behavior, it will be forthcoming.

While work incentive is likely to be something of a problem during the early stages of SuperStock, we will have to make an even more difficult adjustment in our basic concept of working. Even when SuperStock stimulates the economy with fresh purchasing power, there probably won't be enough work to go around. Some states have already adopted "work sharing" to enable companies to shorten the work week and thereby avoid layoffs. In those states, for example, when a company cuts its work force by 20 percent, it does not lay off 20 percent of its employees, but instead reduces the work week to four days; for the fifth day, workers receive pro-rated unemployment payments from the state. These changes in work patterns are not likely to disappear. In fact, when the robots come, the four-day week, and then the three-day week, will become the norm, and people will retire at earlier ages.

SuperStock can facilitate these changes. Right now, most people view work-week cutbacks and early retirement with alarm because such measures signal a loss in spendable income. But if those losses were made up by income from SuperStock dividends, we would create an ideal bridge to the new age of the shorter work-week. And that age must come, if only because a shorter week, early retirement, job-sharing, and similar measures will enable us to reduce unemployment by spreading available work more evenly throughout the work force. Under our present system, these "future shock" changes are likely to cause great resistance and social upheaval. But if workers can count on a substantial capitalist income, the transition to new employment patterns can be both peaceful and productive.

All of these changes can, in turn, offer us exciting opportunities to expand our culture and improve the quality of our lives. In generations to come, freed from the crushing burden of economic insecurity, millions of people will be able to engage in the work of humanity. For example, there is pollution control, which is the work of both industry and humanity. If industry expands as I believe it will under SuperStock, it will take plenty of humanitarian work to preserve our environment and resources. And for the first time, we'll have the kind of affluent society that can deal with these and other problems. Every ghetto and slum, every decaying urban waterpipe and sewage system, every polluted river, can become a golden opportunity instead of a dead weight. We already have the brains, the computers, the technology—and SuperStock will allow us to reap the full benefits these resources can provide.

SuperStock, Big Business, and Wall Street

Since big business will be directly affected by SuperStock, what kind of response might we expect from the corporate sector? A few enlightened business leaders who are familiar with SuperStock realize it is probably our best hope of saving the American economy. Others, however, will need to be persuaded. Those who favor the plan are executives of large corporations whose stock ownership is already widely diffused. They view SuperStock as a means of making capitalism work for everyone, but they also recognize the dangers of allowing SuperStock shares to be traded freely. The potential for exploitation by groups of political and social activists who know nothing about running a business is, in fact, the main reason I have suggested that SuperStock be non-voting and non-transferable. These features should make the plan more attractive to business leaders who might otherwise worry about losing corporate control.

Such concerns apart, SuperStock does offer business leaders a very important benefit: the ability to raise the trillions of dollars American industry will need for new plant and equipment over the rest of this century. Under the present system, nobody really knows where this money will come from. The United States has already fallen way behind other industrial nations in the percentage of Gross Domestic Product (the yardstick used for international comparisons) devoted to fixed investment. In 1981, for example, our investment was 15.4 percent of GDP; Japan's was 31.8 percent. Reaganomics was supposed to spur capital investment, but it has had the opposite effect. Business leaders also worry about the extent of foreign stock ownership in our major corporations, including large blocks held by Arab nations.

Then there is the crying need for innovative research in private industry. Economic pressures have forced many businesses to hold the line with yesterday's products, instead of trying to replace them by expensive scientific breakthroughs. The number of patents granted to Americans fell very sharply during the 1970s, as did the number of innovative American products appearing on the market. As a consequence, we have been forced to import a lot of new technology from abroad. Only an affluent society will be able to fund the kind of research and development needed to increase productivity and economic growth.

A case in point: the need for new energy sources led to the government's Synfuel plan—taxing the oil companies' windfall profits and using that money for grants and government-sponsored research. Unfortunately, that research is not likely to yield positive results because the plan seems unpromising and has virtually been abandoned. Through SuperStock, however, the oil companies would have the necessary capital to research and develop new sources of energy. They would also have the support of the American public. After all, with everybody sharing the dividends, who is likely to complain about excessive profits? The friction between "big" oil and the "little" energy consumers would disappear, and with it, the need to impose an inefficient excess-profits tax. SuperStock, then, would enable us to fight the energy crisis via the real strengths of private enterprise, instead of struggling with the kind of government programs that have never really worked in the United States.

If this facilitation of capital funding were not incentive enough, SuperStock provides corporate executives with another important tool: a weapon in their fight against labor union interference. Some business leaders are aware of the ominous possibilities raised by Sweden's Meidner plan, which would open the way for union control of major corporations. They are also keeping a wary eye on the movement toward pension fund socialism here at home, which began with the AFL-CIO's 1980 decision to back "social investing" of such funds.

Clearly, SuperStock can be of great service to American business. But what about Wall Street—the bankers, brokers, and financiers who traditionally have played large roles in raising the $300 billion spent annually on new capital additions? At first blush, Wall Street might appear to be one of the few losers under SuperStock: its traditional financing services would not be needed to raise funds for capital expansion of our 2,000 leading corporations, nor could it expect to reap any direct benefit from SuperStock shares since they would not be traded publicly. But Wall Street need not be shut out of the SuperStock process, and I have no doubt that ingenious investment bankers will devise ways to take part in the underwriting and distribution of SuperStock. In any case, regular shares of stock will continue to be traded, as part of an expanded economy that is bound to be bullish for Wall Street.

The resurgence of national unity and morale should also give Wall Street a big lift, since it runs on emotional as well as statistical fuel. But the biggest boost—perhaps the largest single dose of good news in financial history—would be the elimination of the corporate income tax, an essential part of the SuperStock plan. In the wake of such a move, we could expect a dramatic rise in corporate profits, and a lot more money flowing into the economy, all of which would stimulate growth and open the way for many new ventures. This would create lots of potential business for investment bankers and securities brokers, since the new ventures would not be eligible for SuperStock financing. Wall Street has always been proud of its role in creating new industries, and SuperStock would enhance that function.

Thus, SuperStock will not mean the end of the stock market. In fact, it could mean a new beginning—a real capital market based on performance and dividends rather than speculation and hype. And a chance for Wall Street to lead the rebirth of American industry by helping to create and finance many new businesses.

Present Stockholders and the Rich:
What's In It For Them?

If Wall Street initially appears to be a loser under SuperStock, so too do the present stockholders in our 2,000 leading corporations. They could argue, with at least technical justification, that the future value of their shares would be diminished under SuperStock. After all, they bought their stock when the corporate financing system was rigged to assure them ownership of capital the corporation would acquire in the future. This assurance was one of the things they paid for, and it was reflected in the price of their stock. They might also argue that they are being deprived of the benefits of the corporation's credit power.

Right now, as we've seen, debt—in the form of bonds and loans—pays for a substantial portion of new capital investments, which means that current stockholders increase the value of their stock without dipping into their own pockets. SuperStock, however, would put this credit power into new hands, using it to finance stock ownership for SuperStockholders. For this reason, while SuperStock is based solely on *new* capital investments, it is perhaps not entirely accurate to say that this capital is not owned or claimed by anyone now; under the present system it would automatically be owned by current shareholders. So the plan may indeed reduce the future value of outstanding stock, at least temporarily, even though the shares acquired by SuperStockholders would be sold at market value.

However, if we're going to make capitalism work, something has to give. There is no free lunch, as traditional economists are so fond of saying. Moreover, the present system is breaking down, and in the stagnating economy created by welfare capitalism, present stockholders are not likely to see the market value of their shares double or triple, as they did in years past. In fact, as long as we try to revive the economy via traditional methods, their position is likely to be worse than it would be under SuperStock. After all, what will their shares be worth if the government is forced to raise taxes to oppressively high levels, tap the pension funds, or print money indiscriminately in order to sustain the present system?

During the 1970s and 1980s, even with the old plumbing system in place, stock values were eroded by billions of dollars. Thus, the present stockholders' position must be compared with their real future expectations under inflationary welfare capitalism, *not* with meaningless dreams of past glory. Moreover, any reduction in future stock values will be more than offset by the overall benefits of SuperStock to the economy. And when stock is issued at market value for new capital acquisition, its value is not diluted. Certainly, each stockholder would own a slightly smaller percentage of the pie, but nobody would actually lose, since the pie itself would be larger and everything would stay in proportion. Nor would there be any dilution of political control, since SuperStock would be issued as nonvoting stock.

If you're troubled by the concept of using the credit power of our major corporations to benefit 50 million noncapitalist households (as SuperStock does), then consider the latest free market maneuver that uses this credit power to benefit a mere handful of people—the leveraged buyout. Formerly known by the more descriptive term of "bootstrap financing," the typical leveraged buyout will involve a few top executives of a large corporation who want to take over ownership for themselves, using the assets of the corporation as collateral for huge loans with which to buy out the present stockholders. Leveraged buyouts do not create jobs, raise profits, increase production, or improve management. Yet, our major lenders have made billions of dollars available for such bootstrap financing, and nobody questions the legitimacy of using the assets of major corporations to create hundreds of millions in profits out of mere paper transactions.

Although the American public is not now benefiting from capital ownership, it is to a great extent already footing the bill for new capital—in the form of the huge government subsidies and tax breaks offered to big business. Today, a good chunk of the financing needed for new capital comes directly from the government—funded, of course, with taxpayers' dollars. There is, for example, the investment tax credit, which amounts to a free gift from the taxpayers to our businesses. Then there are depreciation allowances, credits for adding new employees, and numerous other tax advantages which we have purposely allowed to businesses to keep them healthy. These tax breaks also help the present stockholders to own new capital without investing any more money.

When it comes to building new plants, there are even more direct government subsidies. When executives of our giant corporations announce a decision to build a new plant, their first move is to shop for government grants and tax breaks. From the federal government they would seek, and probably get, huge grants from the Department of Housing and Urban Development for the acquisition of land and relocation of residents. Such grants may exceed $100 million for a single new plant. The corporation will also shop for state and local grants, subsidies, and tax breaks, so that in the end a large portion of the cost of new plants is borne by the taxpayers.

Once the plant is built, the sale of the products produced in the plant is often financed or subsidized by the government. For example, the large portion of our aircraft output that is sold overseas is financed by low-interest loans granted by the Export-Import Bank in Washington. Without that government aid, our aircraft manufacturers could not compete in the world markets. But this assistance doesn't come cheaply. In opposing the 1984 budget cuts in social welfare programs, Public Citizens' Congress Watch pointed out that five major "corporate welfare" items (the Synthetic Fuels Corporation, the investment tax credit, accelerated depreciation, the Export-Import Bank, and oil industry tax breaks) cost American taxpayers $65 billion a year. And in 1982, American businesses benefited from the issuance of more than $40 billion worth of "industrial development bonds," another federally-subsidized, low-interest loan program that provides financing for new business projects through tax-exempt bonds.

So if anybody tells you SuperStock will interfere with "private enterprise," or that low-interest government-guaranteed loans will disrupt our banking system, don't believe them. Our major corporations don't take the kind of entrepreneurial risks they did 50 years ago. Their capital outlays are substantially subsidized and financed by the public treasury. Since the public is already paying much of the bill, why should all that new capital automatically be owned by the present stockholders?

This trick of retaining full ownership of capital paid for by the government has not endeared big business to most Americans. In 1965, the Opinion Research Company surveyed Americans' attitudes about business, asking whether the corporate sector was making too much profit, a reasonable profit, or not enough profit. Fourteen percent of the people polled at that time believed corporate profits were excessive. By 1979, however, that figure had swelled to 51 percent. Clearly, the average noncapitalist does not look kindly on business profits, even though profits have actually been shrinking and have virtually disappeared in major industries like coal, steel, and housing. Yet if all Americans were receiving dividends, it would probably be hard to find anyone willing to complain that business was reaping excessive profit. Nor would we see the kind of political tug-of-war that now puts most of our citizens in an adversarial position against the major corporations. Today most Americans want our major corporations to achieve the impossible: more jobs, higher wages, higher corporate taxes, higher pension contributions, lower prices, and better products. Under SuperStock, these pressures would be eased, and for the first time it would be politically feasible to eliminate the corporate income tax. That would benefit present stockholders enormously, and would more than compensate for any imagined dilution in the value of their shares.

Like the present stockholders in our major corporations, the very rich probably won't welcome SuperStock with much enthusiasm. But, in fact, SuperStock offers them protection against the possibility of confiscation through a wealth tax or even more drastic measures. As long as welfare capitalism fails to provide an adequate income for most Americans, capitalism itself is in danger. As Senator Russell B. Long has pointed out in many speeches, people who are already wealthy will be much more secure in their wealth when capitalism becomes a good deal for everyone. Otherwise, as tax expert Long puts it, "They're going to wind up at a minimum having their eyeballs taxed off them." Beyond that minimum is the risk that the failings of welfare capitalism will lead to socialism. Instead, via SuperStock, the rich could finally utter the word "capitalist" without whispering. Receiving income from MOP ownership would become acceptable behavior in a capitalist society, if everyone gets the chance to become a capitalist.

The broad picture, then, looks very promising. Now let's narrow the focus to examine how SuperStock can benefit specific segments of the American population.

SuperStock At the Grass Roots: What's In It For Various Groups of Americans?

Women: Despite recent legislation, equal treatment in hiring, salary, and promotion remain largely in the hands of top management, which is still very much a man's world. So very few women have the chance to become entrepreneurs or shareholders, except through inheritance. Stock ownership, however, would give women real economic independence for the first time, and what better way to achieve such ownership than through a plan that would distribute it to all American households without regard to gender.

Blacks: For more than 20 years, the government has tried to bring blacks and other minority groups into the mainstream of society via training and affirmative action programs. Unfortunately, their efforts have proved largely unsuccessful. Some black leaders believe these programs simply perpetuate the welfare mentality. And many blacks who get jobs through these programs feel they are being forced to work in a white man's world under a white man's rules—in an environment that's not likely to give them a fair shake no matter how hard they work. This attitude often affects their performance, so they remain at the bottom of the economic ladder, all of which feeds their belief that they would be better off on welfare.

Doubts about the value of government programs are not limited to working-class blacks. In recent years, black intellectuals have begun to oppose programs like busing and affirmative action because they stir up a lot of resentment among whites without providing many real benefits for blacks. And the old liberal faith in education as a cure-all for social problems is fading. Indeed, the unemployment rate among blacks today is higher than it was in the 1960s when education, training, and affirmative action programs were launched. The problem is that anti-inflation policies hit the blacks first because they result in layoffs that start at the lowest economic level. While this is not usually a result of racial prejudice, it certainly has the same effect.

Are jobs the answer? Our politicians still seem to think so, but none can deliver on their campaign promises of employment because the system itself can no longer create enough jobs—for blacks or whites. Entrepreneurship is not the answer either. Venture capital and starting up new businesses are games for the rich, who can afford to take losses on most of their investments and make them up on the one out of ten that hits the jackpot. What blacks really need is a piece of the action—shares in existing successful enterprises, which are now almost entirely owned by white people. SuperStock would, therefore, bring blacks and other ethnic minorities into the mainstream of capitalism and make them full participants in American life for the first time.

Youth: It's difficult to generalize about any group that runs the gamut from committed careerists to revolutionary activists to dropouts. But with our youth, we seem to have moved beyond the self-indulgent "me" generation, and most young people are looking for a new idea, something they can take hold of and use to build a new American dream. But what do they have to work with? Middle-class youths face downward mobility for the first time in our history, and under our present system, they are not likely to equal their parents' standard of living. So it's not surprising that they are loath to bring children into such a world and see little point in saving for a brighter future. They just don't believe a brighter future will arrive. Nor is their cynicism unwarranted; time and again they've heard politicians promise to make America great again, without having the semblance of a plan that can do so.

Some would argue that the prospect of reduced middle-class wealth is a natural consequence of the twentieth century egalitarian leveling process. As the poor use the ballot box to achieve economic gains, somebody has to pay. And the very rich are too small in number and too well fortified in their tax shelters to foot the huge bill presented in the name of social justice. But whether this process is natural or not, it's certainly not healthy for the future of American capitalism; as more of the non-voting half of our population become voters, socialism is likely to win eventually at the polls.

Our youth has more to lose from the end of the American dream than anyone else. They seem very cynical. But if you sit down with college students and explain SuperStock to them for five minutes, you can see their eyes light up. They are literally hungering after a plan that will give them a brighter future. They've tried everything—drugs, narcissism, religious cults—and they know these are not solutions. But a plan with the scope and daring of SuperStock is made to order for our youth.

Senior citizens and retired workers: Because it will take at least seven years for SuperStock to pay for itself, seniors and retired workers have less to gain from its adoption; many will not reap direct benefits of SuperStock ownership in their lifetimes. However, their financial security is constantly threatened by the potential insolvency of the Social Security system. SuperStock would remove this threat by gradually assuming the financial burden now carried by Social Security. At the very least, senior citizens would no longer be considered millstones around the necks of the young and working Americans. Moreover, they would benefit directly from the strengthening of our economy, as well as the greatly enhanced prospects facing their children and grandchildren under SuperStock.

Consumers: Consumer activists have special reasons for supporting SuperStock. With millions of individuals owning capital, they gain economic power that would be impossible to muster through any consumer organization. This power would represent a strong safeguard against the excesses of big business, big labor, and big government—the three superpowers against whom consumer activists usually fight a losing battle.

But if all Americans become capitalists, won't they root for unlimited corporate profits, which would in turn affect consumers adversely? I don't believe so. A rejuvenated American economy would foster plenty of competition, with the lowest price for the best quality still determining what consumers will buy. And as the economy booms, many new products would appear on the market. Moreover, there is no basis for assuming that consumers who are also stockholders of our major corporations will allow prices to rise unreasonably, because their newly gained dividends would not improve their finances if price inflation ate up the benefits.

The labor unions: It is quite likely that labor leaders would initially shun SuperStock, preferring instead to work for pension fund socialism and Meidner-type plans, which give unions stock control of major businesses. However, the workers themselves would be much better off under SuperStock; not only would they own stock outright, but they would also receive dividend income well before retirement age.

Traditionally, American labor leaders have shied away from worker ownership, fearing that if workers became stockholders, they would be less interested in union representation. Early union leaders even opposed pension plans when they first came on the scene. These fears may be valid when employees own stock in the companies for which they work, because their loyalties are split between labor and management. They may want higher wages, but not if that would mean lower profits. But with SuperStock, workers get a share of American industry rather than stock in their own companies, so there is no reason to believe they would be less interested in having the unions negotiate their wage demands. However, those demands might be less militant since workers would also receive the wages of capital and would have a vested interest in the success of big business.

Farmers: SuperStock would be a bonanza for our farmers. For the first time, they would not be entirely dependent on the vagaries of weather and crop yields for their income. And by making agriculture a capital-owning partner in industry, the long-running friction between these segments of our society would dissipate. Such a move might even serve to reduce our enormous expenditures for agricultural subsidies.

Professionals: SuperStock represents an important opportunity for economists, lawyers, accountants, educators, and intellectuals, whose special skills equip them to shape the plan. Rather than continuing to squander their talents on tax shelters and welfare schemes, they can serve the nation—indeed the world—by educating the public on SuperStock and helping to develop a detailed plan for its implementation.

Lawyers and accountants helped to make the stock corporation an efficient tool of capitalism. But now the corporation is in danger of obsolescence, because the lawyer-designed corporate financing system perpetuates the overconcentration of capital ownership and doesn't distribute purchasing power equitably enough. We need the expertise of a lot more lawyers to perfect the SuperStock plan, and since the concept of justice is the central thrust of SuperStock, this might make lawyers popular for a change.

On a more personal level, SuperStock serves the interests of our professional class. They are, after all, among the economic elite of the nation who have the most to lose if capitalism doesn't survive.

Environmentalists and ecologists: The first reaction of an environmentalist to the SuperStock plan is usually negative, a feeling that the plan would be a disaster for our environment because all Americans would become committed to the success of our major corporations, and there would be nobody left to oppose the exploitation of our natural resources for corporate profit. But concern about pollution is often put aside when we run into inflation, unemployment, and capital shortages under welfare capitalism.

Consider the town with the bucolic name of Naturita, Colorado, which made the news in July of 1982 by announcing that it had won a $10 million industrial project that would create 100 new jobs for the 900 people who live in Naturita. What was the project they so eagerly pursued? Operation of a nuclear waste dump! And why were they so willing to turn their town into an ecological disaster area? Because they had been battling economic depression since the early 1980s, when the uranium industry on which they depended went into a major slump.

Only a truly affluent society can afford to protect the environment against the ravages of industry. Right now, the necessary funds are being channeled into the arms race and our futile struggle to maintain economic growth through wages and welfare. The environmentalists need SuperStock as badly as anyone else; they should climb aboard and start the process of shaping SuperStock so it becomes a force for clearing up pollution rather than increasing it. We must find new methods and new fuels to keep our standard of living high and yet keep our environment safe. This will require huge amounts of new capital that neither government nor private industry can muster without a fundamental policy change like Super-Stock.

Small businesses: SuperStock could represent a potential threat to small business, since it favors large businesses by making huge sums available to them for new capital expenditures. Eventually, we should be able to include smaller corporations in the Super-Stock system, but we will have to begin with our 2,000 largest successful corporations because we are trying to plug our neediest people into the strongest sector of our economy.

Of course, traditional sources of capital would remain available to smaller businesses. In fact, financiers and bankers would take more of an interest in them because the larger corporations would no longer constitute a captive market. This would motivate investment bankers to concentrate on one of their most important functions: helping to develop new businesses, new products, and new jobs through venture capital and other methods of creative financing.

I don't think SuperStock would make the situation any worse for small business than it already is under welfare capitalism, which does little to promote the survival and prosperity of small businesses. Government venture capital programs—giving the small entrepreneur a few hundred thousand dollars to compete with the giants— usually are dismal failures. The government also tries to subsidize small businesses with low-interest loans, free management assistance, and by restricting some procurement contracts to bids from small companies. However, these programs don't have a significant impact on our economy, and most small business proprietors are forced to live by their wits.

While the 2,000 large corporations that participate in Super-

Stock at the outset will gain some advantages, they will not be insulated from the effects of bad business decisions. They will have to justify outlays for capital additions just as before, demonstrating to their directors, shareholders, and bankers that the new capital will pay for itself out of its own earnings. These corporations will lose just as much from unsuccessful projects as under the present system. If Peerless Pizza's new plant turns out to be a ten-million-dollar lemon, Peerless will lose the $10 million it invested in the plant, for which it issued that amount of stock to the SuperStock fund. While the federal government guarantees payment of the $10 million lent by banks to pay for the Peerless shares that are distributed to Super-Stockholders, the government guarantee has nothing to do with Peerless itself or the plant that Peerless built.

In summary, then, SuperStock may seem to benefit poor Americans more than rich ones, but that in itself is the great need of *all* Americans—a way of socializing capitalism without going to socialism. Of course, we can't be sure it will work, but we do know that it is the *only* fundamental policy change in the American economic system that promises to solve so many basic problems. So we can't afford to pass up any reasonable chance of making it work. That's how high the stakes are for all Americans.

Chapter 9

SuperStock And The Religious Community: *An Ethical Alternative*

Merely taking these means of production (capital) out of the hands of their private owners is not enough to ensure their satisfactory socialization. . . . We can speak of socialization only when . . . each person is fully entitled to consider himself a part-owner of the great workbench at which he is working with everyone else.

—POPE JOHN PAUL II
Laborem Exercens (On Human Work), 1981

True peace is not merely the absence of tension; it is the presence of justice.

—REV. MARTIN LUTHER KING, JR.

If the clash between capitalism and communism has divided the secular world, it has had an even more devastating impact on the world's religious leaders. Indeed, for a growing number of clergy, it is a contest between two morally unacceptable alternatives: on the one hand, atheistic communism, which threatens the very survival of organized religion; on the other hand, materialistic capitalism, which throughout its history has allowed the few to exploit the many in the name of free enterprise. Addressing this moral dilemma in his 1971 encyclical, *Octogesima Adveniens (A Call To Action),* Pope Paul VI wrote:

Therefore, the Christian who wished to live his faith in a political activity . . . cannot adhere to a Marxist ideology, to its atheistic materialism . . . denying all transcendence to man and his personal and collective history; nor can he adhere to the liberal [capitalist] ideology which believes it exalts individual freedom by withdrawing it from every limitation, by stimulating it through exclusive seeking of interest and power . . . [No. 26]

For historical and geographical reasons, the Roman Catholic Church has been thrust into direct conflict with both ideologies to a greater extent than other religions. But the Roman Catholic concern for a humane alternative is certainly shared by the Protestant, Jewish, and Moslem clergy. SuperStock, then, represents a unique opportunity for the religious community: a program through which they can achieve a union of their theological teachings and their commitment to social justice, regardless of differences in religious beliefs. Certainly, as we shall see in this chapter, such a union is not possible under capitalism or communism. And in the absence of such an ethical alternative, the clash between these systems is likely to intensify the dilemma of religious leaders and cause further internal friction within religious denominations.

The Roman Catholic Church

The ideological clash between Catholicism and Marxism is as old as Marxism itself. Whereas Marxism holds that human beings can achieve salvation only through their own efforts to improve their lot in the world, Christianity embraces the theological principle of transcendence—a belief in the Deity as greater than, and independent of, the material world, where salvation is possible only through God's grace. Perhaps the most emphatic Roman Catholic statement of this incompatibility was made by Pope Pius XI in his 1931 encyclical, *Quadragesimo Anno (Reconstructing the Social Order):*

If, like all errors, socialism contains a certain element of truth (and this the Sovereign Pontiffs have never denied), it is nevertheless founded upon a doctrine of human society peculiarly its own, which is opposed to true Christianity. "Religious socialism," "Christian socialism" are expressions implying a contradiction in terms. No one can be at the same time a sincere Catholic and a true socialist. [No. 120]

As recently as 1980, a similar theme was expressed by the American Catholic bishops in their pastoral letter, *Marxist Communism.* After reexamining the fundamental differences between Christianity and Marxism, they concluded:

As a spiritual phenomenon Marxism, for all its clear affinities, stands at the opposite side of Christianity. The Marxist ideal of a surpassing future intrinsically differs from an object of Christian hope—that goes beyond our future achievements as well as our present ones. Marxist transcendence is a form of *self*-transcending: it remains within the scope of human attainment. Christian transcendence consists in being assumed into an order totally beyond the reach of human endeavor. To the Marxist the ideal future contains more than man can conceive today, but not more than he will achieve tomorrow. To the Christian the promised future descends as a gift from God's mercy. . . . In fact, contemporary Marxism appears as the final stage of a secularizing movement that, begun more than two centuries ago, has gradually substituted the search for the absolute with the search for adequate social structures. Its secularized vision attempts to *comprehend* in its totality what the Christian view left open to transcendence.

Yet the Catholic opposition to Marxism has not been limited to ideological differences. In a 1937 encyclical, for example, entitled *Atheistic Communism,* Pius XI expressed the conflict in political as well as theological terms, seeing in communism not simply a threat to the Church but also to society itself. He called it ". . . Bolshevistic and Atheistic Communism, which aims at upsetting the social order and at undermining the very foundations of Christian civilization" (No. 3).

Pius XI was succeeded by Pius XII, who served from 1939 to 1958, and who shared his predecessor's implacable stance against communism. His successor, however, was John XXIII, who believed the Church needed a broader view of world economics. Although he opposed Marxism, he was receptive to new ideas, and in Vatican Council II, he threw open for re-examination almost the entire program of the Church. John died in 1963, before the Council finished its work, leaving Paul VI to cope with the great upheaval created by the Council. Thus, Paul was the first Pope who really had to come to grips with the need for Catholic-Marxist dialogue and cooperation.

While the Church was still formally condemning Marxism, the Pope and clergy could no longer ignore the fact that most of their 565 million followers lived in countries where capitalism was an oppressive yoke around the necks of the poor, who constituted the overwhelming majority of the population. The 50 million Catholics in the United States could still remain aloof from Marxism, but this could hardly be done in Latin America, where wealthy businessmen and political strongmen conspired to keep the masses in a perennial state of poverty and hopelessness. Thus, for many Latin American Catholics, Marxism seemed to represent the only hope for liberation from poverty, despair, and inhuman existence.

These pressures forced Paul VI to make some concessions to the Marxists. He was the first Pope to receive President Tito of Yugoslavia on a state visit, and he held audiences with many other communist and socialist leaders. By 1972, he was talking and writing about the kind of "democratic socialism" espoused by the Eurocommunists, who claimed they could maintain democratic elections and religious freedom after installing Marxist economic systems. And although Paul remained implacably opposed to Marxism as a substitute for religion, he was forced to recognize that it might provide an acceptable solution to the economic problems of his flock.

Paul had to deal with many anticapitalist factions in the Church, the strongest of which were the priests who espoused a "liberation theology." They believed the Church should be a living institution, working in the field with the people, which meant in the ghettos and shacks of the poor. Their evangelism was not limited to converting the unbelievers—it also extended to *liberating* people from oppressive economic, political and social conditions. They wanted social justice for all, and many saw no way of getting this without taking the first step of replacing capitalism with Marxism.

During the 1970s, numerous North American priests, especially Jesuits and Maryknollers, joined the assault troops of Latin American liberation theology, serving as missionaries and teachers and putting their lives on the line along with their Latin American brethren. Although traditionally the Church in Latin America had been identified with the aristocratic elite and the status quo, this was soon to change. Many of the Latin American clergy gave away the Church's land holdings as a symbol of their solidarity with the poor. More than a thousand bishops, priests, and nuns were murdered or severely persecuted for their support of the poor during this period, and many priests and nuns left the comparative comfort of big city parishes to work in the slums and rural areas at great risk and privation.

Imagine for a moment the dilemma of an American priest sent to serve in Latin America. He has been taught that Marxism is the scourge of mankind, but he must bury babies who died because there was no food or medicine for them under the capitalist regime. And who is working to overcome this inhumane situation? Only Marxists and other groups espousing various shadings of communist ideology. It is not surprising therefore that many dedicated priests came to view Marxism as an attractive alternative. It was, after all, the only popular movement that actively sought to improve the lives of the overwhelming majority of Latin Americans.

By the time Pope John Paul II assumed office in 1978, most of his clergy believed that some accommodation with Marxism was both necessary and desirable. Indeed, many felt that capitalism was no longer compatible with Catholic principles, thus leaving socialism and communism as the only viable alternatives. And like his predecessors, John Paul II faced particular difficulties in Latin America and the Philippines, where many of his priests and nuns had to align themselves with Marxist movements in order to aid their poor parishioners. Often this meant closing their eyes to violence, or even collaborating in it, since force was the only effective weapon in countries too repressive to permit peaceful political change. For many, demographics alone signaled the need for a change in the economic order. Between 1950 and 1980, the population of Latin America had more than doubled, rising to a total of more than 350 million people. How could capitalism possibly produce enough jobs to feed these masses?

John Paul's visit to Brazil in 1980 crystalized this conflict. The Catholic Church in Brazil was the largest in the world. Most of its 335 bishops were liberals who opposed the repressive military regime. They supported workers' strikes and pushed for land reform in a nation where most of the useful rural acreage was owned by less than 2 percent of the population. But these activities created an internal schism, pitting the liberal clergy against those who believed the Church should remain above political controversies. To meet the developing crisis, the Pope attempted to clarify the Church's position. He denounced the exploitation and repression of the poor and affirmed the Church's duty to provide aid; at the same time, however, he directed the clergy not to back any political parties, and he rejected violence and class struggle. In a famous statement made at the 1979 general assembly of Latin American bishops in Puebla, Mexico, he declared, "This idea of Christ as a political figure, a revolutionary, as the subversive man from Nazareth, does not tally with the Church's catechesis." And under even greater pressure during his hectic eight-day visit to Central America and Haiti in 1983, he stood by this position: the Church must press Latin American governments for social justice, but the clergy must avoid political alignments.

While these dramatic events were taking place, the Church faced an even more complicated dilemma in Europe. With France, Italy, Spain, and Portugal expected to elect communist governments before the end of the century, the Church had to find a way of allowing Catholics to vote for communist candidates without being excommunicated. Eurocommunism provided the solution. By characterizing itself as "social democracy" or "democratic socialism," it offered a label that the Church could live with. Thus, by the 1980s, the strongest anticommunist force in Western Europe was heading toward collaboration—or at least coexistence—with Marxism. Yet this move was not universally applauded; the more sophisticated clergymen, and those who had actually lived under Marxist-Leninist governments, saw in Eurocommunism a trap that could destroy the Church in Europe.

Yet, even those who feared such a trap had become convinced of Russia's ability to dominate Europe, and so they had little choice but to support some form of democratic socialism in the hope of making Marxism compatible with Christianity and stemming the spread of Russian-style atheistic communism. Many Italian and French cities had already elected communist governments, and there had been surprisingly little friction between the communists and the Church in those areas. Indeed, they shared a common enemy in Italian terrorist groups who had little sympathy for the communists' stand on law and order. In the wake of this growing trend toward cooperation, several organizations dedicated to uniting Marxists and Christians have sprung up and are becoming increasingly influential in Italy and other European nations, especially among intellectuals and professionals.

In Eastern Europe, the Catholic Church has arrived at a *modus operandi* with communist governments, Poland being the most notable example. There the Church walks a tightrope by allying itself with Solidarity for purposes of social reform, and by cooperating with the Communist Party in order to prevent bloodshed or invasion by the Red Army.

The Catholic shift from fervent anticommunism to collaboration has been well publicized. Less well understood is the Roman Catholic tradition of opposition to capitalism. It was expressed by the French bishops in their commentary on Pius XI's 1937 encyclical, *Atheistic Communism:*

> By condemning the actions of communist parties, the Church does not support the capitalist regime. It is most necessary that it be realized that in the very essence of capitalism—that is to say, in the absolute value it gives to property without reference to the common good or to the dignity of labor—there is materialism rejected by Christian teaching.

The Church's criticism of capitalism goes back to the early days of the Industrial Revolution and was strongly expressed in Pope Leo XIII's famous 1891 encyclical, *Rerum Novarum (The Condition of Labor).* Forty years later, Pope Pius XI attacked capitalism in *Quadragesimo Anno (Reconstructing the Social Order),* which affirmed the traditional Catholic view that labor is not a mere commodity. It also discussed many of the grave abuses perpetrated against workers in the name of property rights and economic freedom. Concluding his position on capitalism, Pius XI noted that:

> . . . the right ordering of economic life cannot be left to a free competition of forces. For from this source, as from a poisoned spring, have originated and spread all the errors of individualist economic thinking . . . Therefore it is most necessary that economic life be again subjected to . . . a true and effective governing principle. [No. 88]

Pope John XXIII continued this theme in his 1961 encyclical, *Mater et Magistra (Christianity and Social Progress)*. And his successor, Paul VI, made increasingly vigorous appeals for reform in a system that reduced so many millions to living in misery. In his 1967 encyclical, *Populorum Progressio (On The Development of Peoples)*, he condemned the harsh side effects of capitalism, referring to it as "liberalism":

> But it is unfortunate that on these new conditions of society a system has been constructed which considers profit as the key motive for economic progress, competition as the supreme law of economics, and private ownership of the means of production as an absolute right that has no limits and carries no corresponding social obligation. This unchecked liberalism leads to dictatorship rightly denounced by Pius XI as producing "the international imperialism of money." One cannot condemn such abuses too strongly by solemnly recalling once again that the economy is at the service of man. [No. 26]

Four years later, he returned to this theme in a new encyclical, *Octogesima Adveniens (A Call to Action)* in which he reiterated the Church's opposition to both Marxism and capitalism and took special note of the evils of the multinational corporation:

> Under the driving force of new systems of production, national frontiers are breaking down, and we can see new economic powers emerging, the multinational enterprises, which by the concentration and flexibility of their means can conduct autonomous strategies which are largely independent of the national political powers and therefore not subject to control from the point of view of the common good. By extending their activities, these private organizations can lead to a new and abusive form of economic domination on the social, cultural and even political level. The excessive concentration of means and powers that Pope Pius XI already condemned on the fortieth anniversary of *Rerum Novarum* is taking on a new and very real image. [No. 44]

For some members of the American clergy, the failings of capitalism are a daily reality that they see firsthand in the urban slums and in the hopelessness of millions of their own parishioners. To deal with these problems, the American bishops created in 1970 an important social action arm called the Campaign for Human Development (CHD), which is struggling to find a way to make structural changes in capitalism. Since its inception, the CHD has distributed some $97 million to groups of poor people who are trying to help themselves by eliminating the cause of their poverty.

Most of this money has gone to social development projects, usually grassroots community organizations that challenge the policies of public and private authorities. The CHD also sponsors economic development projects, some of which involve the acquisition of businesses by employees. All of CHD's funds are allocated to projects that enable the poor to develop a means of self-support; charity handouts play no part in the CHD's programs. In fact, as described by CHD, these projects are designed to fulfill three important objectives of the American Catholic Church: preservation of the right to own property; distribution of ownership to those who own nothing; and socialization of property ownership.

Thus, a major social instrument of Catholicism has been trying to use ownership as a means of making capitalism work for the poor as well as the rich. And their experience of more than a dozen years can be a valuable tool in developing SuperStock. It seems appropriate, therefore, to take a closer look at their accomplishments and plans.

In 1974, the CHD published *Poverty in American Democracy: A Study of Social Power,* which focused on the unequal distribution of wealth and overconcentration of capital ownership in the United States. Although it was an excellent overview of the problem, it did not suggest an overall solution. Then in 1982, the National Conference of Catholic Bishops began preparing an important statement on Christianity and capitalism, to be adopted in 1985. Two representatives of the CHD were invited to testify, and their presentations provide an excellent summary of the CHD's achievements, as well as their outlook on the use of capital ownership.

In one of the CHD papers, Associate Director James Jennings urged the bishops to consider the question of MOP ownership, pointing out that it was a goal first adopted by the American clergy in 1919, in a pastoral letter entitled *The Bishops' Program of Social Reconstruction.* As Jennings noted:

> More than 60 years ago, the American bishops set out a vision for American society. Many of the programs called for have be-

come institutionalized: legalized minimum wage, unemployment insurance, old age pensions and legal enforcement of the right of labor to organize. However, one major program has had virtually no implementation. The bishops specified that "The majority of wage-earners must become owners of the instruments of production" (p. 29). In 1939, the 20th anniversary of the Bishops' Program, Cardinal Mooney, chairman of the NCWC Administrative Board, observed that very little progress has been made in the need to distribute ownership of productive wealth: "Effective ownership," he said, "has become less, rather than more, widely distributed."

In candor, it must be said that the concentration of the ownership of wealth-producing property in the United States has not received the attention of the National Conference of Bishops that might be expected. While the bishops have addressed substantively a variety of critical social issues, the concentration of ownership and the growth of corporations, and their consequent power, have virtually gone unnoted and unchallenged.

In a second presentation, the Reverend Erskine White of the CHD education staff eloquently debunked the myth of capitalism's trickledown effects by describing the grave problems facing the low-income groups funded by the CHD. As White pointed out, Adam Smith's invisible hand theory remains the principal moral justification for capitalism, although its current proponents couch it in semireligious tones: Growth in the wealth of others is good for oneself; when the creators of wealth do so for their own gain, even the poorest among us are helped in the process. How did these claims play out in the real-life work of the CHD? White is specific:

> The experience of the poor provides an important "reality check" on such sweeping moral generalizations . . . On the supply side of the economy, we know coal miners with Black Lung disease because their employers were free not to pay the costs involved in running safe, healthy mines. . . . We know places where the freedom to pay low wages for farm-workers force two and three generations into the fields, just to put food on the family table. . . . On the demand side of the economy, the same relationship emerges between economic faith and reality. In all the poor neighborhoods we know . . . bank executives must reinvest the money they get from the neighborhoods in the suburbs, overseas, or wherever it will earn the greatest rate of return. . . . It is easy to see how all this helps the economy in general. It is not easy to see how such practices help the poor.

As White so perceptively noted, the invisible hand theory may have some relevance to overall economic performance, but what's good for the economy is only good for those in a position to participate in the economy, which the poor are not. The system itself remains unresponsive to the needs of the poor, and that inherent flaw is precisely why capitalism cannot realize its claim to morality. In White's own words:

> . . . the key point is that because of their economic vulnerability, poor people are exposed to harm at the hands of others *who are doing nothing more than what they are supposed to do in a free market economy.* This is becoming more visible to the nation and the media because much of the middle class is now experiencing a similar vulnerability. [Italics mine]

White's point about capitalism's structural defects was echoed in a February 1982 report issued by the National CHD Committee, which examined the CHD's failure to alleviate the plight of the poor through ownership projects. The report concluded:

> The general view was that the imbalance (i.e., rich and poor) was not due merely to flaws that needed to be remedied; rather they were integral to the functioning of the system. A large population of poor and unemployed is built in as a necessary element of the capitalist system. . . . General agreement surfaced around the proposition that Christianity and capitalism are not compatible.

The conclusion that Christianity and capitalism are incompatible was also reached by the Canadian Bishops' Episcopal Commission for Social Affairs in a report entitled *Ethical Reflections on the Economic Crisis,* released in 1983. The Canadian Catholic bishops attacked the system of fighting inflation by creating unemployment as immoral, even though it is capitalism's only weapon against inflation. The Canadian bishops concluded:

> The patterns of domination and inequality are likely to further intensify as the "survival of the fittest" doctrine is applied more rigorously to the economic order. This, in our view, is morally unacceptable as a rule of life for the human community.

The pastoral letter on Christianity and capitalism that the National Conference of Catholic Bishops is scheduled to publish in November of 1985 will probably contain similar attacks on the morality of capitalism. But where does this leave the Catholic clergy? They have consistently condemned both capitalism and Marxism, but have not specified an alternative that would be both morally acceptable to the Church and workable in the real world. The modification of American capitalism by SuperStock does, I believe, provide us with such an acceptable and workable system.

Indeed, since 1891, the papal encyclicals on social justice have adopted the major premises of SuperStock, and the Catholic Church stands just a short step away from finding its own way to a form of capitalism that is morally compatible with its teachings. In his 1891 encyclical, *Rerum Novarum (The Condition of Labor)*, Pope Leo XIII proclaimed:

> The law, therefore, should favor ownership, and its policy should be to induce *as many people as possible to become owners.*
> Many excellent results will follow from this; and first of all, property will certainly become more equitably divided. [No. 35; Italics mine]

These principles were reaffirmed by succeeding Popes, most dramatically in Pope John XXIII's 1961 encyclical, *Mater et Magistra (Christianity and Social Progress)*:

> It is not enough, then, to assert that man has from nature the right of privately possessing goods as his own, including those of productive character, unless at the same time, a continuing effort is made to spread the use of this right through all ranks of the citizenry. [No. 113]

In 1981, on the ninetieth anniversary of Pope Leo's encyclical, Pope John Paul II issued an encyclical entitled *Laborem Exercens (On Human Work)*. In it, he renewed the Church's commitment to broader ownership of the means of production, and he distinguished it very sharply from Marxism:

> Merely taking these means of production (capital) out of the hands of their private owners is not enough to ensure their satisfactory socialization.... This group in authority may carry out its task ... badly by claiming for itself a monopoly of the administration and disposal of the means of production and not refraining even from offending basic human rights....
> We can speak of socializing only when ... on the basis of his work each person is fully entitled to consider himself a part-owner of the great workbench at which he is working with everyone else. A way towards that goal could be found by associating labour with the ownership of capital, as far as possible ... [No. 14]

Clearly, Pope John Paul's striking metaphor of the great workbench to be owned by everyone cannot be realized under either Marxism or traditional capitalism. His goal of "satisfactory socialization" of the means of production can only be achieved by a system such as SuperStock, which puts MOP ownership in the hands of all the people so that democracy and freedom (including freedom of religion) can be preserved.

In September of 1982, I appeared before the committee of the National Conference of Catholic Bishops which was drafting the pastoral letter on Christianity and capitalism. I pointed out that despite the moral shortcomings of capitalism, capitalist nations are more democratic and offer a greater degree of religious and social freedom and a higher standard of living than do Marxist nations. And I tried to convince them that there is a way to make American capitalism a morally just system. I called their attention to the 1976 Joint Economic Report of Congress, which urged a national policy of distributing the ownership of newly created capital broadly throughout society. I suggested they include that section of the Joint Economic Report in their pastoral letter, along with the following statement:

> Unfortunately, the Congress has not followed up on this initiative. Such a program of distributing the ownership of newly created capital throughout American society would do much to alleviate the inequities of capitalism.
>
> The Joint Economic Committee's use of the words "newly created capital" is significant, because American companies are creating new capital (plants, equipment, computers, etc.) at the rate of more than $300 billion per year. It is estimated that during the next twenty years, the total amount of this newly created capital will be $5 trillion, a sum large enough to provide capital ownership of $100,000 to each of 50 million American families who do not own significant amounts of capital now.
>
> Such a wide diffusion of capital ownership would move us much closer to social justice. It would also make American capitalism consistent with the teachings of the Roman Catholic Church [*Laborem Exercens:* 14; *Mater et Magistra:* 113–115; *Rerum Novarum:* 35].
>
> By thus socializing ownership of the means of production, the United States would remove the principal cause of ideological conflict between capitalism and Marxism.

If you are a Roman Catholic and you believe SuperStock should be considered, I urge you to make your views known to your church organization. I believe it is pointless for the Catholic clergy to debate the pros and cons of the old systems. Choosing between the two can only further split the Church and bring us closer to nuclear war. But by seizing the opportunity to lead the way through the minefields of capitalism and communism to a third path, the Catholic Church can solve the dilemma of liberation theology and bring the world a giant step closer to peace.

The Protestant Churches

Not surprisingly, Protestant churches in the United States and throughout the world face the same capitalism-communism dilemma as the Roman Catholic Church. Protestantism, of course, has been popularly identified with capitalism ever since the Reformation, notably through the "Protestant ethic," which glorified hard work, thrift, and efficiency in the name of eternal salvation. Certainly these are qualities any dedicated capitalist would aspire to. As the noted German sociologist Max Weber interpreted Protestantism in his 1904 book, *The Protestant Ethic and the Spirit of Capitalism,* the ethic was an important factor in the economic success of Protestants during the early stages of European capitalism. However, Protestant theologians such as Luther and Calvin never really embraced the capitalist ethic in that way, and in recent years, some Protestant church officials have turned away from capitalism. Like their Catholic counterparts, they have found no alternative but to embrace some version of Marxist ideology.

The main vehicle for Protestant-Marxist relationships has been the World Council of Churches (WCC), an ecumenical body founded in 1948 to promote unity among the world's many Christian churches. Its membership presently consists of 295 Protestant and Eastern Orthodox denominations in over 100 countries. By the mid-1970s, the WCC had developed its own liberation theology that brought it closer to Marxism. In fact, an August 1982 *Reader's Digest* article saw the WCC as being more than "close" to Marxism. Entitled "Which Master Is the World Council of Churches Serving—Karl Marx or Jesus Christ?" this attack on the WCC by Joseph A. Harriss said, in part:

> . . . countless World Council supporters were shocked in August 1978 when the WCC announced that its Program to Combat Racism had given $85,000 to the Patriotic Front, a Marxist guerrilla organization then fighting the white-dominated regime in Rhodesia. At the time of the grant, the Patriotic Front had murdered 207 white civilians and 1712 blacks, and only weeks before had slaughtered nine white missionaries and their children.

* * *

> The Third World viewpoint is incarnate in General Secretary Philip Potter, a 61-year-old West Indian Methodist clergyman. Potter . . . makes no bones about his anti-Western, anti-capitalist attitude in his writings and speeches. . . .
>
> Predictably, many WCC senior staff officers share Potter's

views. Says Uruguayan Emilio Castro, head of the council's Commission on World Mission and Evangelism, "The philosophical basis of capitalism is evil, totally contrary to the Gospel."

The *Reader's Digest* article went on to charge that the WCC does not send any money to dissident groups in the Soviet Union, even though some of those groups are victims of religious persecution; that Marxist governments get "kidglove treatment" by the WCC; that backlash against WCC social activities has caused the American churches affiliated with WCC to reduce their financial support; and that the United Presbyterian Church, which gives the WCC more financial aid per capita than any other American church, has suffered a loss of nearly one million members in the last decade.

While the *Reader's Digest* article served to alert Protestant church members to WCC activities they might not wish to support, it said nothing about the economic reforms that *should* be supported. The article concluded:

> The world's Christians today generally agree that the church must be present with its unique witness on the troubled international scene. For the best example of how to do that, however, WCC officials need turn not to Karl Marx but to Jesus Christ.

Does this mean that Jesus Christ would accept for the poor whatever trickled down from traditional capitalism? We have already seen that many Christian clergymen who have followed in the footsteps of Jesus Christ find capitalism morally unacceptable. But neither the WCC nor its critics have come up with a morally acceptable alternative.

The WCC's American counterpart, the National Council of the Churches of Christ (NCCC), has also taken its share of lumps for sending funds collected in the United States to foreign church organizations which allegedly turned some of this money over to Marxist and terrorist groups. In a January 1983 segment of the television program *60 Minutes,* entitled "The Gospel According to Whom?" both the NCCC and the WCC were charged with supporting Marxists, terrorists, and anti-American groups with funds collected in American churches. The NCCC was quick to deny any anti-capitalist, anti-American bias, and stated that it did not fund or otherwise support communist or terrorist movements anywhere in the world. Again, the critics of the NCCC did not suggest any alternative means of solving the crushing problems of a world that must choose between two defective economic systems.

Can SuperStock be that alternative for the Protestant Churches?

There is no centralized body to speak for all the Protestant churches, as the Vatican does for Catholicism. Neither the WCC nor the NCCC has the teaching authority or power to set policy for any of its member churches in this manner. Therefore, to assess the prospects for widespread Protestant support of SuperStock, we must look to the leading individual theologians and to the causes that have moved Protestant church members over the years.

The evangelical tradition of mainline American Protestantism included spiritual revivals that paved the way for the Revolutionary War and the abolition of slavery. After the Civil War, this energetic spirit became increasingly directed toward questions of labor and capitalist values. Laissez-faire capitalism as practiced in America placed the rights of capitalists and property owners above all other rights. This facilitated industrial expansion, but also brought us sweatshops, child labor, monopolies, robber barons, cruel company towns in the coalfields, and Upton Sinclair's "jungle" in the stockyards.

Within American Protestantism there arose a group of preachers who recognized that Christianity had to address new social issues created by capitalism's abuses. In an age of pulpiteers, there were powerful preachers of national reputation who had the ear of presidents, captains of industry, and the laboring classes for whom they were advocates. The crusade they formed became known as the Social Gospel Movement. Emanating essentially from the middle-class membership of the evangelical churches—mainly Baptist, Methodist, Congregationalist, and Presbyterian—the Social Gospel Movement developed into a national political force, playing a key role in Theodore Roosevelt's Progressive and Bull Moose campaigns, and helping to win the regulatory changes that forced big business to begin assuming some degree of social responsibility. In fact, some of the issues of social justice that have endured to this day were first formulated by the Social Gospel Movement.

In grappling with capitalism's abuses, the Social Gospel Movement had a formidable enemy—the Gospel of Wealth—which relied on its own brand of religious morality to justify capitalism. Essentially, the Gospel of Wealth claimed divine approval for free enterprise capitalism and the rich men it produced. Andrew Carnegie expressed its philosophy in an essay on wealth published in 1889, in which he maintained that civilization depended on three iron-clad principles: free competition, free accumulation, and the sacredness of private property. Although Carnegie recognized that these principles "may sometimes be hard for individuals," he nonetheless believed "it is best for the race because it insures the survival of the fittest in every department" and produces "a wonderful material development" to the benefit of all.

While this self-serving view of "the true gospel concerning wealth" hardly bears comparison to the Sermon on the Mount, it was immensely popular. In 1915, for example, Russell Conwell addressed this theme in a booklet called *Acres of Diamonds,* which went on to sell 10 million copies, a staggering feat matched by only a handful of books in all of history. Here is the flavor of the lecture Conwell delivered countless times to audiences across the country:

> I say that you ought to get rich, and it is your duty to get rich. Some men say, "Don't you sympathize with the poor people?" Of course I do, or else I would not have been lecturing all these years. But the number of poor who are to be sympathized with is very small. To sympathize with a man whom God has punished for his sins, thus to help him when God would still continue his punishment, is to do wrong, no doubt about it.

This sentiment was expressed in the churches as well, although less blatantly, and was also usually accompanied by a reminder that no one needed to go poor or hungry in the vast richness of America. For example, in 1870, *The Congregationalist* newspaper noted that there were thousands upon thousands of acres of magnificent soil beyond the Mississippi to be secured at a nominal price, ensuring that "no man who is blessed with health and a willingness to work, be his family large or small, need come to the poorhouse." Gradually, however, the frontier began to close, and the safety valve that the historian Frederick Turner popularized as the "frontier thesis" was no longer able to delay the day of moral reckoning. Then did the battle for biblical integrity between the Social Gospel and the Gospel of Wealth begin in earnest.

There are too many diverse voices and movements to detail here, but one of the leading nineteenth century Social Gospel preachers was the Reverend Washington Gladden, a Congregationalist minister. Gladden opposed both socialism and capitalism, seeking instead to apply "Christian law" to social problems. In a long career that included 40 books and hundreds of articles, he denounced American capitalism and its leading lights, including the Harrimans and the Rockefellers. He even tried to get his church to turn down John D. Rockefeller's gift of $100,000 as "tainted money." In his view, as recounted in Robert Ferm's book *Issues in American Protestantism,* the problem with capitalism lay in its basic principles:

That self-love is the mainspring of human action, and that all rules of conduct must be adjusted to this as the supreme controlling motive, has been the assumption of all our political and practical philosophy.... That this principle has not worked very well through the old days of absolutism and aristocratic feudalism we could see.... What we are witnessing is nothing other than the culmination and collapse of the existing social order which rests on moral individualism. And the Church of Jesus Christ is called to replace this principle of selfishness and strife with the principle of goodwill and service. [pp. 252–3]

Walter Rauschenbusch, perhaps the most influential of the Social Gospel preachers, held a similar view of the essential immorality of capitalism's basic principles. As a Baptist minister among the poor in New York's "Hell's Kitchen," he saw firsthand the bitter fruits of laissez-faire capitalism, and came to these conclusions about the root causes of the poverty he faced daily:

Our scientific political economy has long been an oracle of a false god. It has taught us to approach economic questions from the point of view of goods and not of man.... Man is Christianized when he puts God before self; political economy will be Christianized when it puts man before wealth. ["Christianity and the Social Crisis" in *The Progressive Movement*, ed. Richard Hofstadter, p. 82]

This criticism of capitalism's "root and branch" did not mean the Social Gospel preachers embraced Marxism or socialism. On the contrary, these foreign ideologies had little appeal in the reformist American churches, and many preachers accurately foresaw the problems inherent in socialism and communism. As Congregationalist minister Charles Reynolds Brown noted in his 1911 book, *The Social Message of the Modern Pulpit:*

"Give us government ownership and government control of all the resources and machinery of production," the socialists say, "and these men who are now selfish, narrow and false will be public-spirited, generous and faithful." But will they? What is to reach the springs of action, renew the heart, purify and ennoble the affections, correct and strengthen the will? [p. 249]

And from Washington Gladden's *Recollections* comes this succinct appraisal: "The Socialistic solution, applied as a panacea, would not give us solitude, but it might give us stagnation" (p. 306).

Most of the Social Gospel preachers, in fact, sought to reconcile capital and labor within a market economy. As Rev. Brown put it in *The Social Message of the Modern Pulpit:*

The right to manage [one's] own business in his own way ... is modified by his obligation to manage it in such a way that his prosperity shall include a fair measure of prosperity for the men whose destinies are bound up with his own in that enterprise. [p. 206]

There was great optimism in the Social Gospel Movement, with the reformers coming to think that poverty and war would be eradicated from the face of the earth. These delusions were shattered by World War I and the Great Depression. But this important strain of Protestantism, adapted to post-Depression conditions, was carried on and led by Reinhold Niebuhr, probably the most influential Protestant theologian of the twentieth century. Born in Missouri in 1892, he was ordained a minister in the Evangelical and Reformed Church (now a part of the United Church of Christ) in 1915.

As a pastor in Detroit from 1915 to 1928, Niebuhr came to embrace Christian socialism, attacking capitalism forcefully in many books, articles, and speeches. But Niebuhr was as skeptical of socialism as a panacea, as he was critical of capitalism's flaws. After World War II, he became a leading opponent of Soviet expansionism in Eastern Europe, and in his later books he rejected both systems, using the evangelical tradition to denounce their shortcomings. In his 1944 book, *The Children of Light and the Children of Darkness,* he wrote:

A conservative class which makes "free enterprise" the final good of the community, and a radical class which mistakes some proximate solution of the economic problem for the ultimate solution for every issue of life, are equally perilous to the peace of the community and to the preservation of democracy. [p. 148–9]

In Niebuhr's mature judgment, capitalism and communism both err in failing to view life as the Bible portrays it: a dialectic between freedom and sin. Capitalism errs in misunderstanding human freedom: individuals and societies cannot morally be dedicated solely to their selfish interests, nor is God a mechanistic "invisible hand" regulating these competing self-interests. Marxism, on the other hand, errs in misunderstanding human sin. It presumes to end injustice by rearranging institutional relationships, but it fails to see that those institutional injustices are the *consequences* of human sin, not the cause.

Thus the works of the greatest Protestant theologian of our time form a foundation for the reforms of SuperStock, which can surmount the economic obstacles to social justice and peace in a way no other system can. At the same time, SuperStock makes no pretense of ennobling or changing human nature, as do the Marxists and proponents of the Protestant ethic. Indeed, SuperStock is based on acceptance of human nature in its imperfect state and merely provides a more logical and just system for organizing economic life.

Despite the charges of Marxist influence on the National Council of Churches of Christ and the World Council of Churches, when those organizations deliberate on the options available for moral reform of economic systems, they do not stray far from the Niebuhr tradition. Thus, in 1954, the NCCC General Board adopted a policy statement entitled *Christian Principles and Assumptions for Economic Life*, which included the following provisions:

> In some situations Christians have had the misconception that the one sure road to economic justice is the socialization of all the major means of production. . . . Today we have enough knowledge of what happens under a thorough-going collectivism to realize that uncritical recourse to the state to remedy every evil creates its own evils. It may easily become a threat to freedom as well as to efficiency. The union of political and economic power is a dangerous road, whether it leads toward complete state control of economic life or toward control of the state by private centers of economic power. A wide distribution of centers of power and decision is important to the preservation of democratic freedom.
>
> ***
>
> Since private ownership of many forms of property is a stimulus to increase production of goods and services, and a protection to personal freedom, wider ownership among our people should be encouraged.

The most recent indication of the Protestant commitment to pursuit of a more logical and just economic system can be found in a report presented to the World Council of Churches sixth general assembly at Vancouver, Canada, in August, 1983, by Archbishop Edward W. Scott of the Canadian Council of Churches, who served as the conference moderator. In his report, Archbishop Scott branded both capitalism and communism as failed ideologies, and called upon the delegates from more than 100 nations to develop "fresh Christian initiatives." His report went on to say:

> Both [capitalism and communism] are on the defensive, and in the present struggle between them, involving power of a magnitude previously unknown in human history, there lies the possibility of destruction not only of civilization as we know it but also of life on this planet. I believe that both of these ideologies, although they remain powerful, are no longer adequately responding to the challenges which confront us. An era is ending. [p. 15]

It is particularly appropriate to include Archbishop Scott's eloquent statement in this book because he recognizes the importance of fresh initiatives, not only in solving the moral dilemma of the churches, but also in ending the struggle between capitalism and communism before it destroys the earth.

Thus, we see that both the Catholic and Protestant churches have been critical of capitalism as well as Marxism. Neither church has found a satisfactory third path, and neither would look upon any single economic reform proposal as the key to a just world. To do this would be to deny the transcendent foundation on which religion is based. Yet within the range of material-world possibilities, what is the third option for the Christian churches? The lofty papal encyclicals and NCCC policy statements do not specify any way out of the dilemma of working with the two defective systems. Super-Stock is a concrete plan that would bring society into line with the principles Christian churches have been advocating for over a century, and would open a way out of the nuclear nightmare which remains both a spiritual and practical problem for the churches.

To my Protestant readers, then, I would make this plea: If you believe SuperStock should be studied, make your views known to your church organization.

Judaism

Judaism as a religion has not become involved in the crossfire between capitalism and communism to the extent Christianity has. Nevertheless, I believe the Jewish people have an important stake in bringing the two economic systems together, and that Judaism's tradition of philanthropic service provides a firm foundation for Super-Stock.

According to Rabbi Marc H. Tannenbaum, national inter-religious affairs director of the American Jewish Committee, the Jewish tradition has always been more concerned with direct aid to the poor than with the more abstract issue of economic systems. When he appeared at the 1974 hearings of the U.S. Senate Ad Hoc Committee on World Hunger, he was asked how the American Jewish Committee could get involved in the problem of world hunger when the needs of the Jewish community were so great. He explained that this was the essence of Judaic tradition as exemplified by Maimonides' belief that "the highest degree of charity is to put the poor person where he can dispense with other people's aid." Rabbi Tannenbaum went on to testify:

Nothing is more fundamental in Biblical and Rabbinic ethics than the moral obligation of *tzedakah,* a Hebrew term which means both "charity" and "to do justice."

***

The Biblical laws of charity in Palestine relating to "gleaning," the "forgotten sheaf," and "the corner of the field," implied the underlying idea that national territory belongs to the public as a whole. In accordance with Jewish law, landowners used to lay open fences surrounding their fields and vineyards, and during certain hours of the day, the needy were allowed to eat from the produce of the harvest. There was also a thrice-yearly allocation of *Maaser Ani* (poor man's tithe) from the threshing floor.

Thus, there arose the charitable traditions and institutions of the Jewish people which have remained a religious-communal characteristic ever since. These customs of charity, which were foreign to the pagan frame of mind of the Greeks and Romans, also had an abiding impact on the nature of the Christian "caritas."

The world's largest Jewish community is not in Israel but in the United States. SuperStock would seem to be in harmony with American Judaism, which is based on philanthropy and kinship within the framework of private property, free enterprise, and independence of the individual. This commitment to social action is particularly evident in the work of the United Jewish Appeal and the Jewish federation movements, which have raised and distributed billions of dollars throughout the world to alleviate the suffering of Jews and non-Jews alike. The Hebrew Free Loan Society, a tradition brought to New York from European Jewish communities in 1892, provides similar services to the needy, although on a smaller scale. Today there are more than 40 such organizations in the U.S., under such names as Jewish Free Loan Association and Jewish Family Service. They lend money without interest, in accordance with the biblical injunction, "If thou loan money to my people thou shalt not lay upon him interest" (Exodus 22:25). The money used for these loans comes from contributions, and although most loans are made to new Jewish immigrants, the societies are nonsectarian.

Thus, Judaism has a long history of service to the poor. In fact, Catholic liberation theologians find support for their "living Church" philosophy in the Old Testament's numerous references to liberation from economic and political oppression. Of particular interest to them, and certainly relevant to SuperStock, is the ancient Jewish custom of the sabbatical year, a period during which all debts were canceled, thus providing everyone a fresh start.

While Jewish biblical and philanthropic traditions afford fertile ground for the planting of SuperStock, there are even more compelling reasons why it should receive strong support from the Jewish community worldwide. Because Israel has had to devote so much of its resources to military expenditures, it has had very little chance to build a stable economy. Notwithstanding this burden, Israel has not shown much economic aptitude, which has certainly surprised those who believe in folklore. According to mythology, the Jewish people would never make very good soldiers or farmers, but had a natural flair for business. But since the establishment of the state in 1948, the Israelis have performed feats of arms to rival any in history, and they have turned an arid sandlot into an agricultural miracle. At the same time, they have managed to construct an economic system so monstrous that even a Rube Goldberg cartoon could not possibly portray all of its conflicting forces.

Many of the organizers of the Jewish state were Russian socialists, and this is reflected today in the position of the Histadrut, which is the Israel federation of trade unions, as well as Israel's largest private employer and capital owner, since it actually owns many of Israel's large businesses. One might assume therefore that labor relations would be ideal, and that it would be a simple matter to obtain the consensus needed to control inflation. But Israel has one of the world's worst strike records, even though the Histadrut would seem to be striking against itself, and Israel's rate of inflation is one of the highest in the world.

Thus, in Israel we have an example of a nation united in religion, in national purpose, and in dedication to a classless society, and yet beset by serious economic problems which appear insoluble under their present system. In view of these conditions, it would appear that SuperStock could be a particularly attractive and practical alternative for Israel and, by extension, Judaism.

Another strong reason for Jewish support of SuperStock is the fact that the religion of Islam has its own latent SuperStock principles, which could be developed into a foundation for peaceful Arab-Israeli relations. These principles are described in a major article by M. Abdul-Rauf entitled "The Ten Commandments of Islamic Economics," which was published in the August 1979 edition of *Across the Board*. In it, Abdul-Rauf notes:

> Islam has some affinities with both socialism and capitalism, but it departs from each in certain basic ingredients of its own. Islam is not so rigid or so radical, so tough or so cruel, nor is it so materialistic or so limited. . . . Not unlike capitalism, Islam believes in human freedom and individual liberty and encourages the en-

trepreneur's initiative. Yet, it does not resent limited state intervention when necessary, as a lever against boundless greed and corruption and at times of a special need.

The Islamic system takes into account certain essential moral objectives that call for social justice based on mutual responsibility.

***

Two Islamic injunctions work against the concentration of wealth in a few hands: the obligation of *zakat*, the annual payment of alms in income and savings, in trade commodities, in crops, and in certain other properties; and *haqq*, the right of the poor to receive charity. The law of inheritance, which breaks up the estate of a deceased person among all the heirs (normally numerous), also works in this direction. Moreover, as already indicated, since ownership ceases on a person's death, he is restrained from making a will involving more than a third of his estate.

Accordingly, if Israel installed SuperStock, it would be in a better position to establish trust and trade with its Muslim neighbors, whose Koran commands them to brotherhood in economic as well as spiritual matters.

A Proposed Declaration of Religious-Economic Principles

With the world's major religions seeking an alternative to continued domination by two defective, destructive, and antagonistic economic systems, I believe it is time religious leaders meet to discuss a joint declaration of religious-economic principles. As a starting point, I suggest the following declaration, which I believe is consistent with the moral and spiritual principles of the world's major religions:

DECLARATION OF RELIGIOUS-ECONOMIC PRINCIPLES

I. Most human beings live in subhuman conditions, and there is little hope that any of the world's present economic systems will improve their lot.

II. The world's population stands in grave peril because of the confrontation between the major economic systems: capitalism and communism.

III. This confrontation threatens daily to erupt into nuclear warfare between the United States and the Soviet Union, the principal proponents of these antagonistic systems. Even without the eruption of warfare, the confrontation itself consumes a major portion of the earth's resources in the escalating arms race and the maneuvering for power and advantage throughout the world. Should it erupt, such nuclear warfare would spell doom to human life.

IV. For centuries, religious groups have worked and prayed for changes that would remove the threat of warfare based on economic conditions, for changes in the distribution of wealth and income, and changes in human nature that would eliminate greed, intransigence, and other causes of conflict. But such changes in human nature have not occurred, and refinements in the systems of capitalism and communism have intensified rather than removed the causes of nuclear confrontation.

V. The capitalist and communist nations have attempted to avoid economic strife by providing jobs or welfare benefits for their inhabitants; but neither system can deliver enough jobs or welfare benefits to satisfy people's increased expectations of social justice, and neither system offers any substantial hope of alleviating the poverty that oppresses three-fifths of the world's population, those who live in the "Third World."

VI. Injustice reigns when those who have only their work to offer are left in poverty and destitution by the prevailing economic systems; but in their quest for social justice, governments in both capitalist and communist nations have largely ignored the potential benefits of broadening the ownership of productive capital to include all of humankind.

VII. The right to own property is founded in human nature and is conducive to the welfare of the individual, the family, and society. The desire for ownership of productive capital is a natural attribute of humankind. It will not wither away, and it is not to be condemned unless it is used as an instrument of injustice. The world and its resources were created by God for the use and welfare of all human beings. God intended these natural resources to help people live a good life and to contribute to the betterment of society.

VIII. Economic systems that subordinate the needs of human beings to the needs of the system are immoral and are to be condemned by all religions.

IX. At this moment in history, many socialist and communist nations are moving from state ownership of capital toward greater use of private ownership, and capitalist nations are moving toward greater state participation in private business activities. The leaders of the world's religions should recognize that in their work they must deal with the world's economic and social problems, and should seize this moment to lead their followers toward a system which combines the best features of capitalism and communism, taking advantage of what may be the last opportunity to eliminate the causes of nuclear confrontation.

X. A system that provides all people with the opportunity to own productive capital, regardless of whether they have savings, holds the promise of achieving social justice and removing the causes of nuclear confrontation. These objectives are so vital that access to long-term credit and the self-liquidating power of productive capital, as well as the right to work, must be made available to all people.

XI. *The world's religions should devote their resources to the adoption and perfection of such a system immediately.*

Whatever your religious affiliation, you can help the cause of SuperStock by passing along this proposed declaration to your local church or synagogue leader.

Chapter 10

Making SuperStock a Reality: *What You Can Do*

What can be conceived can be created.

—Auto designer ENZO FERRARI

Greater than the tread of mighty armies is an idea whose time has come.

—VICTOR HUGO

Men and nations will act rationally when all other possibilities have been exhausted.

—Katz's Law

Throughout this book, I have pointed out that SuperStock is by no means an ideal or fully-realized plan. Nor is it a magic panacea for the nuclear nightmare and our grave economic problems. It is, however, the broad outline of a program that can get us moving in the right direction; at the moment, it is the *only* foundation on which we can begin to build a real solution to these problems. Since 1975, my activities have drawn some attention to the idea, but our professional economists and finest political minds have hardly begun to study its feasibility. The real purpose of this book, therefore, is to demonstrate the need for immediate and in-depth study; to suggest some of the elements that should be considered; and to gain public support for a crash program aimed at developing a truly ideal plan.

Spreading the SuperStock Message

Public support will be crucial, and yes, you *can* make a difference. By supporting the effort to develop a program like Super-Stock, you can play an active role in solving the gravest problem in our history, one that threatens the life of every one of us. It is a role none of us can afford to abdicate on the mistaken assumption that individual action is useless or that the government is the only body equipped to deal with a problem of this magnitude. In fact, history indicates that the establishment and the government always tend to resist fundamental changes, and many of humanity's real advances have come about through the crusading efforts of individuals outside the establishment.

Often it is the outsider who successfully challenges long-standing assumptions on which prestigious careers have been built. Louis Pasteur, for example, was not a physician, and when he suggested that French doctors were literally killing their patients by transmitting germs to them, the entire medical establishment denounced him as a charlatan. But Pasteur was not so easily dismissed, and eventually he prevailed because he was right. Consider too what Ralph Nader did for auto safety and consumer protection in many fields in which he had no professional experience. And remember how outsider Howard Jarvis successfully limited taxation and government spending in California, creating a movement that spread throughout the nation.

The point is that individuals are *not* powerless, and people outside the power structure can indeed change the course of American history. To a great extent, the success of SuperStock will depend on individual effort, particularly during its early stages of development. Right now, the idea is not neatly packaged and ready for legislative or presidential action. It needs further study, discussion, and development, and this effort should involve the entire nation: economists, scholars, financiers, bankers, stockbrokers, business executives, foundations, writers, students, politicians, religious groups, lawyers, labor leaders, government officials, consumer activists, environmentalists—everyone concerned about the future. There is a role for all Americans in the molding of a new form of American capitalism, and your support will help to break through the iron ring of advisers which surrounds American presidents.

SuperStock can become a reality only through federal legislation that authorizes the necessary changes in our corporate finance system. The public cannot wish this plan into existence. And even if corporations wanted to implement SuperStock voluntarily, they could not do so effectively without federal legislation. So we must get the SuperStock message across to the White House and Congress.

I therefore urge each of you to write to the President and your congressional representatives, expressing support for *study* of the SuperStock plan as a tool for nuclear disarmament and economic recovery. Please take every opportunity to talk to your Washington representatives and others who can influence them. Many senators, members of Congress, cabinet members, and high-level executive aides will receive advance copies of this book.

SuperStock is too radical a change to get serious consideration unless it is supported by the White House. It is my hope though that we can begin to act on such a program while Ronald Reagan is in the White House. Whatever you think about his politics, he has a special talent for pulling people together to support a basic change of direction. It is also easier for a Republican president to win broad support for a move toward greater friendship with communist countries, as shown by Richard Nixon's historic breakthrough with Red China, an action that might have branded a Democratic president as "soft on communism." Then, too, Ronald Reagan has already skirted around the edges of the SuperStock idea, although he has not been able to develop a specific strategy for broadening capital ownership. For these reasons, it would be most appropriate if he undertook leadership of this capitalist revolution. The most important reason for beginning action as soon as possible, however, is that we are running out of time. If Reagan does not immediately embrace the idea, it is up to the rest of us to make him realize that there is a viable alternative to Reaganomics and cold war diplomacy.

It will also be important to start a grassroots movement for the study of SuperStock. We should, for example, initiate an intensive research and discussion program in our schools, religious organizations, antinuclear organizations, civic groups, magazines, and newspapers, as well as on radio and television. Many channels of communication must be opened, and we can do this through seminars, books, articles, essay contests, debates, and university courses on capital ownership. To date, our educational institutions and economic think-tanks have largely ignored the concept of stock ownership as a tool for solving macro-economic problems and creating a fairer distribution of income. Indeed, many professional economists believe equitable income distribution is a political question rather than an economic one. Yet, they can always be recruited to shoot down new ideas on income distribution—even though they have not developed the tools needed to test such new ideas. As MIT Professor Lester Thurow points out in *Dangerous Currents: The State of Economics:*

> The profession, the discipline of economics, is on its way to becoming a guild. Members of a guild, as we know, tend to preserve and advance traditional theories rather than trying to develop new ways of thinking and doing things to solve new problems. [p. xviii]

Thus, educational programs, public debate, and media involvement are crucial if we hope to create an atmosphere in which the SuperStock idea can flourish. Specifically, we must remind economists that our present policies may well lead to pension fund socialism or to a variation of the Meidner plan, giving union leaders virtual control of the stock of major businesses. Let us also convince economists that the capital ownership revolution has already begun; indeed, Congress has already set what amounts to a national policy of capital diffusion through TRASOP and PAYSOP, using billions of tax dollars to finance stock giveaways to corporate employees. Thus far, these new policies have not appreciably increased academic interest in the question of broad capital ownership, and if economists continue to ignore this issue, they are sure to be cut out of the policy-making process. But if only a tenth of our 66,000 professional economists involved themselves in a plan like SuperStock, we could build a ground swell that would help to galvanize Congress and the White House into action.

There is little doubt that such prodding will be necessary. Congress tends to be wary of global remedies like macro-economic solutions; too often, such broad and seemingly simple schemes create more problems than they solve. It is also much harder to sell a fundamental policy change than it is to make minor adjustments. Moreover, many grandiose plans have unforeseen consequences. The classic example is Prohibition, which was adopted for the strongest of moral reasons: to save the American family. Its only lasting effect, however, was to spur the development of organized crime. It is not surprising, therefore, that Congress and the White House are somewhat gun-shy.

However, SuperStock should not be haunted by the ghost of Prohibition. The Eighteenth Amendment was an overnight policy reversal which outlawed one of humanity's age-old pleasures. In contrast, SuperStock attempts to revitalize our economic system and to make it *consistent* with human nature and democracy. Although its psychological impact will register immediately after its enactment into law, the actual changes in our financial system will be implemented gradually over at least a decade, and it will take a whole generation before the plan is fully operative. During that time, any unanticipated side effects can be controlled and its operation improved in light of practical experience. Thus, there should be no need for financial speakeasies once SuperStock goes into effect.

While we may not be able to predict all of the consequences and ramifications of SuperStock, we do know some of the traps it will allow us to avoid. For example, since it is not based on the employment relationship, we won't have to deal with many of the problems associated with ESOP and other employee ownership schemes. Nor will SuperStock come between workers and their union. And because employer's stock is not channeled to workers or unions, it will not create an opportunity for union leaders to assume control of our major corporations. Finally, SuperStock does not favor corporate officers, executives, or people working for our most successful corporations, as do ESOP, TRASOP, and PAYSOP. Indeed, it can be tailored to favor anybody we want to help. And, most important of all, it is the kind of a structural change needed to make capitalism consistent with the professed ideals of Marxism.

The ideal plan should probably include a synthesis of several forms of ownership, income, and security. The whole area of pensions, for example, is related to capital ownership, even though the rights held by workers in pension plans do not actually make them owners of corporate stock. Then there are the existing capital ownership schemes based on employment, such as profit-sharing plans, ESOPs, TRASOPs, PAYSOPs, and the European wage-earner investment funds (WEIFs). In addition, Social Security and government transfer payments should be synthesized with SuperStock so that benefits do not overlap and recipients are given an incentive to progress from the welfare system to participation in capitalism. And the insurance industry should be encouraged to synthesize present and future forms of life insurance with SuperStock.

Clearly, making SuperStock a reality will be a long and difficult job—which means it is very important that we all join in the effort. You can help by talking to your friends and colleagues about SuperStock; bring it to the attention of the organizations you belong to now or might join in the future, especially those devoted to nuclear disarmament.

Organizations Working for Nuclear Disarmament

The great Central Park rally of June 1982 demonstrated the strength of public support for nuclear arms limitations and disarmament. But until we can find a way to improve Soviet-American relations, that support will continue to have little practical impact. The dedication and energy of millions of people in the antinuclear movement will be wasted as long as our case is based primarily on accusations that our government officials are warmongers.

There were more than 90 national organizations working for nuclear disarmament by the end of 1982. These organizations have more than 20 million members and cover a broad spectrum of special concerns, such as labor, religion, public health, education, civic betterment, and environmental protection. Most favor a bilateral nuclear freeze, but beyond that, there is no specific program on which they agree. Many want to politicize the antinuclear movement in a leftward direction, combining disarmament with social justice issues. Others want to keep the focus solely on nuclear disarmament for fear of splintering the movement. They point to the British Campaign for Nuclear Disarmament and the European Nuclear Disarmament Organization, both of which moved toward the left, became anti-American, and adopted the platforms of socialist and labor parties.

Unless its constituent organizations agree on a political agenda, the American antinuclear movement is likely to lose its momentum. Future Central Park rallies could become mere outlets for emotional opposition to the existence of nuclear weapons or worse, leftwing mob scenes. To avoid such a possibility, I believe we must convince the antinuclear organizations to consider SuperStock (or a similar plan) as a specific political program that all 20 million antinuclear activists can support.

Therefore, I urge each of you to join one or more of the organizations now promoting the cause of nuclear disarmament. Then work within those organizations to promote SuperStock as a viable route to improved Soviet-American relations and disarmament. Suggest that each organization set up groups or committees to explore the economic approach to nuclear disarmament. Encourage public debate at meetings, and use the organizations' newsletters as a forum for discussion. The point is to spread the message through all available channels, because right now few of those involved in the antinuclear movement realize that changes in our economic system could lead to disarmament. But once they do, they can help to assure that no more wars will ever be fought over the differences between capitalism and communism.

The following is an alphabetical listing of major national organizations devoted to reducing or eliminating nuclear weapons.

Artists for Survival, 144 Moody St., Waltham, MA 02154.

Clergy and Laity Concerned, 198 Broadway, New York, NY 10038.

Coalition for a New Foreign & Military Policy, 120 Maryland Ave., NE, Washington, DC 20002.

The Committee for National Security, 2000 P St., NW, Suite 515, Washington, DC 20036.

Communicators for Nuclear Disarmament, 44 Hunt Street, Watertown, MA 02172.

Council for a Livable World, 11 Beacon St., Boston, MA 02108.

Educators for Social Responsibility, 639 Massachusetts Ave., Cambridge, MA 02139.

Fellowship of Reconciliation, Box 271, Nyack, NY 10960.

Ground Zero, 806 15th St. NW, Suite 421, Washington, DC 20005.

High Tech Professionals for Peace, c/o Davis, 52 Walker St., Newtonville, MA 02160.

International Physicians for Prevention of Nuclear War, 635 Huntington Ave., Boston, MA 02115.

Lawyers Alliance for Nuclear Arms Control, 43 Charles St., Suite 3, Boston, MA 02114.

Musicians Against Nuclear Arms, 2161 Massachusetts Ave., Cambridge, MA 02140.

National Committee of the National Nuclear Weapons Freeze Campaign, 4144 Lindell Blvd., St. Louis, MO 63801.

Nurses' Alliance for the Prevention of Nuclear War, Box 319, Chestnut Hill, MA 02167.

Physicians for Social Responsibility, Box 295, Cambridge, MA 02236.

SANE, 711 G St. NW, Washington, DC 20003.

Union of Concerned Scientists, 1384 Massachusetts Ave., Cambridge, MA 02238.

United Campuses to Prevent Nuclear War, 1346 Connecticut Ave. NW, Washington, DC 20036.

World Federalists Association, 1011 Arlington Blvd., Suite W219, Arlington, VA 22209.

There are, of course, hundreds of other antinuclear organizations. For lists, including those outside the United States, write to: World Conference on Religion and Peace (WCRP), 777 United Nations Plaza, New York, N.Y. 10017, or Housmans Diary Group, 5 Caledonian Road, London N1 9DX, England.

As far as I know, Ground Zero is the only national organization that concentrates on improving Soviet-American relations as a prerequisite to disarmament. But as we have seen, their program is limited to educating Americans about the Soviet Union and fostering individual contacts between American and Soviet citizens. So if you believe in SuperStock's potential, join Ground Zero and try to convince them that they must go beyond their present program and work toward perfecting SuperStock or a similar plan that attacks the roots of Soviet-American enmity.

The Burden of Proof

In a court of law, the burden of proof rests with the prosecutor who must prove beyond a reasonable doubt that the accused is guilty. So, too, does the burden of proof rest with those who will try to debunk SuperStock. In other words, in your efforts to promote the idea, think of yourself as SuperStock's defense attorney, and ask the skeptics what proof *they* have that SuperStock will *not* work. Ask them, too, what other options are available to us—Lew Lehrman's gold standard proposal? Reaganomics? More Great Society welfare capitalism? Socialism, through the ballot box or a revolution?

Certainly, there is no proof that SuperStock *will* work. However, there is a lot of proof that welfare capitalism isn't working, and few would deny that we need to make *some* kind of change. And how can we do this without venturing into the unknown? After all, economics is still a trial-and-error business, and any plan with a chance of working remains untried, simply because so far we have only tried the standard options of welfare capitalism—all of which have been found wanting. Therefore, those who refuse to open their minds to SuperStock must be the ones to demonstrate why it cannot work and why it is not worth a try. Remember, too, that a group of 35 economists, financiers, and government officials spent a full day in 1977 at the Brookings Institution discussing the concept, and they found no obvious flaw or reason why the plan could not work.

Among the ranks of the disbelievers will be those disturbed by the thought of changes in our economic system. But should they not be more disturbed by the continuing ideological battle between capitalism and communism that is likely to cause a nuclear war? They should realize that our welfare capitalist system is changing anyway, and right now it has nowhere to go but straight to socialism, since it has no safety valve without SuperStock.

As for the cynics among us—those who believe anything that is both logical and humane is doomed to fail—let them remember Victor Hugo's words: "Greater than the tread of mighty armies is an idea whose time has come." If they don't believe the time has come to attack the nuclear crisis at its root—ideological warfare—then ask them what other change could possibly bring an end to the nuclear nightmare.

Finally, let no one dismiss SuperStock as utopian, for utopian ideas rest on changes in human nature, while SuperStock accepts human nature as it is. And the most utopian dream of all is that the rivalry between capitalism and communism will remain peaceful indefinitely while MAD and NUTS keep the missiles safely in their silos.

The $10,000 SuperStock Essay Contest

To date, only a few dozen people have studied the SuperStock plan in depth and tried to debunk or improve it. So the plan presented in this book is little more than a Wright brothers model of universal capitalism. We will need something more like a supersonic Concorde model if SuperStock is to achieve its goals.

Therefore, I have decided to begin the search for the best plan by sponsoring an essay contest through the Council on International and Public Affairs. A prize of $10,000 in cash will be given for the best essay on the following topic:

How can we, without adopting socialism or giving up our treasured freedoms, make American capitalism compatible with Marxism and use our modified economic system to end the nuclear nightmare?

The essays submitted can consist of comments and suggestions relating to the SuperStock plan presented in this book; they can recommend fundamental changes in the SuperStock plan; they can even propose an entirely different plan designed to make American capitalism compatible with Marxism. Although I believe that any such plan would have to provide for MOP ownership by all the American people, I would certainly like to hear from anyone who can come up with another way of creating the necessary compatibility between capitalism and Marxism.

I know there are many good ideas out there because I have already received some from readers of my previous writings on this subject. For example, a former Senate aide suggested that the ideal plan should provide for direct ownership of America's natural resources and other government property by individual Americans. This would include the Tennessee Valley Authority, the national parks, post offices, and other property now owned by the federal (and possibly state) governments. And a factory worker from Iowa, who has been trying to design a system of interest-free loans patterned after the Hebrew Free Loan Societies, suggested that interest-free loans be made available to finance the purchase of SuperStock shares. I don't have the skills or facilities needed to assess these ideas, but there are many such modifications that can be evaluated by our universities, think-tanks, and government agencies if we devote just a small fraction of our attention to SuperStock.

One of the objectives of this essay contest is to inject SuperStock into the mainstream of academic and public discussion. To this end, I plan to publish a collection of the best essays submitted. The contest is being administered and judged by the Council on International and Public Affairs. For further details about the contest and publication plans, please write to the Council on International and Public Affairs, 777 United Nations Plaza, New York, N.Y. 10017.

Chapter 11

Final Exams

I've been advocating the SuperStock plan since 1975, so I have had many opportunities to discuss it with people from all walks of life, in person as well as on radio and television programs. Naturally, many questions have been raised about the feasibility of such a novel plan, and since you may share some of these doubts, I will summarize the most searching questions as well as my responses.

Some Tough Questions for the Author

Q. Your idea for ending the nuclear nightmare assumes we can remove the basic cause of enmity between the U.S. and the USSR by making American capitalism compatible with Russian Marxism. But isn't Marxism in the Soviet Union today merely used as a pretext to keep the Kremlin group in power?

A. Although many observers have said that Marxist ideology is irrelevant in the USSR today, practically all admit that ideology is still the very foundation of the Kremlin's power. If the Kremlin leaders abandoned Marxism-Leninism, they would eliminate their own *raison d'être*. Therefore, pretext or not, Marxist ideology is what we must confront when dealing with the power struggle between the U.S. and the USSR.

Q. If we change our system of ownership of the means of production (MOP) so as to remove its conflict with Marxism, can we be sure this will pave the way for friendlier relations with the Soviets—and eventually, disarmament?

A. No, we can't be sure of this. But we *can* recognize that there will be no real hope of improving Soviet-American relations if we don't make capitalism compatible with Marxism. Since we cannot be certain that socializing American MOP ownership will end the nuclear nightmare, we must first make certain that SuperStock is worth doing on its own—that it will help the American economy rather than harm it, regardless of its ability to end the nuclear arms race.

Q. The only real alignment with Marxist ideology in the SuperStock plan is that the ownership of the means of production is opened to the entire population, thereby eliminating the exploitation of the nonowning class by the owning class. But isn't there a lot more to Marxism that we could not accept without abandoning our democratic principles?

A. No. Leading Marxist authorities from the time of Lenin have agreed that the class struggle to overcome exploitation is the central core of Marxism. Thus, there are no other elements significant enough to stand in the way of Soviet-American entente if we broaden MOP ownership, thereby eliminating exploitation and the class struggle.

Q. Even if we eliminated the ideological conflict, wouldn't the threat of war be just as strong because of nationalism and the political differences between American democracy and Soviet dictatorship?

A. No. Nationalism and the differences in political systems *might* cause enmity, but we have maintained friendly relations with many countries that are strongly nationalistic and have undemocratic political systems. It is only the constant global conflict between American capitalism and Soviet communism that *compels* us to be enemies, because each system requires destruction of the other in order to survive. And of all the potential causes of enmity—ideology, nationalism, political systems, and human lust for power—ideology is the only one we can remove.

Q. Couldn't we accomplish the desired changes in MOP ownership by broadening employee ownership plans? Wouldn't that be simpler, less radical, and more practical than SuperStock?

A. It would be simpler, less radical, and much easier to implement, but unfortunately it would not accomplish our purposes. It leaves in place the classes of exploiter and exploited that Marxism insists on eliminating. It would certainly broaden the owning class, but not enough to remove the conflict between capitalism and communism. Furthermore, it would not solve our massive economic problems.

Q. Are you opposed to Employee Stock Ownership Plans (ESOPs) and other employment-based ownership schemes?

A. No. I think they are a step in the right direction because they do broaden MOP ownership. However, they have some drawbacks. They can be used by wealthy owners of closely-held corporations to gain tax advantages, in which case they provide no public benefit.

They transfer considerable sums which would otherwise be tax revenue for the Treasury to a segment of our society that doesn't need help—namely, to people with stable jobs in large corporations. Also, these plans create a large cache of employee-owned stock that would facilitate union takeovers of large businesses under pension fund socialism or the Meidner Plan.

Q. According to your scenario, $5 trillion worth of corporate stock will be owned by SuperStockholders about 20 years after the SuperStock plan goes into effect, and they will receive dividends of about $1 trillion per year. But the total profits of all American corporations right now, even before taxes, do not add up to $1 trillion a year—so how can those figures be correct?

A. $5 trillion is the generally accepted figure for our total new capital requirements over the next 20 years. That money will be invested only in companies that can make a good case for a return of about 20 percent before taxes; otherwise, investors would be better off putting the funds into the money market. Therefore, this annual return of 20 percent should produce $1 trillion in dividends to SuperStockholders. Remember that SuperStock is based upon the *future growth* of the American economy (stretching into the twenty-first century) and neither disturbs nor depends upon the return on presently owned capital. Also, corporate profits will be greatly increased by elimination of the massive interest payments now required under the present system, which uses debt to pay for most capital additions.

Q. But most American corporations pay out no more than 30 percent of their earnings as dividends. How would you get them to pay out the entire $1 trillion?

A. Federal legislation would have to specify full payment of earnings as dividends. Indeed, when Senator Mike Gravel put together his own SuperStock-type plan in the late 1970s, he called it "Full-Return Stock" for that reason.

Q. If corporations paid out their entire SuperStock earnings as dividends, they could not pay corporate income tax on those earnings. Wouldn't that cause a massive loss of federal revenue?

A. No. Right now, corporate income taxes bring in less than 10 percent of federal revenue. Compared to individuals, most large corporations have very low tax rates, and quite a few major corporations pay virtually no taxes at all. SuperStockholders, on the other hand, would pay taxes on their dividends at regular personal rates. Thus, the total amount of tax revenue collected on SuperStock dividends would probably be greater than the amount of corporate income tax payable under the present system.

Q. What about the *real* shares of stock that investors buy and

sell in the stock market; won't their value be watered down by the SuperStock plan?

A. No, there will be no dilution. SuperStock shares will be issued at market value in payment for the new capital items added to a corporation's balance sheet. The corporation will have more stockholders, but there will be a larger pie for them to share, since its new assets will be fully paid for and will thus add nothing to the debit side of the balance sheet.

Q. But today's regular stockholders expect the value of their holdings to grow through the addition of new capital, as you've shown in the Figure 2 bathtub diagram. Aren't you depriving them of a growth factor they had a right to expect when they bought their shares?

A. That growth factor is largely an illusion in an economy ravaged by recurring inflation, oppressive interest rates, and unemployment. Those stockholders took a chance anyway, hoping their investments would increase in value through the traditional corporate financing system. But for many, this didn't happen, and our present system isn't likely to provide substantial growth in the future either, even if we don't install SuperStock. However, the phasing out of the corporate income tax and the revitalization of the entire economy that is likely to accompany SuperStock should benefit every shareholder, old or new, through increased production, profits, and financial stability. Thus, we need not fret about the position of the old stockholders.

Q. What overall effect will SuperStock have on the stock market?

A. I think it will have a very positive effect. SuperStock will not be traded publicly, so it cannot depress the regular stock market. SuperStock will supply our economy's missing link: mass purchasing power to match our huge productive power. This should increase production and profits and raise stock prices. It should also create a political climate in which everyone will be pulling for the major corporations to increase profits, instead of the present tug-of-war which puts most of our citizens in an adversary position against business. A nation composed entirely of capitalists should be a boon to Wall Street. And once we install SuperStock, the corporate income tax becomes superfluous. Therefore, SuperStock is bullish.

Q. Wouldn't there be inequities in parceling out the stock, with some SuperStockholders getting better stock than others?

A. No. Each SuperStockholder will receive the same thing: a certificate of ownership in the pooled shares of about 2,000 major corporations. Each corporation would contribute to the pool the number of shares needed to pay for its new capital expenditures.

Q. How would you get the SuperStockholders to sign notes for their stock?

A. They would not sign any notes. The bank loans needed to finance SuperStock would be secured by bundles of shares of our leading corporations. The financing would be self-liquidating and nonrecourse, with repayment guaranteed by the federal government.

Q. If our 2,000 leading corporations were not allowed to use retained earnings or debt to pay for new capital additions, how would they pay for their new plants and equipment?

A. They would sell their shares to the SuperStock fund for cash, and would use that cash to pay for their capital additions. The cash would come from bank loans equal to the cost of the shares issued.

Q. How can you be sure that the banks will agree to lend billions of dollars at low interest to pay for SuperStock shares?

A. I can't, but if the banks don't agree, the government can finance the program directly, shutting the banks out of the capital financing process that is one of their key functions now. All the bankers I have talked to are more concerned about being shut out than about the risks involved, especially since the government would be guaranteeing the loans.

Q. How would we determine which corporations are eligible to participate in the SuperStock plan?

A. Congress would establish the guidelines. There are some very simple ways to do this. For example, we could start with corporations that have publicly traded shares, annual sales of $100 million or more, and a net profit in two of the three preceding years. We might also want to build in some safeguards, such as requiring these corporations to justify proposed capital additions by submitting certified projections to the Securities & Exchange Commission, in much the same manner as they would have to satisfy their bankers now.

Q. Won't SuperStock get us more deeply involved in government planning and lead to a command economy like that of the socialist countries?

A. No, I don't see how SuperStock will involve us in any more extensive government planning than we have today. To a large extent, we already have a planned economy. Very few important business decisions can be made without some government involvement, although permission is not always required in advance. SuperStock will not bring the kind of rigid command economy that freezes initiative in socialist nations. The planning and decision-making for capital additions will still be done by each individual corporation, but some degree of government participation is necessary in any successful industrial economy. Henry Kissinger and others are urging us to copy the Japanese system, which is built on massive government planning and economic intervention. SuperStock would involve less government planning than the Japanese or the German system, and it would eventually decrease government intervention by eliminating welfare-state handouts that require huge bureaucracies.

Q. How do we know that we can build the apparatus and acquire the skills needed to make a radical plan like SuperStock work?

A. As the noted auto designer Enzo Ferrari said, "What can be conceived can be created." We already have the main ingredients: the most sophisticated credit and stock corporation systems in the world. Moreover, since SuperStock is a more logical system than welfare capitalism and is more consistent with our national goals, it should be easier to manage than the present system.

Q. How does SuperStock differ from George McGovern's old proposal of a $1,000 Treasury handout to every person who needs it?

A. That would have been *socialist* income—transferring tax funds to private individuals. SuperStock is based upon *capitalist* income—giving every American a chance to share in the profits of our leading corporations. It ties everyone into the capitalist system, so that the welfare benefits as well as the dividends are paid from what all of us, working together, make the system earn.

Q. If SuperStock made all Americans shareholders in corporations that have been damaging our environment, how would we ever control pollution?

A. As dependent as we are on jobs today, we cannot afford to close down factories that are causing pollution; that just makes things tougher for the struggling workers. Only a truly affluent society can afford to protect the environment while keeping production and living standards high. We must find new methods to safeguard our environment while we maintain high consumption. This will take huge amounts of capital that neither government nor private industry can muster without a fundamental policy change like SuperStock. Therefore, SuperStock would actually help us to control pollution.

Q. The financing of SuperStock calls for creating massive credit, which is just like printing money. Won't this be inflationary?

A. No. Even under our present system, much of the money for new plant and equipment is borrowed. SuperStock merely changes the ownership—it does not create entirely new credit demands. Nevertheless, if the creation of credit does turn out to increase inflation, we can control it by implementing the plan gradually. And as Wharton Professor Lawrence Klein pointed out during a discussion at the Brookings Institution, since this credit would be used to increase national productivity, its long-term effect should actually be counterinflationary. Little is known about how to stop inflation in a humane way, but it certainly requires a national will that can no longer be mustered under welfare capitalism, except possibly in time of war. Thus, the psychological effect of SuperStock should be so positive that it will give us the will to do whatever is necessary to halt inflation.

Q. How much will it cost us to put SuperStock into operation?

A. Nothing. In the long run, SuperStock will actually save us money. It will reduce government expenditures for Social Security, welfare, armaments, and foreign aid, and enable us to save billions of dollars now spent on the hopeless task of job creation.

Q. SuperStock would make massive amounts of capital available to our largest corporations, which would become the darlings of the nation. Wouldn't this be harmful to the smaller businesses, which would still have to scramble for new capital?

A. This is a potentially undesirable side effect for which I do not have a complete answer. However, the present sources of capital would still be available to the smaller businesses. With a little ingenuity, we should also be able to work out a method of eventually including smaller corporations in the SuperStock system, although I think we would have to begin with only our 2,000 largest successful corporations. Remember, the point is to plug our neediest people into the strongest part of our economy.

Since the financial community will have less involvement with big business, they will be able to develop better methods of financing smaller corporations, particularly those engaged in promising research and development that can increase productivity. Under SuperStock, we should be eager to increase the number of participating corporations as soon as possible, for this will keep our economy growing and spread the benefits of SuperStock more rapidly throughout American society.

Q. How can you justify handing out stock to people who won't have to pay for it and perhaps never did a day's work in their lives, while millions of Americans have saved their hard-earned money to buy shares in the same companies?

A. People who are able to save money would still be able to buy shares, and their old shares should be worth a lot more if we have a healthy economic system. The only real change is that SuperStock opens long-term credit to everyone, instead of limiting it to those who need it least. While this may not square with Milton Friedman's philosophy of capitalism, it is time to face the fact that capitalism is not likely to survive unless we make it consistent with our political democracy. In my opinion, no other change can save capitalism, and certainly no other change can end the nuclear nightmare.

Q. Don't we already have "democratic capitalism"?

A. No. We have a democratic electoral process and a capitalist economic system, which makes us a "capitalist democracy" rather than a "democratic capitalist" state. This important distinction is spelled out in Chapter 5.

Q. Will SuperStock be more appealing to Democrats or to Republicans?

A. It should appeal equally to both parties, because it combines important features of liberal and conservative economics.

Q. If every family is going to get $20,000 per year in dividends without working, how can we preserve the work incentive?

A. Even under our present system of welfare capitalism, millions of people have no incentive because work would provide them with little more money than welfare or other transfer payments. However, SuperStock can be designed so it actually encourages work and other socially desirable behavior. We could, for example, make those who are unwilling to work ineligible.

Q. Won't SuperStock make it easy for activist groups to collect voting proxies and take control of major corporations?

A. No. SuperStock need not be voting stock, and in my opinion, it should not be.

Q. If SuperStock is not transferable and has no voting power, would its holders really be capitalists?

A. They will be capitalists in the sense that they will receive a substantial part of their income from ownership of the means of production. That is all we can hope to accomplish through Super-Stock. If we also made it transferable voting stock, we might create problems that would wreck the system before it got off the ground.

Q. Is SuperStock a scheme for redistributing the wealth of the nation?

A. No. It does not redistribute present wealth, but it will distribute future wealth more equitably. It will give the disadvantaged sector of our society the same access to long-term credit that has always been held exclusively by the wealthy.

Q. Are you sure SuperStock will expand our economy and deliver more jobs, more income, and more growth than we have now?

A. We can't be sure, since economics is a trial-and-error game. What we *can* be sure of is that welfare capitalism can no longer provide the growth we need to keep our economy from eroding. It seems clear to me that by funneling a new stream of income to the millions of people who need it most, SuperStock is bound to create new customers and increase economic growth for a generation or more.

Q. You seem to have high hopes for reviving American morale through SuperStock. But isn't it true that people tend to put a low value on things they do not pay for?

A. In an important way, each person must earn the right to SuperStock, by obeying the law and doing his or her best to contribute to the well-being of American society. It would be preferable to make everyone earn SuperStock benefits more directly, but I have not been able to come up with such a plan. Perhaps others will be able to.

Q. Do you really think that a utopian, pie-in-the-sky idea like SuperStock is worth discussing and has any chance of being enacted?

A. Yes, because the nuclear nightmare is a problem that *must* be solved, and there is no apparent solution among all the standard remedies that have been tried. No plan other than SuperStock has the potential to end the nuclear nightmare and preserve capitalism, freedom, and democracy.

Q. SuperStock almost seems too good to be true. How can one plan solve most of our economic problems and end the nuclear arms race as well?

A. It frightened me at first to discover that a change in our capital financing system might solve so many of the world's grave problems. Then I came to realize that practically all of our major problems, both in our domestic economy and in our relations with the USSR, stem from the forces unleashed by our inequitable distribution of income and MOP ownership. Therefore, it should not be surprising that a laser beam aimed at the source of these maladies should be capable of burning all of them out at once.

Q. But isn't SuperStock too radical a plan to take seriously?

A. SuperStock is radical, in that it cuts to the roots of the problems it is aimed at: the nuclear arms race and America's failing socio-economic system. If there were any easy or nonradical solutions, they would have been found by now. It is time for us to look beyond such palliatives and consider a solution that matches up to the staggering scope of these problems. Besides, after you get used to the idea that it is possible to make our capitalistic economic system consistent with our political democracy and to improve Soviet-American relations without nationalizing our MOP, SuperStock doesn't seem all that radical.

Q. If SuperStock succeeds in revitalizing capitalism, isn't it

possible that the Soviets would see us as a greater threat and view a nuclear war as the only possible way to save their own system?

A. Yes, that is possible, but I do not think it is likely, especially if we make it clear to the Soviets that SuperStock is not another ploy in the global slugfest between capitalism and communism. It must be designed as an invitation for the Soviets to participate in a world-wide partnership that will end the nuclear nightmare and bring great benefits to both nations—far greater than anything that might be accomplished by continuation of the rivalry between capitalism and communism.

Q. When do you think SuperStock will get serious attention from the White House and Congress?

A. Like the overwhelming majority of the world's people, Americans are fed up with their own economic system. The world is ready for the next big economic idea, and only the United States has the flexibility to pioneer it. How soon Washington gives SuperStock serious consideration will depend on how quickly it becomes a topic of public discussion. We have tried all the conventional solutions, so I am counting on the operation of Katz's law: "Men and nations will act rationally when all other possibilities have been exhausted."

Q. What can I do to get the White House and Congress to consider SuperStock seriously?

A. (1) Pass this book along to someone else who might be interested in helping. (2) Enter the SuperStock essay contest if you are so inclined, and urge your friends and associates to enter, especially those who are connected with a university. (3) Urge your colleagues in antinuclear organizations to consider the economic approach to nuclear disarmament. (4) Tell your own senators and congressional representatives to open their minds to the SuperStock concept. (5) If you believe in prayer, please pray.

Easy Questions for the Reader

I've finished my homework; now it's your turn. The following multiple choice questions cover the major points in this book. In my mind, there is only one correct answer to each question, but the subjects treated in this book are so controversial that reasonable minds may differ. Therefore, please feel free to select more than one answer to each question. Indeed, you may find all of the answers to a particular question unsatisfactory—some may even irritate you, since some are designed to demonstrate how ridiculous our present system can be, or to force you to make choices between unpleasant alternatives because they are the only ones available. If you find no satisfactory answer to a question, please draft your own answer and send it to me at 200 Park Avenue, New York, N.Y. 10166.

1. Who is competent to decide how many and what kinds of nuclear weapons the United States should deploy?

a. The President and his advisers, including knowledgeable senators and members of Congress, since only they have access to the secret information on which such a decision must be based.

b. Sociologists, journalists, and writers who study the subject, because all of our presidents from Truman through Reagan have succumbed to pressure from warmongers and cannot be trusted to make the proper decision.

c. It should be decided by popular vote, since it affects the safety of every person in the United States.

d. This question is academic, because we have enough nuclear warheads already to blow up the USSR and the rest of the world many times over, provided that our weapons or communications systems are not knocked out by a Soviet first strike or a new Soviet weapons system.

e. Nobody, since no one can answer this question with any reasonable degree of certainty.

2. What is our best hope for ending the nuclear nightmare?

a. Deterrence by Mutual Assured Destruction (MAD).

b. Going beyond MAD deterrence to the nuclear war fighting posture as espoused by the Nuclear Use Theorists (NUTS).

c. A verifiable bilateral freeze on the testing, production, and deployment of further nuclear weapons.

d. Mutual pledges of "No First Use" of nuclear weapons.

e. The establishment of nuclear-free zones.

f. Negotiating further arms control and disarmament treaties in the present atmosphere of mutual distrust.

g. Unilateral nuclear disarmament.

h. Nongovernmental solutions, such as marching to Central Park, civil disobedience, elimination of national sovereignty, and establishment of a holistic world picture.

i. Getting rid of the American governmental officials who are prolonging and accelerating the nuclear arms race in the tradition of all of our presidents from Truman through Reagan.

j. Improving Soviet-American relations by removing the causes of enmity where possible.

3. Is it worthwhile for us to consider trying to improve Soviet-American relations by modifying our economic system so that it no longer conflicts with Marxist ideology?

a. It is *not* worth considering, because neither the Soviet government nor its people believe in Marxist ideology any longer, and therefore such a modification could not possibly reduce Soviet-American enmity.

b. The idea is *not* worth considering, because the conflict between Soviet Marxism and American capitalism is a peaceful rivalry between two economic systems, and this rivalry is unlikely to destabilize either nation or lead to nuclear warfare.

c. The idea is *not* worth considering, because the conflict between these economic systems is not a significant obstacle to improvement of Soviet-American relations.

d. The idea is *not* worth considering, because Soviet-American enmity can be significantly reduced by the pairing of cities, by education, cultural exchanges, trade, and other current measures that do not require any change in American economic ideology.

e. The idea is worth considering, for some or all of the following reasons: Marxist ideology is the basis of the Kremlin's power, regardless of whether anyone in the USSR still believes in the ideology; Marxist ideology is the basis of worldwide revolutionary movements, which the Kremlin uses to destabilize or overthrow capitalist governments; this clash of economic ideologies has been a major cause of Soviet-American enmity since 1917; and economic ideology is the only Soviet-American difference that can be removed, since we cannot change our nationality and we do not wish to change our democratic political system.

4. Would a change in the MOP ownership system of American capitalism make it compatible with Marxism?

a. It would not be compatible with Marxism unless we nationalized MOP ownership, the method of socialization specified by Marx and his followers.

b. It could not make America's economic ideology compatible with Marxism, because there would remain other essential points of difference, such as the Marxist insistence on atheism and dialectical materialism.

c. This change would make American capitalism compatible with Marxism, for several reasons: Marx said the stock corporation and the credit system could bring about socialization of MOP ownership; Marxism does not require state ownership, since the state was to wither away in Marx's classless society; the class struggle between owners and nonowners of MOP is the central core of Marxism; and socialization of MOP ownership by making all Americans owners would leave no class to be exploited by any other class.

5. What would be the result if we did modify our economic system by making MOP ownership available to all Americans?

a. It would require socialization of ownership of the means of production, which would be intolerable, even if this socialization does not take the form of nationalization.

b. It could not possibly end the nuclear nightmare, because the basic cause of Soviet-American enmity is the incorrigibly bad character of the Russian people, whose history (both before and after the Bolshevik revolution of 1917) has been one of unbridled nationalism, expansionism, and imperialism, and who are incapable of understanding that their self-interest is better served by entente with the U.S. than by continued ideological warfare.

c. It would automatically improve Soviet-American relations and open the way for disarmament, cooperation, and partnership.

d. It would not automatically improve Soviet-American relations, but it would remove the main roadblock to such improvement, and is therefore a precondition to opening the way for disarmament, cooperation, and partnership—a bridge that would link Soviet self-interest with American self-interest.

6. What purpose would it serve if we socialized MOP ownership by having corporations issue stock to their employees?

a. That would be the only acceptable way to socialize our MOP, because it would make American capitalism compatible with Marxism while adhering to the American way of earning or paying for capital ownership.

b. It would be the best way to make American capitalism compatible with Marxism, since such employee ownership plans as ESOP, TRASOP, and PAYSOP are already in existence and have proven that employee ownership increases productivity.

c. It would not bring compatibility with Marxism, because its benefits would be restricted to the long-term employees of stable corporations, leaving most MOP ownership in the hands of an elite minority, albeit a larger minority than under the present system; therefore it would not socialize MOP ownership broadly enough.

7. American welfare capitalism is plagued by many tough problems: recurring inflation, high interest rates, business and farm failures, unemployment, capital shortages, more tax dependents than private sector workers, onerous transfer payments, huge budget deficits, erosion of the work ethic, threatened insolvency of the Social Security system and of state and local governments, and insufficient resources to assure national security and environmental protection. These problems appear to be insoluble whether Democrats or Republicans are in office, because:

a. Our economists and politicians are so stupid that they don't know how to use the safeguards built into our economic system to solve these problems.

b. The system itself needs some changes.

8. How would *you* solve the problems of American capitalism?

a. Allow the free market to function with a minimum of government interference, and let Reagan's supply-side economics encourage savings and investment.

b. Return to the remedies of the New Deal, the Great Society, and other liberal Democratic programs of government intervention.

c. Adopt the Japanese form of planned economy in which the government controls credit, capital investment, employment, and competition.

d. Return to the gold standard, which pegs the money supply and the growth of the American economy to the amount of gold stored at Fort Knox.

e. Change to a system of democratic socialism, as did some other democratic countries where, as in the United States, the overwhelming majority of voters had no hope of becoming MOP owners.

f. Continue to use the three methods of support now open to all Americans: wages, welfare, and cheating.

g. Rely on the present American system of democratic capitalism, which is composed of a democratic electoral process and a capitalist economic system, and therefore embodies in our economic system the principles of democracy.

h. Recognize that the present system, which is rigged to reward destruction of jobs, can no longer create enough jobs to keep the economy growing; recognize that welfare is inherently inflationary; and recognize that it is time to open the fourth method of support (return on invested capital) to all Americans because it is the only method not yet tried and is the only way of using capitalism to save capitalism.

9. What will happen to the ownership of the means of production if we do not attempt to socialize it through a plan like Super-Stock?

a. The MOP will remain permanently under the ownership of the pinnacle class which has the savings to buy stock, even though this class represents no more than six percent of the population.

b. The MOP will come to be owned by labor unions because we would end up with pension fund socialism or the Meidner plan.

c. The MOP will come to be owned by the federal government because we would end up with democratic socialism.

d. The MOP will come to be controlled by the Communist Party of the United States because we would end up with communism.

10. During the next two decades, American corporations will spend about $5 trillion on new capital items that are projected to

pay for themselves in a few years through extra income which the corporations will receive from their operation. Who should own this newly created capital of $5 trillion?

a. It should be owned by the present owners of most of the stock of American corporations, even though: They make no additional payment for acquisition of this capital; this will perpetuate the corporate finance and tax-rigging that encourages corporations to create new capital without creating any new stockholders; this will aggravate the existing concentration of capital ownership and income in a pinnacle class, which further reduces the mass purchasing power needed to buy what the economy produces and further widens the rich-poor gap, perpetuating class struggle and ideological warfare between capitalism and communism; and even though no law or constitutional provision mentions this system.

b. It should be owned by a handful of corporate executives who, under the present system, have access to long-term credit which enables them to make "leveraged buyouts" of all the stock of the corporations they work for, using the assets of these corporations as security for long-term loans to buy out the present stockholders.

c. It should be owned by wooden Indians.

d. It should be owned by the poorest 50 million American households, provided that a practical means can be found to: issue new corporate stock to them; pay the issuing corporations for the stock immediately; and finance the payment of the stock price over a period of years out of dividends paid by the corporations from their future earnings—thereby socializing ownership of the means of production in the United States, equalizing the productive wealth of the United States in one generation, ending class struggle in the United States, and opening the way for cooperation and friendship with the Soviet Union.

11. Should we finance the new plant and equipment of major corporations through SuperStock?

a. SuperStock is not worth studying because it smacks of socialism.

b. SuperStock is not worth studying because it smacks of capitalism.

c. SuperStock is not worth studying because it is utopian, is not supported by any big-name economists, and would create serious problems of work incentive and eligibility priorities.

d. SuperStock is not worth studying because we already have democratic capitalism, which is composed of a democratic electoral process and a capitalist economic system and therefore embodies in our economic system the principles of democracy.

e. SuperStock is not worth studying because there are *proven* ways of making American capitalism equitable, consistent with our political democracy and our religious heritage, and compatible with Marxism.

f. SuperStock is worth studying, along with any other suggested methods of achieving universal capitalism or socializing MOP ownership without going socialist or giving up our treasured freedoms.

12. Religious institutions concerned with the quest for social justice:

a. Should attempt to choose capitalism or Marxism as the best economic system, and support that system.

b. Should condemn capitalism and Marxism, because each has materialistic or immoral elements that are incompatible with religious principles in some degree.

c. Should search for a new path which seeks to combine the best features of capitalism and Marxism in order to achieve social justice and bring an end to the confrontation between American capitalism and Soviet communism, thus opening the way for nuclear disarmament.

13. If we do *not* try to remove the ideological basis for enmity between the United States and the Soviet Union:

a. Nothing will be lost, because the Soviets are intent on nuclear confrontation as part of their plan for world conquest.

b. It will make no difference, because the belligerency of human nature will eventually cause a nuclear holocaust no matter how we try to prevent it.

c. We will avoid nuclear war despite the clash of ideologies, because both sides know that neither side can win.

d. We will miss the best chance of avoiding nuclear war by improving Soviet-American relations.

14. How would Soviet communism affect us once we have socialized American MOP ownership?

a. It would still be a threat to us, because its political system of dictatorship might be adopted by the United States.

b. Soviet communism would still be a threat to us, because its atheism might be adopted in the United States.

c. Soviet communism would still be a threat to us, because its system of dialectical materialism might be adopted in the United States.

d. Soviet communism itself would no longer be a serious threat to the American way of life, because our self-administered socialization would immunize us against the effects of all other methods of ending the class struggle (such as Soviet communism) and make all such other methods irrelevant.

15. If we socialized American MOP ownership, what would be our attitude toward Marxist groups in Latin America and other foreign nations?

a. It would have to remain unchanged, since we could not tolerate the spread of Marxism.

b. Our attitude would change to indifference, since the spread of socialized MOP ownership through Marxism would no longer be a threat to the American way of life, as long as Marxist groups did not seek to launch military forces against us.

16. How might the Soviets react if we socialized MOP ownership and made it clear to the USSR that we had taken that step in order to remove a major cause of Soviet-American enmity, and then followed up by offering to make the Soviet Union an equal partner in world leadership, covering such spheres as energy, space, Third World development, and curbing of terrorism?

a. The Soviets would undoubtedly cling to their paranoid distrust of the United States and would believe it to be in their self-interest to continue the dangerous, expensive arms race and their partnerships with the likes of Cuba and the PLO.

b. It would clearly be in the self-interest of the Soviets to open their minds to the possibility of friendship, cooperation, and partnership with the United States; and we can assume with a reasonable degree of certainty that the Soviets will act in their own self-interest.

Bibliography

Abdul-Rauf, Muhammed. "The Ten Commandments of Islamic Economics," *Across the Board.* Washington: American Enterprise Institute for Public Policy Research, 1979.

Barnet, Richard. *Real Security.* New York: Simon & Schuster, 1981.

Barraclough, Geoffrey. *An Introduction to Contemporary History.* New York: Pelican Books, 1967.

Barron, John. *MiG Pilot.* New York: Avon Books, 1980.

Berman, Larry. *Planning a Tragedy: The Americanization of the War in Vietnam.* New York: W. W. Norton & Co., Inc., 1982.

Brown, Charles Reynolds. *The Social Message of the Modern Pulpit.* New York: Charles Scribner's Sons, 1912.

Churchill, Winston. *The Gathering Storm,* Vol. 1 of *The Second World War.* Boston: Houghton Mifflin Co., 1948.

Churchill, Winston. *The World Crisis.* New York: Charles Scribner's Sons, 1931.

Conquest, Robert. *Present Danger.* Oxford: Basil Blackwell, 1979.

Conwell, Russell H. *Acres of Diamonds.* New York: Harper & Brothers, 1915.

Cox, Arthur Macy: *Russian Roulette: The Superpower Game.* New York: Times Books, 1982.

Davenport, Nicholas. *The Split Society.* London: Victor Gollancz Ltd., 1964.

Drinan, Robert. *Beyond the Nuclear Freeze.* New York: The Seabury Press, 1983.

Drucker, Peter F. *The Unseen Revolution—How Pension Fund Socialism Came to America.* New York: Harper & Row, 1976.

Ferm, Robert. *Issues in American Protestantism.* Garden City, N.Y.: Anchor, 1969.

Galbraith, John Kenneth. *Almost Everyone's Guide to Economics.* New York: Bantam, 1978.

Gladden, Rev. Washington. *Recollections.* Boston: Houghton Mifflin Co., 1909.

Green, Mark. *Winning Back America.* New York: Bantam Books, 1982.

Ground Zero. *What About the Russians and Nuclear War?* New York: Pocket Books, 1983.

Hackett, John. *The Third World War: The Untold Story.* New York: Macmillan Publishing Co., Inc., 1982.

Hamrin, Robert. *Managing Growth in the 1980s: Toward a New Economics.* New York: Praeger Publishers, 1980.

The Harvard Study Group: [Carnesale, Albert; Doty, Paul; Hoffman, Stanley; Huntington, Samuel P.; Nye, Joseph S., Jr.; Sagan, Scott D.]. *Living with Nuclear Weapons.* New York: Bantam Books, 1983.

Hofstadter, Richard, ed. "Christianity and the Social Crisis," *The Progressive Movement.* Englewood Cliffs, N.J.: Prentice Hall, 1963.

Hook, Sidney. *Marxism and Beyond.* Totowa, N.J.: Rowman and Littlefield, 1983.

The Independent Commission on Disarmament and Security Issues. *Common Security.* New York: Simon & Schuster, 1982.

Kahn, Herman. *The Coming Boom.* New York: Simon & Schuster, 1982.

Kahn, Herman. *On Thermonuclear War.* Princeton, N.J.: Princeton University Press, 1960.

Kaiser, Robert. *Russia.* New York: Pocket Books, 1976.

Kautsky, Karl Johann. *Social Democracy vs. Communism.* New York: The Rand School Press, 1946.

Kennan, George. *The Nuclear Delusion.* New York: Pantheon Books, 1976.

Kennedy, Edward M., and Hatfield, Mark O. *Freeze!* New York: Bantam Books, 1982.

Keynes, John Maynard. *The General Theory of Employment, Interest and Money.* London: Macmillan, 1936. Harbinger paperback, 1964.

Larson, Thomas B. *Soviet-American Rivalry.* New York: W. W. Norton & Co., Inc., 1978.

Lekachman, Robert. *Capitalism for Beginners.* New York: Pantheon Books, 1981.

Lifton, Robert Jay, and Falk, Richard. *Indefensible Weapons.* New York: Basic Books, Inc., 1982.

Maital, Shlomo. *Minds, Markets & Money.* New York: Basic Books, 1982.

Marx, Karl. *The Communist Manifesto.* New York: International Publishers Company, 1948.

Marx, Karl. *Capital,* vol. 3. Translated by David Fernbach. New York: Vintage Books, 1981.

Marx, Karl. *Critique of the Gotha Programme.* New York: International Publishers Company, 1938.

Medvedev, Roy. *On Soviet Dissent.* New York: Columbia University Press, 1980.

Mills, C. Wright. *The Marxists.* New York: Penguin Books, 1963.

Niebuhr, Reinhold. *The Children of Light and the Children of Darkness.* New York: Charles Scribner's Sons, 1944.

Novak, Michael. *The Spirit of Democratic Capitalism.* New York: Simon & Schuster, 1982.

Reich, Robert B. *The Next American Frontier.* New York: Times Books, 1983.

Samuelson, Paul A. *Economics,* 11th ed. New York: McGraw-Hill, 1980.

Scheer, Robert. *With Enough Shovels: Reagan, Bush and Nuclear War.* New York: Random House, 1982.

Schell, Jonathan. *The Fate of the Earth.* New York: Alfred A. Knopf, 1982.

Schumacher, E. F. *Small is Beautiful.* New York: Harper & Row, 1975.

Servan-Schreiber, Jean-Jacques. *The World Challenge.* New York: Simon & Schuster, 1981.

Shirer, William L. *The Rise and Fall of the Third Reich.* Greenwich, Connecticut: Fawcett Publications, Inc., 1978.

Smith, Hedrick. *The Russians.* New York: Ballantine Books, 1976.

Sokolovsky, V. D. *Military Strategy.* New York: Crane-Russak Co., 1975.

Solzhenitsyn, Alexander. *The Mortal Danger.* New York: Harper & Row, 1980.

Speiser, Stuart M. *A Piece of the Action.* New York: Van Nostrand Reinhold Co., 1977.

Taylor, A. J. P. *Origins of the Second World War.* Greenwich, Connecticut: Fawcett Publications, Inc., 1961.

Thompson, E. P. *Beyond the Cold War.* New York: Pantheon Books, 1982.

Thurow, Lester C. *Dangerous Currents: The State of Economics.* New York: Harper & Row, 1983.

Toland, John. *Adolf Hitler.* New York: Ballantine, 1977.

Ulam, Adam. *The Unfinished Revolution: Marxism and Communism in the Modern World.* Boulder, Col.: Westview Press, Inc., 1979.

Von Thunen, Johann Heinrich. *The Isolated State.* Abridged and translated from the 2nd German ed. Oxford, England: Pergamon Press, 1966.

Weber, Max. *The Protestant Ethic and the Spirit of Capitalism.* New York: Charles Scribner's Sons, 1980.

Index